UNDERSTANDING MORALITY, FREEDOM, AND CAPITAL

Martin J. Miles

---

[1] E Environments Design Morality XXXI

Acknowledgements

Generally, I dedicate this book to all of the scientists and researchers who discovered information used in this book. Obviously, I couldn't have written this book without them.

Specifically, I am indebted to three of my mathematics professors who deserve recognition for going far beyond what was expected. They did not directly contribute to this book - but indirectly because all three were valuable role models for me and others.

Dr. Edwin L. Crow (1916-2005) was an adjunct professor of mathematics at the University of Colorado and former head of the mathematical statistics branch in the Department of the Navy. We derived the dependence factor for the American National Standard X3.14.1, a function that is called the Freedom function in this book. He was my valued colleague for 35 years, and he was very supportive during my career.

Dr. George W. Morgenthaler (1926-2013) was a Professor Emeritus in the College of Engineering at the University of Colorado and a former Vice President of Martin Marietta Corporation. He was an inspirational teacher and friend.

Dr. Aubrey J. Kempner (1880-1973) was President of the American Mathematical Association (1937-1939) and Chairman of the Mathematics Department at the University of Colorado (1944-1949). He invited me to meet with him before our classes (analysis of a complex variable) so we could discuss the new geometries and their relationships to Einstein's theories of relativity. I was delighted. His knowledge was not only academic - it was personal. His mentor and teacher at the University of Göttingen, Germany was the famed Hermann Minkowski who was also Einstein's teacher.[2] Minkowski conceived the four-dimensional coordinate system of space and time that enabled Einstein to understand and explain his Special Theory of Relativity (i.e., speed of light). Einstein stayed at Göttingen to work with another of Aubrey Kempner's teachers, David Hilbert. Hilbert and Minkowski, were probably the most famous mathematicians of that time. They helped Einstein apply the new hyperbolic geometry that also enabled Einstein to understand and explain his General Theory of Relativity. (Since gravity warps space, it also modifies the Theory of Special Relativity).

Aubrey Kempner loved mathematics, and it was contagious. He was a dear friend and mentor.

I am also indebted to my friend, Thomas L. Carr, of Maplewood, Minnesota for volunteering to review this book and contributing many excellent suggestions.

---

[2] An astonishing 47 persons associated with the university were awarded Nobel Prizes even though its mathematicians and scientists either fled or were removed by the Nazis in 1933, prior to World War II.

Contents

Chapter 6 Measure Moral Behavior, Freedom, Accuracy, and Market Freedom

Introduction

When you want to help people, you tell them the truth.

When you want to help yourself, you tell them what they want to hear.

~ Thomas Sowell

I believe that truth must be more important than desires and feelings. If you agree, I invite you to think outside the "bottle" and consider many important truths about morality, freedom, and capital.[3]

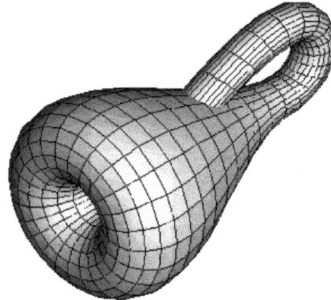

Recently, I decided to explore the relationships between nature and economics and the lessons we might learn from them. I wrote a book entitled *The Nature of Economics*. While writing that book, one of the surprising facts was the frequent references to morality. I knew then that I wanted to understand morality much better. So, when I finished *The Nature of Economics*, I eagerly began to investigate morality, freedom, and capital.

Even though I have an extensive background in mathematics and the sciences, my best attribute for writing books such as these is probably my interest in the truth.

Several Core Concepts

The following concepts are core to this book:

- **Capital.** Capital is knowledge and its manifestations.

- **Entropy.** Entropy is the constant flow of energy to regions of lesser energy. Consequently, life must constantly replace lost energy.

- **Evolution.** There are four types of evolution. By far, the most significant type is natural selection. Natural selection designs living entities to be compatible with their environments - and nothing more.

- **Freedom.** Freedom is the ability to act or behave. Ideally, freedom is the ability to act or behave morally. Freedom coexists with life. Consequently, life is the basic freedom.

---

[3] We are joking about the bottle because the pictured bottle has only one side. The one-sided Klein bottle was conceived in 1882 by the German mathematician, Felix Klein.

- **Market Freedom.** Market freedom is the accuracy of market values as measured by moral behavior.

- **Moral Behavior.** Behavior is moral behavior if and only if it increases the probability of freedom.

- **Morality.** Morality is the system of innate propensities that enables moral behavior.

- **Productivity.** Productivity is a type of efficiency (i.e., output/input) that is applied to producing resources. Capital alone can achieve productivity greater than unity (i.e., greater than the productivity of the food cycle) – thereby, providing increased resources to augment moral behavior and freedom.

This book has four parts:

- **Part I** Entropy and Evolution

- **Part II** Morality and Freedom

- **Part III** Capital

- **Part IV** Summary and Conclusions

Part I Entropy and Evolution

The purpose of Part I is to remind us of several events and phenomena important to the evolution of the Earth and its life.

Entropy

The origin of the Universe apparently occurred 13.8 billion years ago (i.e., the Big Bang), and its Second Law of Thermodynamics (i.e., entropy) states that energy tends to flow to regions of lesser energy. This law requires living entities to constantly replenish their energy. In fact, the flow of energy distinguishes the physical system from the biological system: In the physical system, energy always flows to regions of lesser energy, and the biological system exists only because, approximately 3.5-4.0 billion years ago, some molecules were able to divert energy for a purpose - the necessities of life.

When a life is lost, it cannot be regained. Therefore, the constant availability of necessary resources is necessary for life and freedom.

Evolution

When life began, we moved from the physical system, where the freedom of a rock is zero, to the biological system, where the freedom of life is infinite. Life and freedom must coexist and both must be maintained by moral behavior.

Part I describes the four types of evolution, including, of course, the most important type, natural selection. Several stages of the evolution of humans have led to the current stage, *Homo sapiens*.

We view the human brain as the successive evolutionary layers of the triune brain:

- **Reptilian Brain.** The reptilian brain provides *instinct*.

- **Limbic Brain.** The limbic brain (particularly the amygdala) provides *emotion*.

- **Neocortex.** The neocortex provides *logic*.

Specifically, logic resides in the dorsolateral prefrontal cortex of the neocortex. However, decisions are made in the ventromedial prefrontal cortex of the neocortex when emotions from the amygdala are pitted against logic. The separate locations of logic and decision-making explain why logical individuals can sometimes make (surprisingly) emotional decisions.

Part I relates the three criteria of natural selection to four dependent types of moral behavior: individual, cooperation, competition, and force. It also discusses evidence from recent psychological experiments with infants and adolescents that suggest that morality is innate. (Why do some people exclude morality as the only part of the body that does not evolve – especially since moral behavior is essential to natural selection and freedom?)

Implications of Innate Morality

The implications of innate morality are profound:

- **Countless Moralities**. Natural selection designs humans, including their morality, to adapt to their environments. Consequently, there are countless versions of morality rather than one universal morality.

- **Immature Moralities.** Moral propensities exist *only* for types of situations that were novel more than 7,000 years ago. Approximately 7,000 years ago, capital, which increases exponentially, reached a level of development that whelmed evolution, whose rate is much slower and sporadic. Consequently, there are many inherent situations for which we have no morality – only dilemmas (e.g., interactions with strangers). It is estimated that delays in the evolution of morality have allowed billions of humans to be killed by conflicts and wars. This horrible result is described by the structure in the *Genetic Levels of Morality* (listed below).

Part II Morality and Freedom

Part II of this book discusses the essence of morality and freedom as well as the relationships between them.

Genetic Levels of Morality

We consider four nested genetic levels of morality that were created at progressively later times:

- **Individual Morality.** Individual morality is self-interest morality.

- **Group Morality**. Group morality is magnanimous morality.

- **Species Morality**. Species morality is mundane morality.

- **Ecosystem Morality**. Ecosystem morality is necessary morality.

Individuals feel less empathy for each other as the genetic distance between them increases. The evolutionary states of individual morality and group morality are now mature, but, due to the rapid rate of capital development, the evolutionary states of species morality and ecosystem morality are decidedly less mature.

Relationships between Moral Behavior and Freedom

Freedom and moral behavior are naturally opposing binary states - just as are rights and responsibilities. We discuss four such binary states in Chapter 8. Following are a few precise statements concerning moral behavior and freedom.

Basic Freedom exists if and only if Life exists.

Ideally, Freedom is the ability to Behave Morally.

Behavior is Moral Behavior if and only if it increases the probability of Freedom.

Freedom exists if and only if Moral Behavior can exist.

Moral Behavior is a function of Freedom, and Freedom is a function of Moral Behavior.

A Market is a Moral Market if and only if it is a Free Market.

Precise Definitions of the Most Important Parameters

Chapter 6 introduces what we believe are the most precise definitions of the most important parameters in this book. They are the most precise because we provide a mathematical model for each parameter, and the parameter can be measured:

- **Moral Behavior.** We selected the logical formula to model and measure moral behavior; we call it the Moral Behavior function. It models and measures moral behavior as a function of a sequence of its activities.

- **Freedom.** We derived the widely and long-sought link between morality and freedom that models and measures freedom; we call it the Freedom function. It models and measures freedom as a function of moral behavior and moral behavior as a function of freedom.

- **Accuracy.** We selected the logical formula (i.e., the expected value of the random squared error) to measure accuracy. It is a function of the bias and the precision of its values.

- **Market Freedom.** We derived the formula to model and measure market freedom; we call it the Market Freedom function. It models and measures the moral behavior of a market as a function of the accuracy of its market values. It applies to markets of goods and services as well as to markets of selecting entities. (What does this say about the morality of identity selection to replace merit selection, such as Affirmative Action?)

Countless Moralities

All humans have the same moral characteristics, but each environment designs its human inhabitants with appropriate levels of these moral characteristics – levels that favor their natural selection in their environment. Part II includes several examples showing that morality is designed by environments (e.g., worldwide homicide rates, degrees of political freedom, and degrees of economic freedom).

The Optimum Environment for an Individual is the Environment that designed it.

Our Moral Propensity Space

We define the dimensions of our moral propensity space according to the six interrogatives. This helps us to depict the moral *propensity* space and distinguish it from the moral *dilemma* space (i.e., Figure 4.4-1).

Part III Capital

Productivity

Entropy designs the sustainable food cycle (i.e., Production = Consumption). That is, in the food cycle,

$$\text{Productivity} = \text{Production/Consumption} = 1.$$

Produce-consume is an important type of naturally opposing binary states.

Capital

Capital is knowledge and its manifestations. Scraping tools, the first evidence of capital, were created by humans 2.5 million years ago.

In an earlier book, The *Nature of Economics*, we demonstrated the unique productivity achieved by capital: It is similar to a catalyst. In fact, only capital can increase productivity beyond unity – which is the productivity of the food cycle.

Capital Can Augment Morality and Freedom

Capital has been an unbelievable benefit to humans worldwide for morality and freedom: Resources can be increased greatly by productivity:

- **Morality.** Capital has allowed the human population to increase dramatically (in part, by increasing the probability of human natural selection from about 45% to more than 95% worldwide). Applications of capital can unquestionably be moral.

- **Freedom.** Freedom can be denied in at least three ways:
  - **Death**.
  - **Restraint.** Governments and individuals can restrain the freedom of individuals and markets.
  - **Constraint.** Insufficient resources can constrain the freedom of individuals. Consequently, in the absence of death or restraint, freedom is proportional to an individual's desires and resources.

Section 6.2.3 shows that capital enables morality, freedom, and capital to increase exponentially (i.e., in proportion to the amount present).

Capital Can Alter Environments

Environments design Morality, but Capital alters Environments.

The moral propensity system is a logical system for all types of situations that were novel more than 7,000 years ago – but not after. This time-gap is vast because the rate of evolving moral propensities is very, very slow compared to the rate of capital development! This is a most serious problem because it has affected almost all of us for centuries, and it is not realized!

Approximately 7,000 years ago, capital allowed increased human migrations and mergers – and, consequently, increased interactions with strangers. That is, capital enables novel types of situations to occur, and, because they are novel within the last 7,000 years, we have either no or few moral propensities to guide us. Moreover, it will probably require millennia to evolve the needed moral propensities! Until then, we must live with moral dilemmas - dilemmas that have already allowed an estimated one billion lives to be lost to strangers from conflicts, wars, and associated diseases.

As an example of our missing moral propensities, we do not possess the moral propensities to accurately judge the moralities associated with, say, Christopher Columbus and his interactions with natives in the New World. It is eerie to realize that our judgments are baseless: How can our moral judgments hit the bull's-eye of a target that has not yet evolved?

Capital can also Break the Bonds of Naturally Opposing Binary States

Capital can also allow natural relationships to be broken. One important example of natural relationships is the naturally opposing binary states of rights-responsibilities: Since rights are specific freedoms, and since responsibilities are specific moral behaviors, rights and responsibilities are subsets of freedom and moral behaviors, respectively.

The bond between rights and responsibilities is broken when individuals surrender their responsibilities, say, to the state. Abdicating one's responsibilities is decidedly immoral: It is only a matter of time before these individuals also lose their rights to the state. This is the seemingly inevitable result of socialism. See Figure 8.3.5-1. Any tendency of an individual to be irresponsible is increased by the continuing responsibilities to replace resources lost to entropy.

Another important example of the separation of the naturally opposing binary states is the broken bond between consume-produce. Of course, separation is allowed by the efficiency of capital relative to labor. The result is job loss from labor to capital. Section 8.3.4 shows how to measure the effects of job loss for five of the most important economic parameters: wages, profit, rate of return, production, and productivity.

Chapter 8 of Part III discusses approximately 13 novel types of situations that cause great trouble and dilemmas for us – particularly with regard to strangers and novel environments for some life styles (e.g., abortion, homosexuality, merging of gender roles, etc.).

Part IV Summary and Conclusions

Even though Part IV is an important part of the book, it seems that discussing the summary and conclusions here, in the introduction, is illogical.

We hope the information in this book (e.g., the existence of *countless* individual and group moralities and the *immaturity* of species and ecosystem moralities) will help us understand each other better.

Part I
Entropy and Evolution

Chapter 1 Natural Evolution
(13.8 Billion BC - Present)

The purpose of this chapter is to discuss the physical system, discuss the increasing complexity of the biological system, and review the components and systems of life because understanding natural selection and life are fundamental to understanding morality and freedom.

The sections of this chapter are:

1.1 Thermodynamics

1.2 Origin of Life on Earth

1.3 Evolution

1.4 Principles of Natural Selection

The Big Bang

"Once upon a time" there was a Big Bang. We can say three things about this incredible event:

- It occurred at least once.

- It occurred upon a time - in fact, it undoubtedly coexisted with time.

- It did not make a sound.[4]

The idea that the origin of the universe could be traced to a single point (a mathematical singularity) was proposed in 1927 by Monsignor Georges Lemaître, a Belgian physicist and a Roman Catholic priest. Early theory held that after the universe originated as a single point, it was uniformly dense and had constant curvature.

However, the Ukrainian physicist, George Gamow, believed otherwise. He believed that after the Big Bang, the universe was not uniform but was dominated more by energy than by matter. Consequently, he is the father of the "Hot Big Bang" theory of the expanding universe (so named

---

[4] We know it did not make a sound because it is a matter of definition, not a matter of science: A sound is defined as a sensation *perceived* by the sense of hearing - and life didn't exist then. Often, a mystery or an uncertainty exists not because of an (inherent) characteristic of the phenomenon, but only because we have not defined the phenomenon. See also Section 1.2, *Origin of Life on Earth*.

because of the presumed predominance of energy). His theory prevails today, and most work on cosmology is based on Gamow's theory.[5]

Because the Big Bang occurred 13.8 billion years ago, the universe is thought to be that old.[6]

Early Natural Events of Earth

The Earth is thought to be about 4.5 billion years old. The Earth existed for 1 billion years before the first hint of life, possibly primitive prokaryotic cells. The origin of life is the origin of freedom. Another 1.5 billion years passed before more complex eukaryotic cells evolved. And another 0.5 billion years passed before complex organisms evolved. Table 1-1 lists some significant natural events during the early history of the Earth.

---

[5] I knew George Gamow and his family, and I admired them greatly. As a separate human-interest story, in 1928, while he was at the University of Leningrad in St. Petersburg, George Gamow also explained the theory of alpha decay of a nucleus from quantum tunneling. Simultaneously, at Princeton, NJ, Edward U. Condon (and Ronald Gurney) made the same discovery. Gamow received credit for the discovery because he also provided experimental evidence of the phenomenon. In 1945, President Truman named Condon the director of the National Bureau of Standards - now, National Institute of Standards and Technology (NIST). Gamow and Condon became friends in Boulder while Gamow was a professor of physics at the University of Colorado (from 1956), and Condon was a researcher at the Joint Institute for Laboratory Astrophysics (JILA) (from 1963), a joint effort between NIST and the University of Colorado. Condon attended Gamow's burial service in Boulder in 1968. I knew Gamow as an "oral" personality (i.e., enjoyed eating, talking, smoking, and drinking), so I thought it was humorous that, when leaving the service, Condon fondly remarked to their mutual friend, the mathematician, Stanislaw Ulam (who devised the Monte Carlo method of computing), "I never thought George could go this long without talking." Condon died in Boulder in 1974.

[6] However, the Big Bang (an expansion) might be only the latest in a series of expansions and contractions.

Table 1-1 some significant natural events during the early history of the Earth

Years Ago (Billions)	Early Natural Events of Earth
4.5-5.0	Earth's first atmosphere was gas (i.e., hydrogen and helium)
4.4	Earth's second atmosphere was gas from volcanoes (i.e., ammonia, carbon dioxide, water vapor, etc.). Subsequently, sunlight decomposed ammonia to nitrogen.
3.5-4.0	Life (in an unknown form - probably as macromolecules or cells)
3.5	Prokaryotic Cells
3.0	Earth's third atmosphere is oxygen gas from cyanobacteria. Cyanobacteria began to produce free oxygen from photosynthesis. (The atmosphere is now 78% nitrogen, 21% oxygen, and 1% other gases.)
2.0	Eukaryotic Cells. Endosymbiosis seems to have created the first eukaryotic cell from two prokaryotic cells - one engulfing the other.
0.5-1.0	Complex Organisms

Earth's First Atmosphere: Hydrogen and Helium

The Earth's first atmosphere consisted of hydrogen (H_2) and helium (He). However, these elements did not remain because the Earth's gravity could not hold these lighter elements, and the Earth's immature magnetic field could not counter the Sun's intense solar wind.

Earth's Second Atmosphere: Nitrogen, Carbon Dioxide, and Water Vapor

About 4.4 billion years ago, the Earth's second atmosphere was developing: The cooling Earth developed a crust; internal pressure caused gases (i.e., ammonia (NH_3), carbon dioxide (CO_2), water vapor (H_2O), etc.) to spew from vulnerable regions of the crust, called volcanoes; over a few billion years, sunlight decomposed the ammonia to nitrogen (N_2). The amount of nitrogen was essentially equal to the current amount.

Earth's Third Atmosphere: Oxygen

Earth's third atmosphere is oxygen (O_2), gas from cyanobacteria. Cyanobacteria began to produce free oxygen from photosynthesis. (The atmosphere is now 78% nitrogen, 21% oxygen O_2, and 1% other gases.)

Natural Economy

At a minimum, an economy is a system of living organisms in which energy flows through and matter recycles. Natural economies evolve to become the ecosystem. Technology has since increased the availability of resources, but it has also caused us to take our resources for granted.

1.1 Thermodynamics

Thermodynamics is one of the truly fundamental theories of physics - and the Second Law of Thermodynamics is fundamental to life.

The four laws of thermodynamics describe the relationships between temperature, thermal energy (heat), and other forms of energy.

Temperature

Temperature is a measure of the average kinetic energy of particles in a sample of matter. Temperature depends upon the *velocity* of atoms in the sample.

Heat

Heat is neither created nor destroyed, but it can be transferred. Heat is the energy transferred from one body to another according to the difference in temperature between them - from higher energy to lower energy. The amount of heat transferred depends upon the *number and velocity* of atoms in a sample of matter. Heat can also be converted to other forms of energy (e.g., from heat energy to kinetic energy and from electromagnetic energy to light energy).

Heat Transfer

Heat can be transferred in three ways:

- **Conduction.** conduction is the transfer of heat *through matter* from particle-to-particle;

- **Convection.** convection is the transfer of heat *by the movement of matter*; and

- **Radiation.** radiation is the transfer of heat *by electromagnetic waves propagating through space - either from or to matter*.

The Implications of Entropy for Life

Entropy is the universal slave master of all living organisms.

Entropy causes all living entities to swim against the tide - for as long as they live. We lose energy continuously: That is, our entropy increases continuously, and our disorder increases continuously - until we consume resources and distribute its energy purposefully. This situation continues forever and is fundamental to morality and freedom.

1.2 Origin of Life on Earth

Figure 1.2.1-1 is a Venn-type diagram that depicts two relationships between the physical system and the biological system.

1.2.1 Types of Matter

About 3.5 billion years ago, the Earth spawned a *very improbable system* - a parasite that we call the biological system. Now, the Earth's natural environment is both a physical (abiotic) system and its parasitic biological (biotic) system. Clearly, the physical system does not need the biological system. Indeed, if the physical system is sentient, it must be displeased to have acquired a parasite - because parasites necessarily rob their host of energy - increasing its entropy and causing it to "age" more quickly.

Figure 1.2.1-1 Venn-type diagrams of two views (i.e., types of matter and distributions of energy) of the two systems: physical and biological

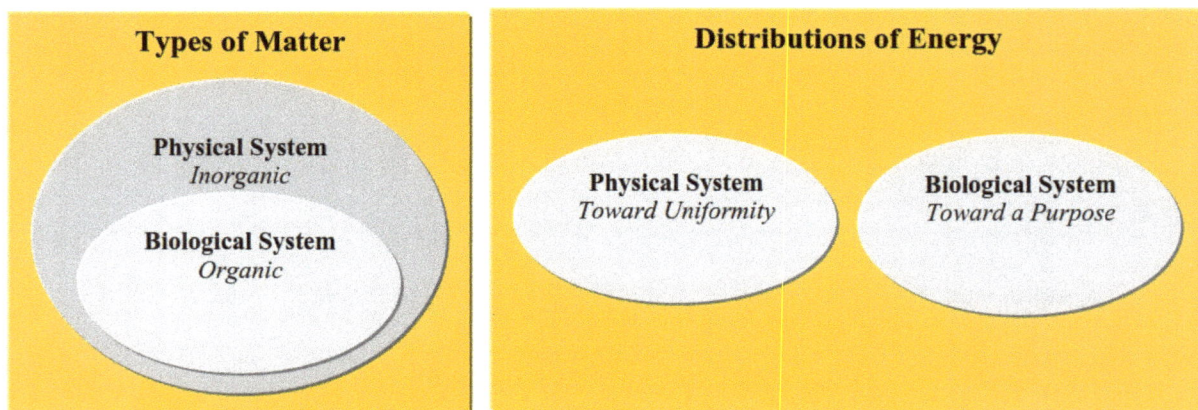

Types of Matter

Physical System
Inorganic

Biological System
Organic

Distributions of Energy

Physical System
Toward Uniformity

Biological System
Toward a Purpose

1.2.2 Distribution of Energy

Perhaps the most fundamental difference between the physical system and the biological system is the manner in which they distribute energy.

Physical System: Uniform Distribution of Energy

The physical system tends to distribute energy along the path of least resistance (i.e., a geodesic) so that energy can increasingly become available to nearby regions of lesser energy.[7]

Biological System: Purposeful Distribution of Energy

Biological processes are highly improbable because they require an *immense* concentration of energy.

There is still no consensus for the definition of life. At least one of the following functions is usually considered necessary for life: metabolism, irritability, reproductivity, adaptability, growth, and organization. Because entropy is a constant factor, all of these functions require the constant acquisition of energy. (Perhaps life could be declared for an entity if its temperature continues to exceed the temperature of its ambient nonliving environment – regardless of which function might be enabled.)

Organisms consist of organized subsystems. *The purposeful distribution of energy (as opposed to a uniform distribution of energy) distinguishes life from nonlife.* While the organism dissipates energy, it becomes progressively less organized, and it requires maintenance. The physical system does not require maintenance. While purposefully distributing energy, biological processes must also acquire energy - to remain distinct from the physical system (i.e., to remain alive).[8]

When an organism assimilates nutritional resources from the environment, the following occurs:

- **Energy.** The organism gains energy, and the environment loses an equal amount of energy.

- **Entropy.** The organism loses entropy, and the environment gains an equal amount of entropy.

---

[7] Energy in physical entities is transferred to regions of lesser energy along geodesics - paths of least resistance. For example, lightening follows the path of least resistance in the atmosphere; and the "great circle" is the path of least resistance between any two points on the surface of a sphere (e.g., the Earth). It is the shortest path in the following way: It is an arc of the circle that is defined by the intersection of the sphere and the plane that passes through any two points on the surface and the point that is the center of the sphere. Any plane that passes through any two points but does not pass through the center of the sphere defines an arc that is longer than the great circle arc (i.e., the geodesic).

[8] A process or an entity could be considered in the state of life *only while* it can reduce its entropy. Perhaps it would be helpful to associate the words, *organ* and *organism*, with the word *organize* because life needs *organization* to mitigate *entropy*.

It is impossible to overstate the importance of continuous energy for life. Specifically, we humans become so accustomed to the continuous struggle to acquire resources that we can forget how the struggle dominates our lives.

Energy is necessary but not sufficient for life, and life is necessary for freedom. In fact, life is the most basic type of freedom. Any level of life requires moral behavior to continue life. Morality and freedom are discussed at length in most subsequent chapters of this book.

1.3 Evolution

Philosophers pondered evolution even before Socrates (469 BC) and also before Carl Linnaeus introduced his classification of species in 1735 AD - 124 years before Darwin's *On the Origin of Species*.

Gene frequencies in a population tend to remain constant unless there are disturbing factors. Without disturbing factors, evolution does not occur. However, there are four independent types of disturbing factors that cause evolution:

- random genetic drift,
- mutation,
- migration, and
- natural selection.

The probability that a species will succeed in its environment depends upon its compatibility with its natural environment. Probably *the optimal (most successful) environment for an individual is the environment that "designed" it.*

1.3.1 Random Genetic Drift

In each generation, the frequency of occurrences of a characteristic or level might increase/decrease when the occurrence of a variant form of a gene, called an allele, increases/decreases *by chance* - rather than because the individual is either more or less *fit*. This is random genetic drift. (There is an unknown cause for the variant, but it is assumed that it is not caused by fitness.)

1.3.2 Mutation

A gene mutation is a permanent alteration of an individual's DNA. The size of mutations range upward from a single base pair of nucleotides to a segment of a chromosome (that would include multiple genes). See Figure 1.4.1-1. Additionally, there are two types of mutations. [9]

- **Hereditary Mutations.** These mutations can be passed to descendants because they are present in a germ cell (i.e., a parent's egg or sperm cell).

- **Somatic Mutations.** These mutations are not passed to descendants because they exist in an individual's body cells - but not in a germ cell.

1.3.3 Migration

Some individuals from a population might migrate and join a population having different traits, thus changing the distribution of the traits of both populations. That is, the genetic variation of the destination population tends to increase. Technology and relaxed social and economic protectionism among societies have allowed migration to increase - and the introduction of exotic species to consequently increase.

Migration and the previous two disturbing and contributing factors of evolution (i.e., random genetic drift and mutation) alter gene frequencies with little regard to the environment or survival in it. Compared to the following fourth factor of evolution, migration and the above two factors are insignificant.

1.3.4 Natural Selection

Natural selection is not random. It is an accurate result of a critical mismatch between an organism and its environment. The variation of environments in the biosphere causes the variation of traits of individuals. That is, the variation of traits in a species (from many environments) is larger than the variation of traits in a group. Charles Darwin considered natural selection to be the key factor of evolution.[10] It is the iterative, non-random process by which

---

[9] The rate of mutations in humans is not known precisely because it can have several causes (some of which might be unknown): environmental toxins, age, copy error, etc. However, it is currently believed that there are 60 mutations for the $6,000,000,000 = 6 \times 10^9$ bases per person per generation. Therefore, for each person there are $(6 \times 10^1)/(6 \times 10^9) = 10^{-8}$ mutations for each generation (i.e., for each person there is one mutation for each 100 million bases for each generation). This means that, if each mutation occurs in a different base, all bases would be mutated once every 100,000,000 years, and an entirely new individual would occur every 100,000,000 years. See http://www.livescience.com/14620-humans-evolving-slower-expected.html.

[10] Natural selection is analogous to successfully passing the baton in a relay race.

9

biological traits become either more or less common in a species as individuals become more compatible with their environment. Natural selection may also vary with differences in fertility and mating success.

Cooperation and competition within and between species are heightened by increases in population density because basic resources become relatively scarcer. Thomas Malthus discussed this in his *Essay on the Principal of Population*. Motivation for Darwin's theory of natural selection seems to have come from, what he called, the individual's "struggle for existence."

Natural selection consists of three parts:

- A. genetic variation,

- B. heredity, and

- C. differential reproduction.

Individuals are said to be selected if they live long enough to procreate. Their genes remain in the gene pool at least until the next generation.[11]

A. Genetic Variation

Genetic variation exists within populations of all organisms. It occurs partly because the disturbances (i.e., random genetic drift, mutation, and migration) occur somewhat randomly in the genome of an individual. The characteristics of individuals of a species have different levels.[12] The occurrence of a specific characteristic can be described by a probability distribution of its levels among individuals in a population. The distribution of a level of a characteristic is defined by:

- **Type of Distribution.** The general shape of a probability distribution can usually be identified as a known type of distribution, such as the normal distribution, log-normal distribution, gamma distribution, etc.[13]

---

[11] Even though natural selection applies to all living organisms, it generally refers to humans in this book.

[12] Each characteristic has multiple levels. However, an individual can exhibit only one level of a characteristic simultaneously. A level can be quantitative or qualitative: Height is a characteristic whose quantitative level could be 183 cm. Eye color is a characteristic whose qualitative level could be blue.

[13] Consider three plausible density functions, f(x), where μ is the population mean and σ is the population standard deviation:

- Normal density: Let X be a random variable whose density is

$$f(x) = \{1/[\sigma(2\pi)^{1/2}]\} \cdot \exp\{-(1/2)[(x-\mu)/\sigma]^2\} \text{ for } -\infty < x < \infty.$$

- **Specific Distribution.** The specific shape of a selected probability distribution can usually be determined by estimating values of two independent parameters, the mean and the variance.

Genetic variation exists in all life. This fact is enormously important to the goal of socialism. The goal of socialism (i.e., to make everybody equal) is unnatural.

B. Heredity

Traits are heritable. Each individual consists of two types of inherent characteristics:

- **Genotype.** The genotype is an individual's genetic material that determines its characteristics and levels. It can be passed through consecutive generations.

- **Phenotype.** The phenotype is the manifestation of an individual's genotype (i.e., characteristics and levels): appearance, structure, functions, and behavior are not passed through consecutive generations because they result from genes of many individuals.

C. Differential Reproduction

Differential reproduction is the executive stage of *natural selection* (and, essentially, the executive stage of *evolution*). It is here that moral behavior and freedom work as a pair. Individuals are not equally capable of passing their genotypes. It is through differential reproduction that the environment, including all individuals in it, acts to select an individual (phenotype) which can then pass its genotype to its descendants.

Natural selection is so important to evolution that it, alone, is the evolutionary subject of the remainder of this book.

Darwin's theory of natural selection clearly comes from the individual's "struggle for existence." However, Darwin also believed natural selection possibly acts upon an individual's kin or its group. The *mechanism* of differential reproduction would be the same in either case. However, the results could be altered if individuals from the group cooperate to allow it to be selected

---

- Log-normal density: Let X be a random variable whose density is
$$f(x) = 0 \text{ for } x \leq c, \text{ and}$$
$$f(x) = \{1/[(x-c)\sigma(2\pi)^{1/2}]\} \cdot \exp\{-[(x-c)-\mu]^2/(2\sigma^2)\} \text{ for } x > c, \text{ where } c \text{ is a constant.}$$
- Gamma density: Let X be a random variable whose density is
$$f(x) = 0 \text{ for } x \leq 0, \text{ and}$$
$$f(x) = [b^p/\Gamma(p)] \cdot x^{p-1}e^{-bx} \text{ for } x > 0, \text{ where } b > 0 \text{ and } p > 0.$$

when it would not otherwise be selected. Alternatives to individual selection are also discussed in Chapters 3 and 4.

Order of Death and Procreation

The order of an individual's death and its procreation determines its contribution to natural selection (i.e., the gene pool):

- **Death after Procreation**. If the individual dies after its procreation is complete, its genotype is passed to its descendants; natural selection occurs.

- **Death before Procreation**. If the individual dies before it procreates, its phenotype is consumed, its genotype is not passed (i.e., neither those genes that are adequate for life in the environment nor those that are inadequate), and natural selection does not occur.

Differential reproduction is an unbiased selector. An individual is said to be selected if it lives long enough to pass its genes to a descendant.

Figure 1.4.1-1 is a structured diagram that, depending upon the relative order of death and procreation, depicts the passage of either an individual's genotype to its progeny or an individual's phenotype to the heterotrophs (that consume it). In structured diagrams,

- processes are depicted by ovals,

- input/output are depicted by rectangles, and

- decisions are depicted by diamonds.

(We use many structured diagrams in this book; these depictions allow them to be easily understood.)

1.4 Principles of Natural Selection

The principles of natural selection are the genetic levels of natural selection, criteria, and probability of natural selection.

1.4.1 Levels of Natural Selection

Although Charles Darwin conceived natural selection as selection of the individual, he wondered if natural selection also operated on the kin or group level. (For the purposes of this book, *group can be* considered to include *kin*.) [14] In *On the Origin of Species*, Darwin wrote:

---

[14] In the 1960s, W.D. Hamilton developed the idea of gene selection because it is logical for related individuals to cooperate. Later George C. Williams published *Adaptation and Natural*

"... One special difficulty, which at first appeared to me insuperable, and actually fatal to the whole theory of evolution by natural selection. I allude to the neuters or sterile females in insect-communities; for these neuters often differ widely in instinct and in structure from both the males and fertile females, and yet, from being sterile, they cannot propagate their kind.

This difficulty, though appearing insuperable, is lessened, or, as I believe, disappears when it is remembered that selection may be applied to the family, as well as to the individual, and may thus gain the desired end."[15]

Selection to further express the idea of gene level selection. Then, in 1976, Richard Dawkins published an interesting contribution to gene selection, called *The Selfish Gene*.

[15] Darwin believed that neuters and sterile females were selected due to their cooperative contribution to the group.

Figure 1.4.1-1 structured diagram of contributions to natural selection from differential reproduction, depending upon the order of death and procreation of an individual

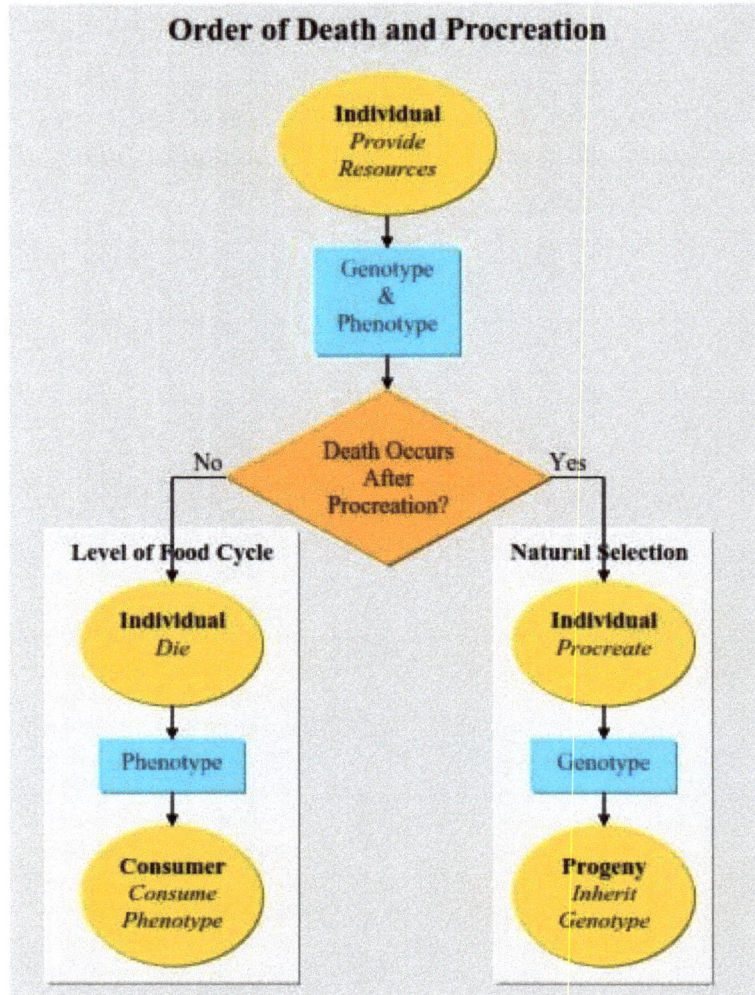

Cooperation (and some competition) naturally exists *within* groups, and competition (and some cooperation) naturally exists *between* groups.[16]

In 1962, the zoologist, V.C. Wynne-Edwards, was such a strong advocate for group selection that evolutionary ecologists began to debate it vigorously. Obviously, social behavior exists, and behavior can affect natural selection. Additionally, group selection has been observed in the regulation of population size. Specifically, a group would cooperate to limit reproduction to avoid exceeding available resources.

---

[16] The "distance" between levels of selection and within levels of selection can be measured by the value of the cross-correlation coefficient for competition and cooperation.

By 1994, some evolutionary models suggested that natural selection may act on even more levels than the individual level and the group level (although there is still debate about this). The hierarchy of possible levels of natural selection is listed in Figure 1.4.1-2, a Venn-type diagram that depicts the range of *genetic* material on Earth.

Figure 1.4.1-2 Venn-type diagram of nested biological entities illustrating how genetic material is contained in them and how natural selection can occur at all biological levels

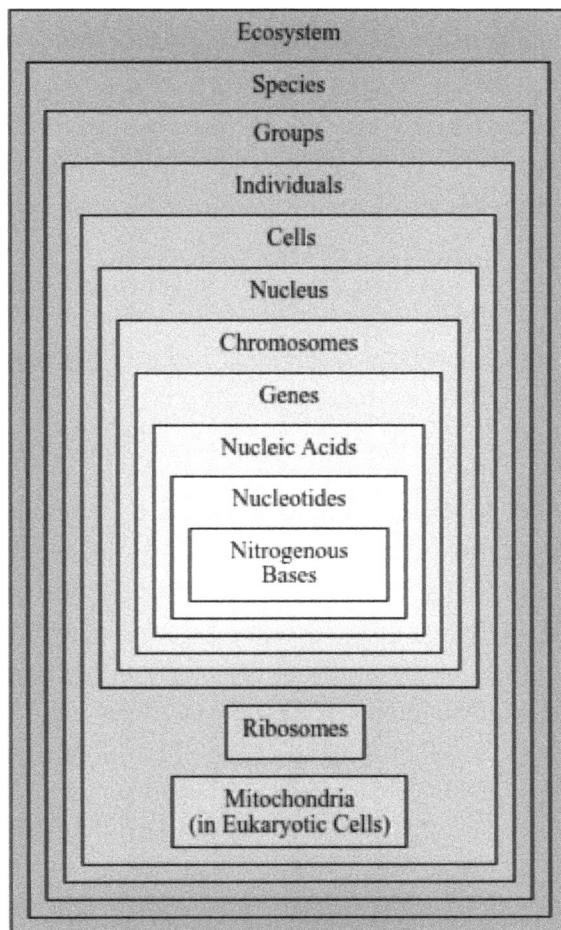

The Four Highest Biological Levels

Our interest in the possible existence of natural selection for the hierarchy of biological levels is limited to the four highest levels because the behavior of the individual becomes less magnanimous (i.e., exhibiting less empathy and less cooperation) toward individuals of levels that are genetically more distant from the individual level.

Each Trait Favors a Specific Level of Morality

Natural selection can favor different levels of morality, depending on individual traits. Natural selection exists at a higher level if cooperation with an individual of a higher (i.e., encompassing) level increases the probability of selection of the encompassing level. That is, individual, group, species, and ecosystem selection can occur if cooperation with an individual from a higher level increases the probability of selection at the higher level. If all traits of an individual are adequate at a certain level, the individual is said to be selected at that level.

Natural selection always selects at the individual level, but natural selection is said to occur at the group level only if the selected individual has traits that favor success of the group more than it favors success of the individual, the species, or the ecosystem. Similarly, natural selection is said to occur at the species level only if the selected individual possesses traits that favor success of the species more than it favors success of the individual, group, or ecosystem.

A. Individual Selection

Individual selection is called Darwinian selection. It clearly exists and is discussed widely.

B. Group Selection

Group selection is believed to exist because enabling a vulnerable member of the group to succeed might increase the probability that the group would succeed (i.e., the group would be more robust). Experiments and simulations have shown that group selection exists. The existence of group selection would be verified by the increased proportion of selected individuals or selected groups. Additionally, the *optimum degree* of cooperation would be indicated by the *greatest number* of selected individuals or groups for each type of cooperative activity (e.g., sharing a needed resource, division of a certain type of labor, etc.). Group selection is logical.

C. Species Selection[17]

Species is a unit of the taxonomical rank (under *genus*). It is usually described as the highest rank of organisms that is capable of reproducing fertile offspring (and usually from sexual reproduction).[18] If a new species were to arise from a parental line, the process would be called speciation.[19] Other means of classification are the similarity of DNA, phenotype, and ecological

---

[17] The species level of natural selection (and higher), appeals to those interested in the holistic Gaia hypothesis, etc.

[18] Presence of specific locally adapted traits may further subdivide species, such as into subspecies.

[19] Even though two species very rarely interbreed, when they do and when the offspring survive, they seem to be less vigorous than either parent.

niche.[20] It should be noted that it is difficult to make definitive statements about species because there are often unknown exceptions lurking. The uncertainty of clearly defining species is known among biologists as the "species problem."

It is clear that environments decide natural selection: Different environments favor different traits. Thomas Malthus noticed that the rate of growth of a biological population would always exceed the rate of growth of the resources in the environment - at least until resources become limited. Darwin added that those individuals that do survive will be those that have the most favorable traits with respect to the environment - even slightly more favorable.[21]

Gene expression is the process by which an organism's genotype creates its phenotype. Gene expression is also the process that implements the central dogma of molecular biology: DNA makes RNA, and RNA makes protein. Some biologists would classify a species by genotype and others would classify a species by phenotype (i.e., physical traits). The biologist, Richard Dawkins, defines any two organisms as being from the same species if they have the same number of chromosomes and each chromosome has the same number of nucleotides. See Figure 1.4.1-2.

Species have an interest in success, just as do other biological levels, but is the probability of success of a species increased by increasing its proportion (i.e., within the population of all species) or by increasing the fitness of selected individuals and/or groups within the species? That is, is the probability of species success from quality or quantity? (It is believed that there are approximately 10,000,000 species.)

D. Ecosystem Selection

The biological system is an extension of the physical system, and it is totally dependent upon it. (If the two systems, instead, were two species, this situation, a type of symbiosis, would be called commensalism.)[22] The ecosystem consists of the interacting parts of the physical system and the biological system.

Evidence of ecosystem selection exists when individuals, groups, or species are selected due to the aid of individuals of another species. *Due to entropy, virtually all proximal species are mutually dependent.* The food cycle is depicted in Figure 8.3.4-1.

---

[20] The classification of species has been profoundly improved by molecular markers that determine relatedness.

[21] *Homo sapiens* that left Sub-Saharan Africa had the remainder of the Earth to find human resources.

[22] Of course, these two systems are not species, but commensalisms are a type of symbiosis that exists when one species is left unaffected, but the other species is benefited.

The highest four biological levels (i.e., individual, group, species, and ecosystem) of multi-level selection are discussed in Section 4.1, relative to their inherent moral behavior.

1.4.2 Criteria of Natural Selection[23]

Natural selection requires that an individual's inherent and/or acquired resources are *constantly* adequate, at least until it procreates.

This book partitions human differential reproduction into three independent types of criteria. Following are the three types of criteria and a mixture of individual, cooperative, competitive, and forced behaviors that affect natural selection (i.e., differential reproduction):

1. **Environment Protection Criteria.** Environment Protection Criteria include the hazards of the physical system, such as accidents, climate, conflicts, extinction events, natural disasters, and/or an immune system that does not adequately repair physical damage. To protect themselves, individuals may also cooperate and/or compete - behaviors that alter the probability of selection.

2. **Predator-Pathogen Protection Criteria.** Predator-Pathogen Protection Criteria include consumption by predators, including an immune system that does not adequately protect against pathogens. Individuals may cooperate to increase the probability of selection. Predator-Pathogen Protection Criteria are necessary because of entropy. Entropy designs the food cycle, and humans are still part of it.

3. **Prey Acquisition Criteria.** Prey Acquisition Criteria include an individual's ability to acquire adequate resources. Individuals may cooperate or compete, behavior that alters the probability of selection. Prey Acquisition Criteria are necessary because of entropy. As stated above, humans are still part of the food cycle.

---

[23] We will usually refer to differential reproduction as natural selection. Even though *natural selection* is not as accurate, but it is common usage.

Table 1.4.2-1 lists the three independent criteria for natural selection. They are organized according to their type of environment, physical or biological.

Table 1.4.2-1 list of the three independent criteria for natural selection

Natural Selection Criteria		
Physical Environment Criteria	Biological Environment Criteria (Entropy Designs the Predator-Prey Food Cycle)	
1. Environment Protection Criteria	2. Predator-Pathogen Protection Criteria	3. Prey Acquisition Criteria

Figures 1.4.2-1 through 1.4.2-3 are structured flow diagrams that depict each of the three criteria.[24] Flow diagrams include decisions that, in this case, lead to either selection or rejection of an individual in natural selection. The results of decisions are shown at the bottom of each figure. The probability of rejection of the individual by each of the three criterion is denoted by R_1, R_2, and R_3, and the probability of selection of the individual by each criterion is denoted by $S_1 = 1 - R_1$, $S_2 = 1 - R_2$, and $S_3 = 1 - R_3$. These probabilities denote the overall probability of rejection, R, or selection, S, by the three criteria of natural selection. They are also shown in Section 1.4.3 and at the bottom of Table 5.5-1.

1. Type 1 Natural Selection: Environment Protection Criteria

The environment protection criteria for the individual could be extreme temperature, wind, flood, earthquake, physical disruptions, accident, or any other physical insult that exceeds the individual's ability to survive. The individual's habitat is sought to mitigate the physical effects.

---

[24] Flow diagrams are a type of structured diagram. As depicted in Section 1.3.4, they consist of three geometric shapes connected by arrows. For example, input to a process and output from a process is defined in rectangles, activities or processes are defined in ovals, and decisions are defined in rhombuses. (A rectangle necessarily occurs between ovals and rhombi).

19

Figure 1.4.2-1 structured diagram that depicts Type 1 natural selection

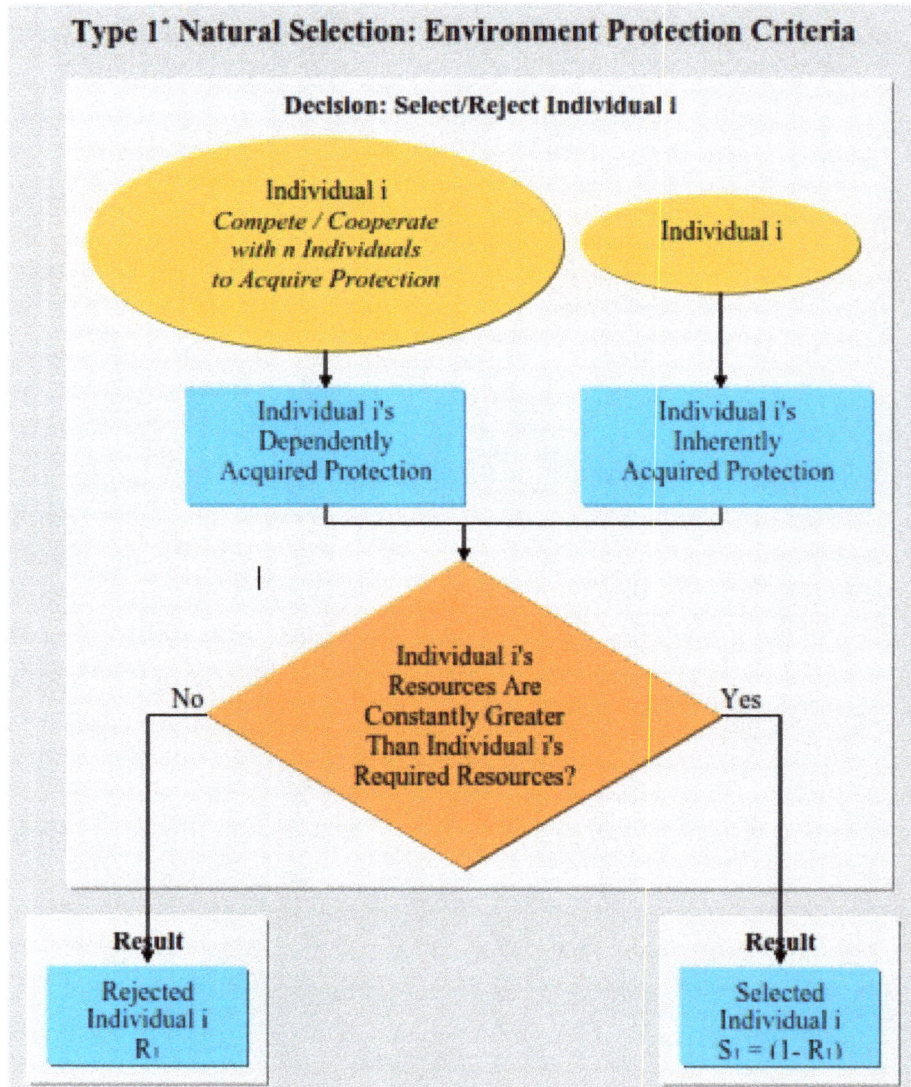

*The character, i, refers to any individual between, and including, 1 and n.

2. Type 2 Natural Selection: Predator-Pathogen Protection Criteria

The criterion for this decision is the individual's resources relative to those of its predators-pathogens. This type of selection involves cooperation for survival that can end in the death of the individual. The individual's inherent ability includes physical ability, mental ability, and behavior. Predation can come from one or more individuals of the same species, but, most often, it comes from individuals of another species.

Figure 1.4.2-2 flow diagram that depicts Type 2 natural selection

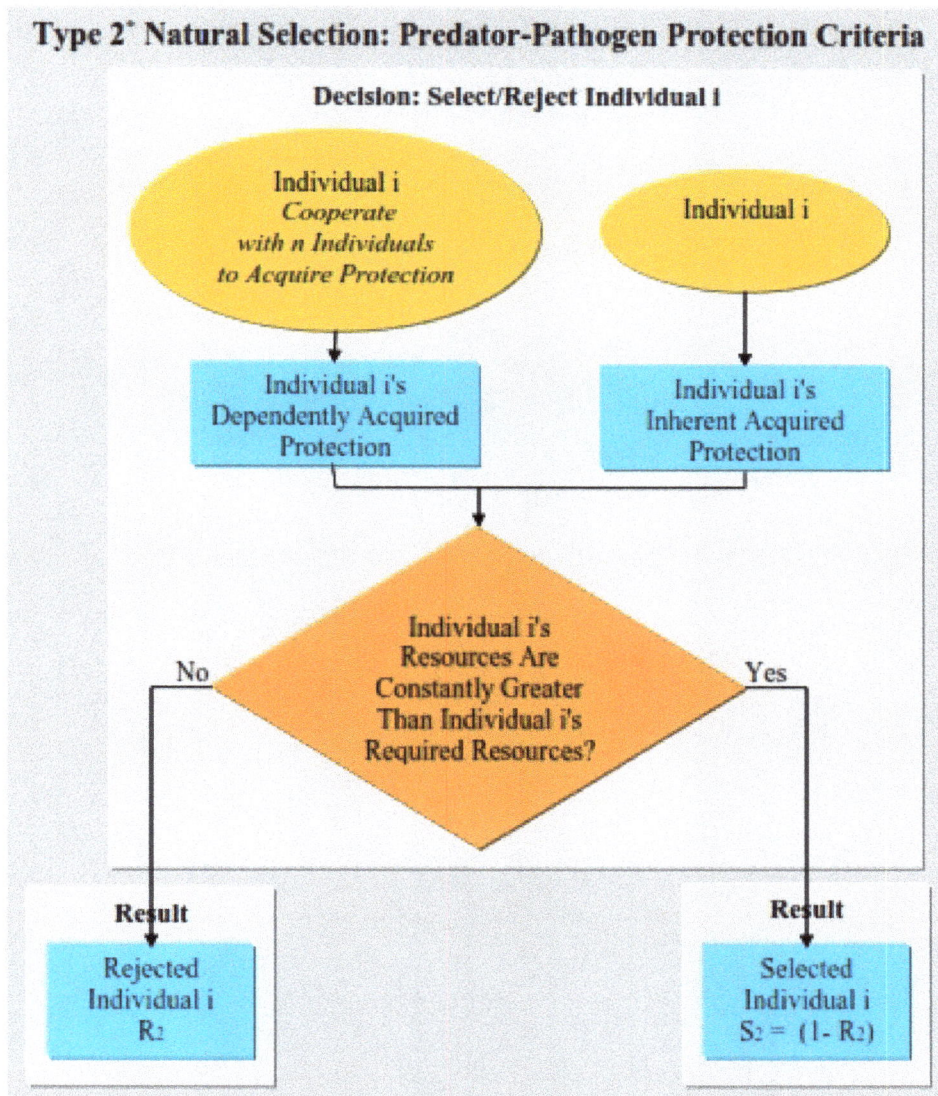

* The character, i, refers to any individual between, and including, 1 and n.

3. Type 3 Natural Selection: Prey Acquisition Criteria

Even though there is frequent competition and some cooperation, the participants must meet the nutritional criteria. (For any individual, say individual i, the acquired resources must constantly equal or exceed the required resources.)

Prey acquisition criteria are more formidable when there is competition. Because competition is frequent, individuals must be unusually capable to exceed these criteria. It is reasonable to assume that individuals also cooperate when they believe it is in their self-interest.

Competition and cooperation within and between species are heightened by increased population density because basic resources are relatively scarcer. Thomas Malthus discussed this situation in his *Essay on the Principal of Population.*

Figure 1.4.2-3 flow diagram that depicts Type 3 natural selection

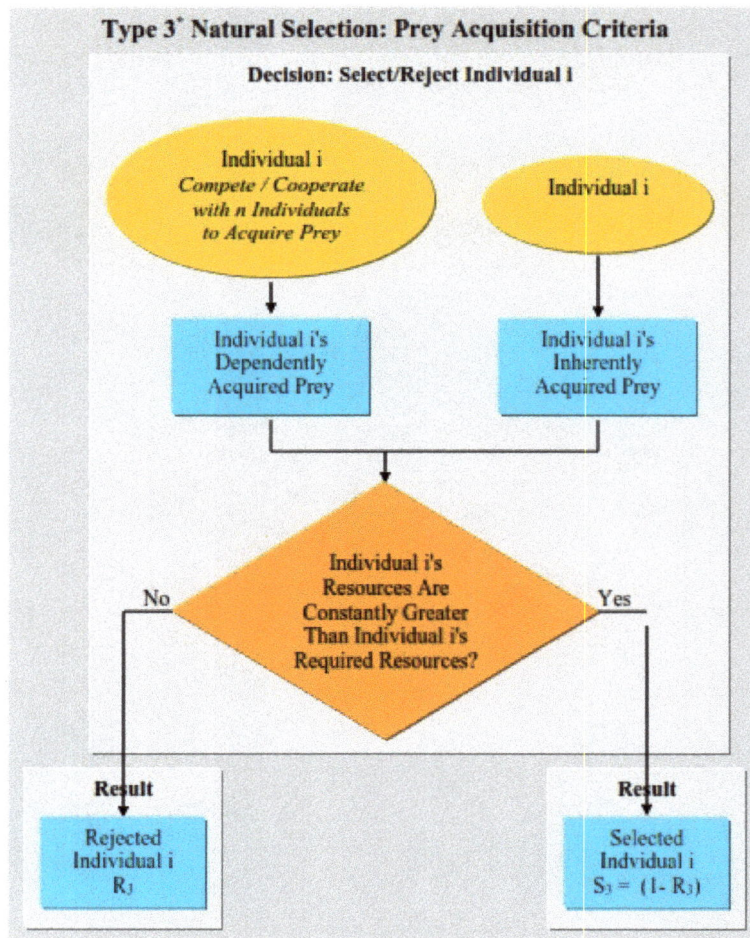

Type 3* Natural Selection: Prey Acquisition Criteria

Decision: Select/Reject Individual i

Individual i
Compete / Cooperate with n Individuals to Acquire Prey

Individual i

Individual i's Dependently Acquired Prey

Individual i's Inherently Acquired Prey

Individual i's Resources Are Constantly Greater Than Individual i's Required Resources?

No — Yes

Result — Rejected Individual i R_3

Result — Selected Individual i $S_3 = (1 - R_3)$

*The character, i , refers to any individual between, and including, 1 and n.

1.4.3 Probability of Natural Selection

Staying alive requires effort (i.e., energy). It doesn't just happen. Natural selection is free (i.e., unbiased); it is not equal; natural selection is survival of those sufficiently compatible with their environment.[25]

Due to natural selection, traits that are necessary for selection are more common in the population than by chance. As natural selection continues (and the environment remains relatively constant), essentially all individuals in the population will have increasingly compatible traits: Selected individuals will be increasingly compatible with their natural environment (i.e., the environment that designed them).

Probability of Selection

We can determine the probability that the individual will be selected if we know (or hypothesize) the probabilities that an individual will be rejected by *each* of the three criteria prior to natural selection.

Specifically, it is possible to determine the probability, R, that an individual will be rejected (i.e., not selected) during any period and in any environment prior to selection. Let R_1, R_2, and R_3 designate the probabilities that the individual will be rejected by each type of criteria, 1, 2, and 3, respectively.[26] Then, *R is the probability that at least one of the three probabilities causes rejection:*

$$R = (R_1 + R_2 + R_3) - [(R_1 \cdot R_2) + (R_1 \cdot R_3) + (R_2 \cdot R_3)] + (R_1 \cdot R_2 \cdot R_3),$$

where each probability is expressed as a decimal (e.g., 0.18 rather than 18%).

---

[25] Some who believe that free markets are immoral believe so because free market decisions are similar to natural selection – necessarily natural and without compassion.

[26] Generally, numbers are combined as we were taught in grade school. However, probabilities are combined in a different way. Recall the duck test: If a bird looks like a duck, swims like a duck, and quacks like a duck, then it is probably a duck. For simplicity, assume all three characteristics resemble those of a duck with the same, 50% probability. If the three probabilities were added as numbers, there would be 150% probability that the bird is a duck – but, because this is greater than 100%, it is impossible. As in the above equation, the probability is slightly greater than 87.5% that at least one of the probabilities is true (that the bird is a duck). From U.S. Patent 6,125,340, issued to Martin J. Miles on September 26, 2000: *A System for Determining the Probability that Items of Evidence Prove a Conclusion* (67 claims)

Example

Suppose that during a specified period, prior to selection, and in a specified environment, there is a probability that a specified individual will be rejected. Each criterion is:

- **Criteria #1.** Probability that the individual's inherent resources will not continually exceed the environment protection criteria: $R_1 = 0.01$.

- **Criteria #2.** Probability that an individual's inherent resources will not continually exceed the predatory-pathogen protection criteria (including the individual's immune system that repairs injuries and protects against pathogens): $R_2 = 0.08$.

- **Criteria #3.** Probability that the individual's acquired resources will not continually exceed the prey acquisition criteria, given the competition from other individuals: $R_3 = 0.20$.

Determine the probability, R, that the individual will be rejected during this period and in this environment.

Solution

Given these conditions and these probabilities,
$$R = (0.01 + 0.08 + 0.20)$$
$$- [(0.01 \times 0.08) + (0.01 \times 0.20) + (0.08 \times 0.20)]$$
$$+ [(0.01 \times 0.08 \times 0.20)].$$

Then,
$$R = 0.29$$
$$- (0.0008 + 0.0020 + 0.0160)$$
$$+ 0.00016.$$

Then,
$$R = 0.29$$
$$- 0.00188 + 0.00016.$$

Now, the probability that the individual will be rejected is
$$R = 0.27136.[27]$$

That is, the probability that an individual will be selected is
$$S = 1 - R = 1 - 0.27 \approx 73\%.$$

---

[27] Since the probability of each type of decision is known only to two significant figures (i.e., decimal places), the probability, R, can also be known only to two significant figures. Hence, R = 0.27.

Chapter 2 Evolution of Humans
(15 Million BC - Present)[28]

The ecosystem is the interacting parts of the physical system and the biological system. Humans were indistinguishable from the ecosystem until they fashioned the first tools (i.e., the first evidence of capital). Practically, the first tool, a knapped stone, was used to *kill or butcher* animals, but symbolically, the first tool moved humans higher among the predators in the food cycle.

A human group is a small number of families and friends - usually fewer than one hundred individuals. Humans essentially traveled only in groups from 15 million BC until 5,000 BC - when events allowed them to migrate, merge, and create larger societies.

Cells, organisms, animals, mammals, and humans make progressively complex decisions. However, the development of tools created abilities and opportunities for human decisions that could not have been imagined. The mind that created tools was capable of instinct, emotion, and reason - and decisions that allocated between emotion and reason.

We define capital to be knowledge and the manifestations of knowledge. We will usually refer to tools or innovations as capital.

Purpose of This Chapter

The purpose of this chapter is to describe the evolution of humans until they eventually merged into societies that are larger than groups of family and friends (i.e., 5,000 BC).

Capital can cause unintended consequences, notably, consequences arising when the rate of innovation far exceeds the rate of human evolution. Capital is creating types of situations in which humans have yet to adapt.

The sections of this chapter are:

2.1 Innovations during the Primitive Capital Era

2.2 Evolution of Humans

---

[28] We include times for humans only if they have persisted (i.e., *Homo sapiens*). We are grateful to all the scientists that have estimated the important knowledge of humans and their history. Even though they have provided so much information, there are still some uncertainties – especially about dates. We believe that the uncertainty about dates does not affect our conclusions.

Primitive Capital Era: 2.5 Million BC - 5,000 BC

In this book, the Primitive Capital Era begins in 2.5 million BC and ends in 5,000 BC. This period also roughly corresponds to both the geological Pleistocene Epoch and the anthropological Paleolithic Age. [29] We introduce and discuss the Primitive Capital Era here because it will help us discuss morality in subsequent chapters.

Beginning of the Primitive Capital Era: 2.5 Million BC

The beginning of the Primitive Capital Era coincides with both the current ice age and the Stone Age: [30]

- **Pleistocene Epoch (i.e., Current Ice Age).** The current ice age began 2.5 million years ago. Glaciations caused lower sea levels that allowed humans to migrate over land from Asia (along the Bering Straits) to the Americas before 10,000 BC, and allowed humans to spread to all continents. Cycles of glaciations (i.e., advancing ice sheets) and inter-glaciations (i.e., retreating ice sheets) occur every 40,000-100,000 years.[31]

---

[29] The Paleolithic Age relates to the early phase of the Stone Age, when primitive stone implements were used. It lasted from 2.5 million BC to 8,000 BC. The Pleistocene Epoch corresponds to the epoch forming the earlier half of the Quaternary Period. It lasted from 2.5 million years ago to approximately 9,700 BC. It was characterized by widespread glacial ice and the advent of modern humans.

[30] Even though dates of primitive and ancient milestones are being known with greater accuracy, there are two caveats: Dates are the current earliest *known* dates and the current *uncertainty* in dating technology.

[31] In the last 2.5 million years, there have been five Ice Ages.

- **Paleolithic Age (i.e., Stone Age).** The Stone Age began 2.5 million years ago with the emergence of humans and the fashioning of stone tools:
  - **Humans Emerged.** The genus *Homo* evolved in Ethiopia and traveled in small groups of approximately 100 family and friends. Humans subsisted by hunting and gathering.
  - **Tools Are Fashioned.** The first tool, a knapped stone tool, for killing or scraping animal flesh, was fashioned in Ethiopia. Other tools, fashioned from plants and animals, might have existed, but no evidence of them could remain.[32]
- **Primitive Capital Era:** We consider the Primitive Capital Era to begin 2.5 million years ago when the current ice age and the Stone Age began. Also, at that time, humans emerged and other tools were fashioned.

Ending of the Primitive Capital Era: 5,000 BC

The events that ended the Primitive Capital Era occurred somewhat after the time that the Pleistocene Epoch ended and the anthropologic Paleolithic Age ended:

- **Pleistocene Epoch (i.e., Current Ice Age).** The Pleistocene Epoch ended in approximately 9,700 BC.

- **Paleolithic Age (i.e., Stone Age).** The Paleolithic Age ended in 8,000 BC.

- **Primitive Capital Era.** We consider the Primitive Capital Era to have ended in approximately 5,000 BC because the human population is thought to have accelerated then:
  - **Humans Merge.** Small groups merged into larger societies around 5,000 BC. The mixing of family and friends with strangers not only ended the Primitive Capital Era, but it created a new human environment (called the Ancient Period). Application of tools and the end of the current Ice Age seemed to allow human groups to coalesce, "outstripping" human evolution, and causing severe emotional disruption and disease to organisms that had not adapted immunity to exotic pathogens.
  - **Tools Allow Populations to Accelerate.** Multiple innovations and possibly the current ice age allowed the human population to accelerate about 5,000 BC.[33]

---

[32] Even though there is some evidence that the beginning of tools and the Stone Age is 3,400,000 BC, we will use the 2,500,000 BC date. The exact date is unimportant for the purposes of this book.

[33] Some believe that the population acceleration caused Neanderthals to become extinct.

Figure 2-1 depicts the relationship among four significant periods for humans. It covers periods from the beginning of the Earth to the present. The period is divided into 10 cycles of a logarithmic scale. Each cycle is a period between consecutive powers of 10 (i.e., a cycle is from 1 to 10, from 10 to 100, from 100 to 1,000, etc.).

Figure 2-1 relationships among four significant periods for humans

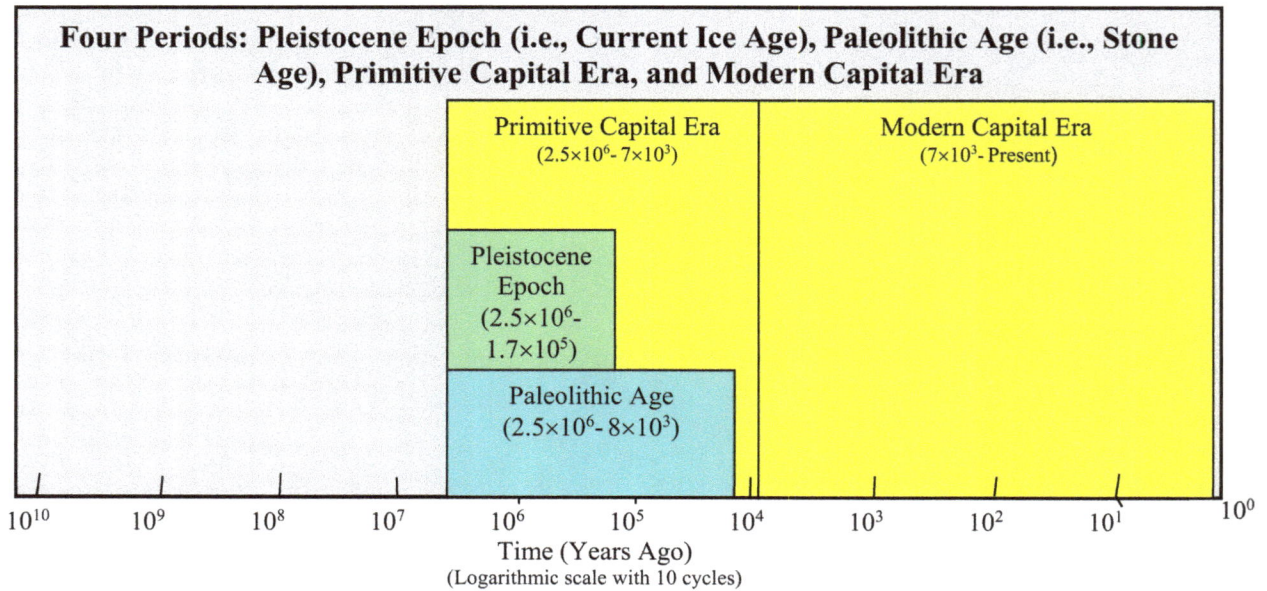

Four Periods: Pleistocene Epoch (i.e., Current Ice Age), Paleolithic Age (i.e., Stone Age), Primitive Capital Era, and Modern Capital Era

Primitive Capital Era (2.5×10^6- 7×10^3)	Modern Capital Era (7×10^3- Present)
Pleistocene Epoch (2.5×10^6- 1.7×10^5)	
Paleolithic Age (2.5×10^6- 8×10^3)	

10^{10} 10^9 10^8 10^7 10^6 10^5 10^4 10^3 10^2 10^1 10^0

Time (Years Ago)
(Logarithmic scale with 10 cycles)

28

2.1 Innovations during the Primitive Capital Era

There is always a delay for the effects (intended and unintended) of tools to be realized. In the modern economy, many years were required for the benefits of electricity and the Internet to be realized. Gradually - very gradually - accretion of innovations and the end of the current ice age allowed groups to merge into larger societies.

Table 2.1-1 lists some significant dates, innovations, milestones, societies, and life spans during the Primitive Capital Era: 2,500,000 BC - 5,000 BC.

Table 2.1-1   dates of some significant innovations, milestones, society types, and life spans:
2,500,000 BC - 5,000 BC

Date	#	Innovation/Milestone	Society Type	Human Life Span (Years)
2,500,000 BC	1	Beginning of Genus *Homo*[1]	Groups 10s-100s	-
	2	Stone Tools (Paleolithic Age)		
	3	Current Ice Age (Pleistocene Epoch)		
1,000,000 BC	4	Domestication of Fire[2]		
380,000 BC	5	Dwellings		
190,000 BC	6	Stone Tools (hand axe, spear, and awl)		
180,000 BC	7	Burial of dead, using some rituals/headstones		
170,000 BC	8	Clothing[3]		15
100,000 BC	9	Migration from Africa as *Homo sapiens*		
25,000 BC	10	Ceramics (and perhaps the first liquid container because ceramics could be fashioned as concave)		18
15,000 BC	11	Domestication of Animals		20
10,000 BC	12	Religions		
9,700 BC	13	Ending of Current Ice Age		
9,000 BC	14	Bow and Arrow		
8,000 BC	15	Domestication of Agriculture (and plow)		
	16	Copper Tools (Neolithic Period)		
5,000 BC	17	World Human Population Accelerates		

1 The lifespan of great apes is currently 35-50 years, but their lifespan 15,000,000 years ago might have been different.

2 Knapping and flaking stones to create scraping tools is similar to using pieces of flint and stones to "spark" fires. Even so, the next known innovation, domestication of fire, came 1,500,000 years after these tools were fashioned.

3 Before money, trade existed in prehistoric time and was known as barter. Early trading was in obsidian and flint during the Stone Age. In Europe, early trading began along the Danube River around 35,000 - 30,000 BC.

2.2 Evolution of Humans

The three domains of life are Archaea, Bacteria, and Eukarya. Humans belong to the domain, Eukarya. Within this domain, humans belong successively to the kingdom Animalia; phylum Chordata; class Mammalia; order Primates; family Hominidae; subfamily Homininae; tribe Hominini; sub tribe Hominina; genus *Homo*; species *Homo sapiens*; and subspecies *Homo sapiens sapiens*.

Table 2.2-1 lists the times of origin, taxonomic classifications, and types of humans. It also includes some information about humans as long ago as 15,000,000 BC.

Table 2.2-1   time of origin, classification, and type of human from 15,000,000 BC

Time of Origin	Classification	Type of Humans
15,000,000 BC	Family: Hominidae	Great Apes (i.e., humans, chimpanzees, bonobos, gorillas, and orangutans)
7,500,000 BC	Subfamily: Homininae	Humans, chimpanzees, bonobos, and gorillas
5,800,000 BC	Tribe: Hominini	Homo and Australopithecina
3,000,000 BC	Subtribe: Hominina	Human branch, including genus *Homo*
2,500,000 BC	Genus: *Homo*	Humans, *Homo habilis*, and their direct ancestors
500,000 BC	Species: *Homo sapiens*	Humans, *Homo erectus*, *Homo habilis*, and *Homo sapiens*
200,000 BC	Subspecies: *Homo sapiens sapiens*	Modern Humans, *Homo sapiens sapiens*

Figure 2.2-1 is a Venn-type diagram that depicts the increasingly specific taxonomic classification of humans, beginning 15 million years ago with the family Hominidae - the great apes - and ending with modern humans, the subspecies *Homo sapiens sapiens*.[34] Essentially, Figure 2.2-1 depicts the data listed in Table 2.2-1.

---

[34] In the 18th century, Carolus Linnaeus devised the method of classifying and naming species: Each species is assigned a binomial Latin name, formed by appending the species name to the genus name; the genus name is capitalized, but the species name is not; both the genus name and the species name are italicized.

Figure 2.2-1 Venn-type diagram of the taxonomy of humans

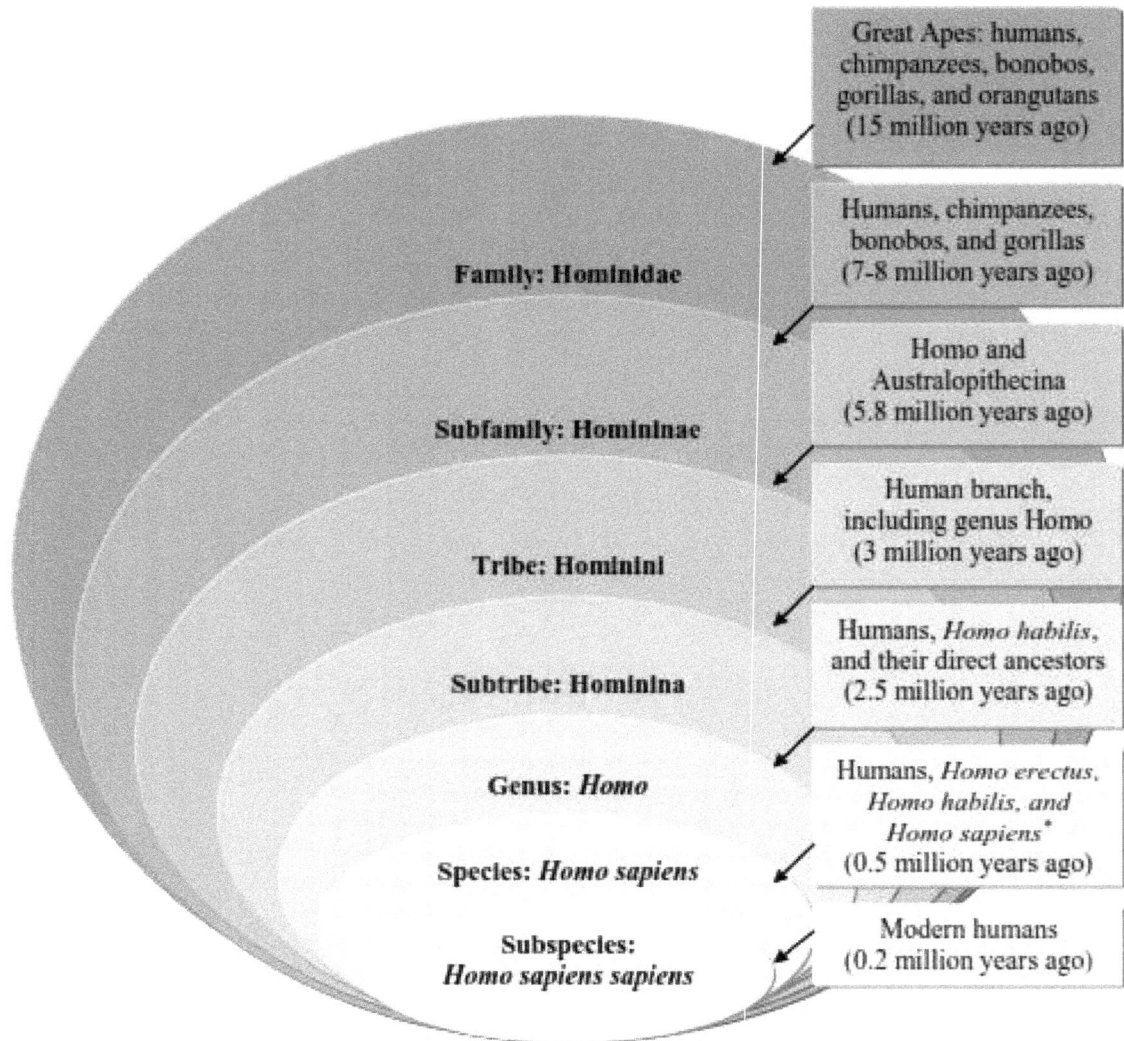

Great Apes: humans, chimpanzees, bonobos, gorillas, and orangutans (15 million years ago)

Humans, chimpanzees, bonobos, and gorillas (7-8 million years ago)

Homo and Australopithecina (5.8 million years ago)

Human branch, including genus Homo (3 million years ago)

Humans, *Homo habilis*, and their direct ancestors (2.5 million years ago)

Humans, *Homo erectus*, *Homo habilis, and Homo sapiens** (0.5 million years ago)

Modern humans (0.2 million years ago)

Family: Hominidae

Subfamily: Homininae

Tribe: Hominini

Subtribe: Hominina

Genus: *Homo*

Species: *Homo sapiens*

Subspecies: *Homo sapiens sapiens*

* Scientists debate whether Neanderthals were *Homo neanderthalensis* or *Homo sapiens neanderthalensis* (i.e., a subspecies of *Homo sapiens*).

2.2.1 Family: Hominidae

Approximately 15 million years ago the family of great apes (i.e., humans, bonobos, chimpanzees, gorillas, and orangutans) evolved; approximately 14 million years ago, humans split from orangutans; approximately 8 million years ago humans split from gorillas; and approximately 7 million years ago humans split from chimpanzees and bonobos; and, finally, these humans walked upright in the plains of eastern Africa. [35]

Approximately 2.5 million years ago, some hominids in Ethiopia (thought to be the species *Homo habilis*) knapped stones to develop the first tools - cutting tools for butchering animals.[36] This event and the evolution of the genus *Homo* initiated the Group Era.

2.2.2 Genus: *Homo*

The origin of the genus *Homo* is not clear; that is, a number of species has been proposed as the origin of the genus *Homo*. *Homo habilis* ("handy man") existed at least 2.5 million years ago in Ethiopia, and *Homo erectus* ("upright man") existed at least 1.8 million years ago. Even though they coexisted for about 0.5 million years in Kenya, it is believed that they evolved independently.[37] *Homo erectus* had a brain whose size was about 74% that of modern humans. *Homo habilis* is generally believed to have been slightly more advanced than *Homo erectus*. Homo fossils were found recently in the nation of Georgia in the Caucuses. This discovery confirmed the presence of either *Homo habilis* or *Homo erectus* near Europe at least 1.7 million years ago.

2.2.3 Species: *Homo sapiens*

Homo sapiens ("wise man") were known to live in the Herto village on the Awash River of Ethiopia about 500,000 years ago. They practiced mortuary rituals, fished, and butchered hippopotami. *Homo sapiens* is the only surviving species of the genus *Homo*. *Homo neanderthalensis*, considered by some to be the last surviving relative of *Homo sapiens*, became extinct about 24,000 years ago.

---

[35] Our closest *living* relatives are chimpanzees and gorillas. After 7 million years of separation, the difference between a modern human and a modern chimpanzee is less than 5% - but this is ten times greater than the difference between two unrelated modern humans.

[36] *The Oldowan* is the term that refers to the earliest stone tool industry.

[37] The oldest known preserved DNA is that of a horse, preserved in the permafrost of the Klondike region of Alaska. That DNA is 700,000 years old.

2.2.4 Subspecies: Homo sapiens sapiens

It is believed that (all) modern humans, the subspecies sapiens, *Homo sapiens sapiens,* emerged from Africa approximately 100,000 years ago. The subspecies *Homo sapiens sapiens*, is the only existing extant of the species *Homo sapiens*. The other subspecies, *Homo sapiens idaltu,* ("Elder wise man") is extinct.

Figure 2.2.4-1 depicts the migration of *Homo sapiens* from Sub-Saharan Africa. *Homo sapiens* left Sub-Saharan Africa approximately 100,000 years ago. They might have left at Suez and gone to the Middle-East. Some 30,000 years later, some of those who migrated out of Africa to the Middle-East migrated east and into Asia. They evolved into the Mongoloid race. Then about 30,000 years later others migrated west from the Middle-East. They entered Europe through the Caucuses and evolved into the Caucasoid race.[38] Genetic data suggest that the Caucasoid and the Mongoloid races are closer to each other than either is to the Negroid race.[39] They gradually populated all continents until they reached South America approximately 11,000 years ago. Because previous migrants (*Homo erectus*) from Africa were extinct, *Homo sapiens* apparently did not encounter other humans. That is, the émigrés had virtually no human competition for 100,000 years while those that remained continued to have significant human competition. As we shall see in Section 8.3.8, this difference in human competition seems to be very significant.

Then 7,000 years ago, capital allowed humans to migrate more easily. This secondary type of migration caused frequent interactions with strangers.

2.3 Evolution of the Human Brain

Great research is being conducted to understand the human brain. But since there is much yet to learn, there is also substantial disagreement. Even though we present facts that seem to be accurate, undoubtedly some will be modified as more knowledge is available.

The functions of many regions of the human brain are known passively, by examining patients who lost the functions after damage to a specific region. Other functions are known actively, by probing with research methods such as attached electrodes, magnetic resonance imaging, etc.

The Hunter-Gatherer Brain

The human brain evolved for success as hunter-gatherers in the plains of Africa, not for success in the modern world created by technology. Social scientists say that we seem to prefer stories

---

[38] Cro Magnon is the name given to the oldest known *Homo sapiens sapiens* to live in Europe - approximately 43,000 years ago. Their average lifespan was 18 years.

[39] https://pubmed.ncbi.nlm.nih.gov/7163193/

to facts, and we prefer anecdotes to statistical experiments. Consequently, relating stories and anecdotes require less energy than analyzing facts and experiments (that require methodical, deliberative, and logical thinking). Thinking as hunter-gatherers (i.e., using instinct, emotion, and minimal reasoning) is the natural mode.

Figure 2.2.4-1 where and when *Homo sapiens* migrated during the last 100,000 years

- Most *Homo sapiens* remained in Africa and continued to evolve as Negroids during this 100,000 period.
- In this primary migration, *Homo sapiens* migrated from Sub-Saharan Africa approximately 100,000 years ago to the Middle-East. Approximately 70,000 years ago some moved east to Asia and evolved as Mongoloids, and approximately 40,000 years ago, some of those migrants moved west to Europe and evolved as Caucasoids. Some Middle-Eastern people remained.
- In many secondary migrations, approximately 7,000 years ago, groups dispersed and caused many strangers to interact – causing human conflicts to begin evolving propensities for species morality.
- From 200-400 years ago, the slave trade brought some Sub-Saharan Africans to the Americas. (This forced migration is depicted by the very, very short line segment, resembling a dot, on the right side.)

Legend
Era of Evolution due to Physical Environments (i.e., Group Era) (100,000-7,000 years ago)

Era of Evolution due to Physical Environments & Conflicts with Strangers (i.e., Species Era) (7,000-0 years ago) (See Section 8.3.2.)

Environments in which *Homo sapiens* have evolved over the Last 100,000 Years

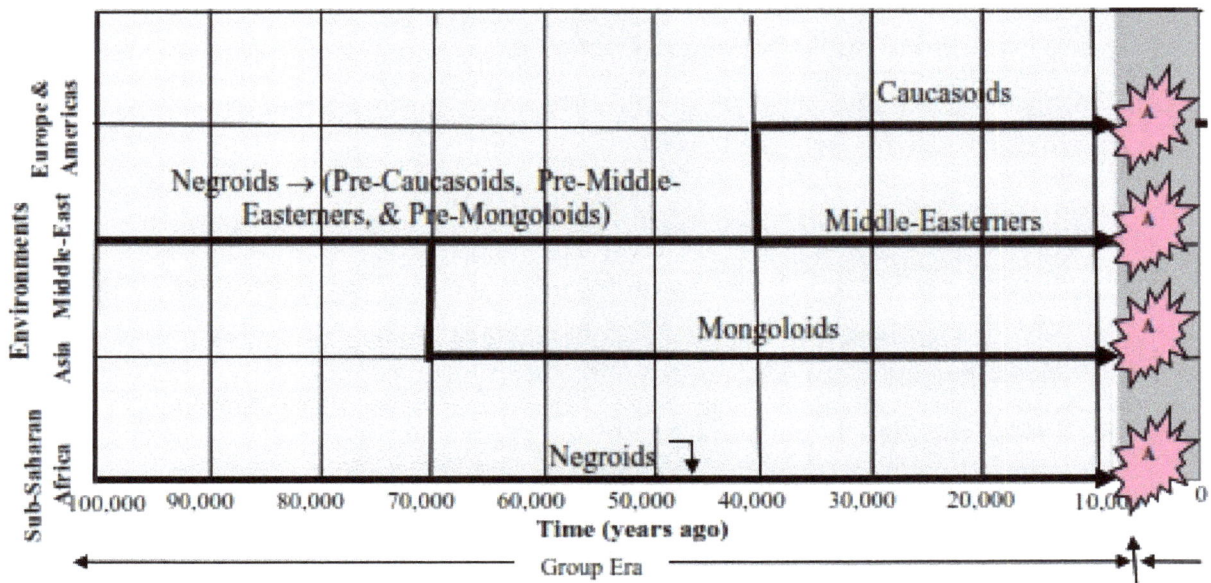

*Sub-Saharan African slaves were brought to the Americas 200-400 years ago. Therefore, they evolved for 200-400 years in the Americas as Caucasoids. The very, very short line segment (i.e. like a dot) could be labeled as Negroids→ Caucasoids.

Beginning of Species Era (7,000 years ago)

The Triune Brain

The brain is the body's control center. It receives, interprets, and sends sensory information throughout the body. The human brain seems to have evolved in three successive layers of functional sophistication, each on top of another - analogous to layers of an archeological digging site. The three-layer human brain is called the triune brain.[40] Beginning at the bottom of the brain (which is the top of the spinal cord) the layers are:

- **Reptilian Brain.** The reptilian brain facilitates instincts and motor control for growth, maintenance, and reproduction.

- **Limbic Brain (i.e., Old Mammalian Brain).** The limbic brain (i.e., also called the limbic system) facilitates emotion, memory, motivation, olfaction, etc.

- **Neocortex (i.e., New Mammalian Brain).** The neocortex facilitates reason, speech, abstract thinking, etc.

Roughly, the reptilian brain provides *instinct*, the limbic brain provides *emotion*, and the neocortex provides *reason*.

2.3.1 Reptilian Brain

Since the reptilian brain is the oldest of the three layers, it formed directly on top of the spinal cord. It is quick, constant, and reflexive. It controls the body's vital functions and motor control. (Reptiles evolved 315 million years ago.)[41]

The two structures of the reptilian brain are the brain stem and the cerebellum.

Brain Stem

The brain stem consists of two parts:

- **Medulla Oblongata.** The medulla oblongata is the part of the brain stem that controls *autonomic functions*, such as breathing, heart rate, and digestion.

- **Pons.** The pons is the other part of the brain stem that controls *sensory information*, primarily bladder control, equilibrium, eye movement, facial expressions, facial sensation, hearing, posture, respiration, sleep, swallowing, and taste. It also contains the

---

[40] The triune brain model was proposed by the American physician and neuroscientist, Paul D. MacLean, in the 1960s and described in his 1990 book, *The Triune Brain in Evolution*.

[41] Earliest evidence of a brain structure dates to 0.526 billion years ago.

small locus ceruleus (i.e., dark blue spot) that aids physiological responses to stress and panic - responses such as homeostasis.[42]

Cerebellum

The cerebellum is next to the brain stem and behind the pons. It controls motor activity such as accuracy and coordination. It receives signals from the sensory system of the spinal cord and from other parts of the brain. It is also thought to contribute to cognitive functions such as attention, fear, language, and pleasure.

2.3.2 Limbic Brain[43, 44]

The limbic brain evolved with the first small mammals approximately 250 million years ago to control fight-or-flight responses. Since it records many types of memories, including "good" and "bad" experiences, it is responsible for emotion in humans. The limbic brain, along with the neocortex, is the seat of our decisions - often unconscious decisions.

The limbic brain is believed to include the following several structures - of which the two amygdala are most important to the subjects of this book because their interactions with the neocortex produce behavior that can be considered moral. (See Figure 2.3.4-1 concerning decision-making.)

Amygdala

The amygdala is two almond-shaped bodies, one on each side of the brain. They have many connections to *warn* of significant situations, particularly those related to memories, the sense of smell, social interactions, and survival:

- **Memories.** The amygdala is concerned with episodic-autobiographical memory (EAM). It decides *which* of these memories are stored and *where* they are stored. (It is thought that these two types of decisions - *which* and *where* - depend upon the emotional intensity of the response to an event.) The amygdala *defines* a stimulus and, therefore, helps an individual respond appropriately.

_____

[42] Homeostasis is the ability of an organism to maintain its conditions when conditions in its environment change.

[43] There are disagreements about which anatomical bodies should be included in the limbic brain. Some scientists believe the concept of the limbic brain should be abandoned, apparently because it has many structures and they are more diverse than those of the reptilian brain and the neocortex.

[44] The many regions of the cerebral cortex are called areas, cortices, fields, gyri, lobes, sulci, etc.

- **Sense of Smell.** The amygdala is involved with the sense of smell and pheromone-processing. It receives information from the olfactory bulb and the olfactory cortex.

- **Social Interactions.** The amygdala and the neocortex cooperate to play an important role in the acceptability of modern life. Specifically, individuals with larger amygdala tend to have greater emotional intelligence:

    o **Acceptability.** They have greater social integration and cooperation.

    o **Judgments.** They exhibit social judgments that are more accurate, including those related to trust and facial expressions.

    o **Social Networks.** They have larger and more complex social networks.

- **Survival.** The amygdala is involved in many of our emotions and motivations, particularly those related to survival. After receiving signals from the thalamus, the amygdala sends signals to other systems in the brain:

    o **Hippocampus.** The amygdala signals the hippocampus (of the limbic brain) regarding *memories* of spatial details surrounding significant situations.

    o **Neocortex.** The amygdala signals the neocortex regarding *significant stimuli* (i.e., aggression, anger, arousal, fear, protecting personal space, and reward).

Other Structures and Regions of the Limbic Brain

- **Anterior Thalamic Nuclei.**[45] The anterior thalamic nuclei modulate alertness, learning, and memory.

- **Basil Ganglia.** The basil ganglia control voluntary motor movements, habitual behavior, procedures, cognition, and eye movement.

- **Brain Stem Nuclei.** Brain stem nuclei are the 12 cranial nerves, including motor and sensory nerves that originate in the brain stem (i.e., medulla, midbrain, and pons).

- **Fornix.** The fornixes carry signals from the hippocampus to the mammillary bodies and to the septal nuclei (i.e., see the last bullet of this section).

- **Hippocampus.** The hippocampus creates long-term memories and cognitive maps for navigation.

---

[45] In the brain, a nucleus is a structure consisting of a *cluster of neurons*. It is one of the two most common forms of nerve cell organization. The other common form of nerve cell organization consists of *layers of neurons*, such as the cerebral cortex.

- **Hypothalamus**. The hypothalamus strongly influences autonomic control, behavioral functions, endocrine functions, and sexual functions.

- **Limbic Lobe.** The limbic lobe has three parts (i.e., three wrinkles that are called gyri). The three gyri are:

  - **Cingulate Gyrus.** The cingulate gyrus regulates blood pressure, heart rate, attentional processing, and cognitive processing.

  - **Dentate Gyrus.** The dentate gyrus aids formation of new memories.

  - **Parahippocampal Gyrus.** The parahippocampal gyrus aids formation of spatial memories.

- **Mammillary Bodies**. The mammillary bodies aid formation of recognition memory.

- **Olfactory Bulb.** The olfactory bulb is a filter that receives information from structures, such as the amygdala, hippocampus, locus coeruleus, and neocortex.

- **Septal Nuclei.** The septal nuclei are a pleasure area.

2.3.3 Thalamus: the Brain's Switchboard

The two thalami are part of the brain, but they don't naturally belong to any one of the three parts of the triune brain. Rather, they are a major switchboard in the brain, particularly between the limbic brain and the neocortex; they decide the transfer of nearly all signals from the structures of the limbic brain to the cerebral cortex. The two thalami resemble two very small eggs, one under each of the two cerebral hemispheres and above many structures of the limbic brain.

Some signals that are sent to the cerebral cortex pass through the thalamus.

Passing through the Thalamus

The following types of information pass through the thalamus:

- **From Multiple Sensory Modality Inputs.** Some sensory information from sensory modality inputs is transferred through the thalami to the cerebral cortex.[46]

- **From the Cerebellum (of the Reptilian Brain) or the Basal Ganglia.** All motor and planning information is transferred from the cerebellum or the basal ganglia through the thalamus to the cerebral cortex.

---

[46] Some modality inputs are auditory (including the vestibular system), olfactory, tactile, and visual.

- **From the Amygdala or the Mammillary Bodies**. Emotional and motivational information from the amygdala of the mammillary bodies is transferred through the thalamus to the cerebral cortex.

Not Passing through the Thalamus

The following types of information pass to the cerebral cortex along other pathways:

- **From the Amygdala.** Some information from the amygdala moves directly to the prefrontal cortex (in the cerebral cortex).

- **From the Olfactory Bulb.** Some information from the olfactory bulb moves directly to the olfactory cortex (in the cerebral cortex).

- **From the Brain Stem Nuclei.** Neuromodulatory projections from the brain stem nuclei move directly to the cerebral cortex.

2.3.4 Neocortex

Since the neocortex (i.e., "new bark") is the newest layer of the cerebral cortex, it is the outermost layer. The neocortex comprises 90% of the cerebral cortex; it is the "grey matter." The neocortex first appeared with the evolution of larger mammals and primates 75,000 years ago. It consists of six layers, labeled from I to VI, where I is the outermost and VI is the innermost (as if there will be no future layers). The neocortex is responsible for abstract thought, attention, consciousness, culture, imagination, information processing, language, logic/reason, and memory. It has almost unlimited learning abilities.

Even though the neocortex has many regions, we shall concentrate on two regions that are most relevant to the subjects of this book:

- **Dorsolateral Prefrontal Cortex.** The dorsolateral prefrontal cortex develops logic.

- **Ventromedial Prefrontal Cortex**. The ventromedial prefrontal cortex decides by weighing the relative importance of logic from the dorsolateral prefrontal cortex and emotion from the amygdala.

Dorsolateral Prefrontal Cortex

The dorsolateral prefrontal cortex (dlPFC) does not mature until adulthood. It is a functional region of the neocortex rather than a clearly defined structure. The dlPFC communicates with the neo-cerebellum, posterior cingulate, posterior parietal cortex, premotor cortex, and retrosplenial cortex. These communications provide mutual regulation between these five structures and the dlPFC. The dlPFC also provides two extremely important types of functions - executive and decision-making:

- **Executive.** The dlPFC provides management of cognitive functions such as

    o cognitive flexibility (i.e., ability to switch attention between two concepts),

    o inhibition,

    o planning,

    o logic, and

    o working memory (i.e., holding information in memory).[47]

Using these executive functions, three types of tasks have been studied extensively:

    o A-not-B,[48]

    o delayed response, and

    o object retrieval.

- **Decision-Making.** Since the dlPFC decision-making does not communicate with (emotions from) the amygdala, its decisions are logical (i.e., not emotional). The working memory executive function is essential for decision-making because a decision compares two types of information - a sequential process. Deciding morally and evaluating risk accurately are essential to survival (i.e., success):

    o **Group Morality.** The dlPFC decides to distribute scarce resources equitably and to suppress greed. (Such decisions are consistent with group selection and with the belief that group morality is inherited.)

    o **Risk**. The dlPFC minimizes risk by

        ▪ knowing values,

        ▪ comparing values, and

        ▪ executing "cost-benefit" analyses.[49]

    See Sections 6.5.1 through 6.5.3.

---

[47] Working memory in the human brain has the same function as random access memory (RAM) in computing devices.

[48] The notation, *A-not-B*, refers to elements of the set A that are *not* in the set B.

[49] Risk can be determined more accurately if values (both cost and benefits) are accurate, as obtained from the equivalent of a free market. The definition of risk is,

$$\text{Risk} = (\text{Probability of Loss}) \cdot (\text{Amount at Risk}).$$

Ventromedial Prefrontal Cortex

The ventromedial prefrontal cortex (vmPFC) communicates sensory information between itself and many structures in the brain - especially the amygdala. It also regulates emotion and decides morally. Specifically, it

- **Communicates Information.**
    - **Receives Information.** The vmPFC receives information from the
        - **Limbic Brain.**
            - amygdala,
            - olfactory system, and
            - ventral tegmental area.
        - **Neocortex.**
            - dorsomedial thalamus and
            - temporal lobe.
    - **Sends Information.** The vmPFC sends information to the
        - **Limbic Brain.**
            - amygdala,
            - hippocampus, and
            - lateral hypothalamus.
        - **Neocortex.**
            - temporal lobe.
- **Regulates Emotion.** The vmPFC regulates emotion received from structures such as the amygdala. It controls physiological responses and behaviors. The subgenual anterior cingulate of the vmPFC is associated with the characteristics of courage and risk (as known from experiments that observed the proximity of humans to poisonous snakes).
- **Decides Morally.** The vmPFC is involved with important decisions: It compares *emotion and logic* to make moral judgments:
    - The vmPFC suppresses negative emotions (e.g., it moderates the emotions of anger and violence).
    - The vmPFC is associated with empathy, responsibility, and good decisions.
    - The vmPFC is important to many levels of decision-making:
        - It performs well, whether the situation is uncertain or certain.

- It handles economic or value-based decisions in which preferences are required.
- Recent experiments verify the cooperation between the amygdala and the vmPFC in reaching moral decisions.
- A relatively inactive vmPFC is associated with antisocial behavior. For example, impulsive murderers have relatively active amygdala compared to their vmPFC.
- Individuals whose vmPFC are damaged are noticeably deficient in decision-making, empathy, and responsibility. Such individuals have difficulty
  - judging morally,
  - choosing between options,
  - recognizing deception,
  - detecting irony and sarcasm (e.g., they are easily fooled by misleading advertising),
  - making decisions consistent with their beliefs, and
  - controlling emotional reactions.

Summary: dlPFC and vmPFC

In summary,

- the dlPFC refines and hones the sense of logic, and
- the vmPFC creates a moral decision by allocating this sense of logic and the sense of emotion from regions of the brain, such as the amygdala.

Location of Morality

Controls of the usual five senses (i.e., sight, smell, taste, hearing, and touch) are located in the brain. Similarly, the sense of morality is located in the brain. Specifically, morality is *known* to reside in the

- dorsolateral prefrontal cortex,
- ventromedial prefrontal cortex,
- amygdala,
- orbitofrontal cortex,
- insular cortex, and
- anterior cingulate cortex.

43

Some of this is known because serious injury to these parts of the brain has caused many previously moral humans to immediately lose this sense.

The vmPFC is known to decide between *logic* received from the dlPFC and *emotion* received from the amygdala.[50] This process is depicted by the structured diagram in Figure 2.3.4-1.[51]

Figure 2.3.4-1 structured diagram of the human brain's decision process between a logical and an emotional response to a sensory stimulus

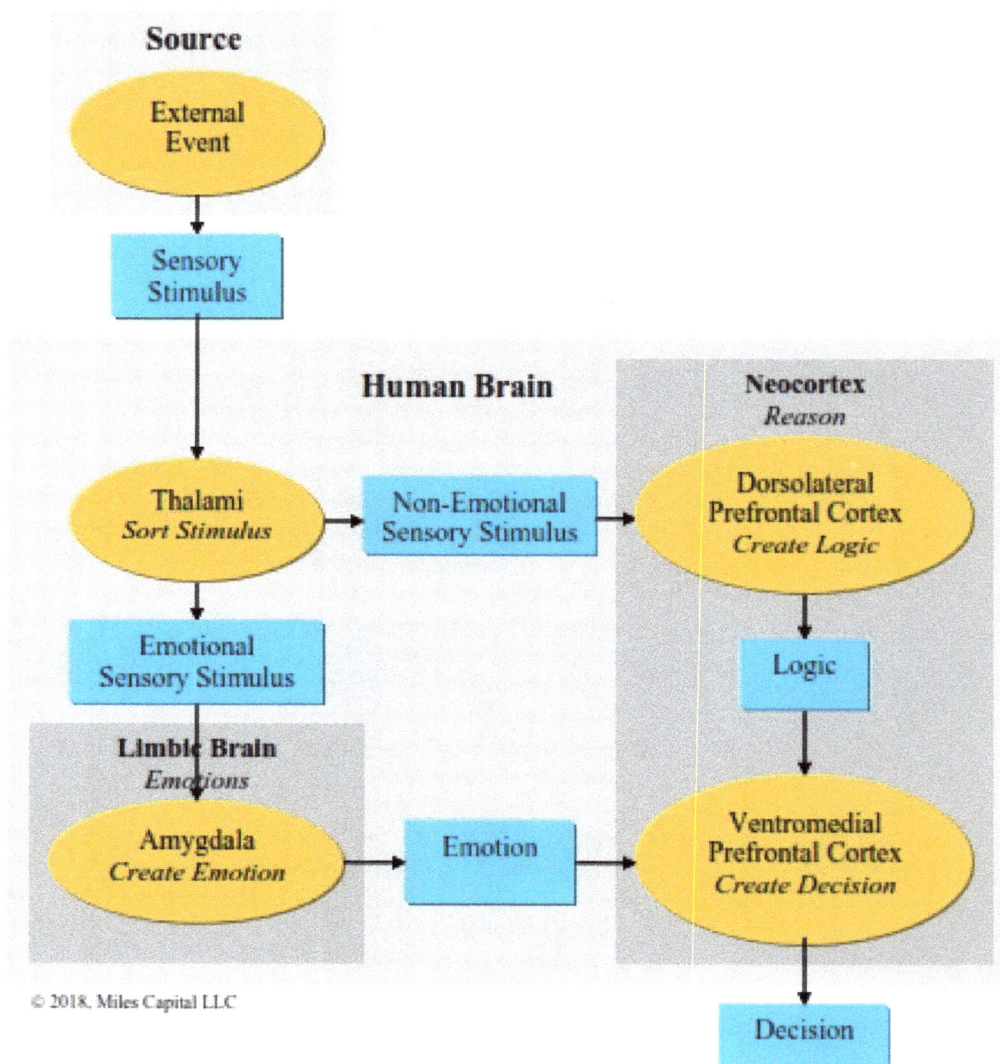

© 2018, Miles Capital LLC

---

[50] This decision is mediated by the anterior cingulate.

[51] Almost everybody has known very intelligent people who make bad decisions. This can happen because logic is determined in the dlPFC and decisions are determined in the vmPFC.

2.3.5 Summary of the Evolution of the Human Brain

Table 2.3.5-1 is a summary of the evolutionary origins, structures, and functions of the human brain. The times at which each of the three layers of the triune brain formed clearly precede the time at which humans first existed as Great Apes (15 million years ago).

Table 2.3.5-1 summary of evolutionary origins, structures, and functions of the human triune brain

		Evolutionary Origin		Structures and Functions	
		Age (years)	Species	Structures	Functions
Evolutionary Layers of the Human Brain	**Reptilian** *(Instinct)*	315,000,000	Reptiles	• Brain Stem • Cerebrum	• Autonomic Functions • Motor Activities • Reproduction • Survival Instincts
	Limbic *(Emotion)*	250,000,000	Small Mammals	• Amygdala • Anterior Thalamic Fornix • Hippocampus • Hypothalamus • Limbic Lobe Mammillary Bodies • Nuclei • Septal Nuclei	• Emotions • Long-Term Memory • Motivation • Olfaction • Social Interaction • Survival
	Neocortex[*] *(Logic)*	75,000,000	Large Mammals & Primates	• Dorsolateral Prefrontal Cortex • Ventromedial Prefrontal Cortex	• Abstraction • Decision-Making • Logic • Regulation of Emotion • Speech

* The neocortex is smooth in small mammals, but it has grooves (sulci) and wrinkles (gyri) in large mammals and primates. The sphere is the shape having the smallest surface area for a given volume; therefore, grooves and wrinkles enable the surface area of the neocortex to increase relative to the fixed volume within the cranium. The six layers of the neocortex are unique to humans, and the ratio, (brain mass)/(body mass), is largest in humans.

Chapter 3 Evolution of Human Morality

The purpose of this chapter is to present evidence that we believe indicates that human morality is innate.

Realizing that human morality is consistent with group selection is fundamentally important to understanding ourselves and human history.

Due to our continual loss of energy (i.e., entropy), sustaining life is the primary purpose of morality, and this requires us to continually replenish the energy and stay on the "winning" side of natural selection. The Earth contains countless environments and species. Natural selection designs individuals to be increasingly compatible with their environments (but not more).

Humans have traveled in small societies (i.e., groups) for approximately 15 million years. Then, after the innovation of tools and toward the end of the last ice age, groups merged into larger societies. Forming groups and larger societies seems to be natural for humans (and for some other social species). It works: Even though there are many problems with larger societies, they are generally more successful. This success could be due to capital, including the division of labor that it enables.

The subjects of this chapter are most important to human success. The sections of this chapter are:

> *3.1 Definition of Morality*
>
> *3.2 Primitive Morality was Practical*
>
> *3.3 Evidence that Morality Is Inherited*

3.1 Definition of Morality

Natural selection seems to act on more than one level. (We assume it *can potentially* act on four levels: individual, group, species, and ecosystem – but individual empathy diminishes with increasing genetic distance of levels from the individual.) This chapter discusses morality and why different levels of morality may be inherited.

Discussing an important concept, such as this, should begin with an understanding of terms. Consequently, we provide dictionary definitions of moral and morality and a traditional definition.

3.1.1 Definition of Moral

A recent Webster dictionary defines moral in two ways:

- of or relating to principles of right and wrong

- conforming to a standard of right behavior

Since we need to know the meaning of *right*, we offer this statement: *A casual observation of moral behavior reveals that virtually all behavior that increases our probability of group success is considered right (or good), and virtually all behavior that decreases our probability of group success is considered wrong (or bad).*

3.1.2 Definition of Morality

The following two dictionary definitions of morality are quite different. The first definition is independent of a society. The second definition is relative to a society and permanent within an individual. The third definition is a traditional classification.

Independent of Society

The Webster dictionary defines morality in two ways; both definitions refer to agreed-upon conduct:

- *a doctrine or system of moral conduct or*

- *particular moral principles or rules of conduct.*

Dependent upon Society and Permanent within an Individual

Another dictionary defines morality more broadly - relative to a society and as being permanent within an individual. It states: *Morality is a code of conduct that regulates interactions within complex societal groups. It is different from rules or laws: It is permanent within an individual. Therefore, it cannot be changed or overruled by an authority.* I believe this definition is consistent with natural law as espoused by many philosophers since ancient times.

Traditional Classification

Social scientists have developed a system to classify morality. The classification is discussed in Appendix C.

3.2 Primitive Morality was Practical[52]

Earlier anthropologists believed primitive people were amoral, but subsequently, they realized that imbedded in their languages are indications that they declared behavior as either good or bad. Correspondingly, primitive people believed that moral behavior was self-validating. Anthropologists, more than philosophers, tend to believe that morality is inherent.

Whether a society is primitive or sophisticated, behavior - such as stealing, cheating, or lying - is universally considered immoral. For example, some Indian tribes believe that these behaviors are immoral because they are impractical. In fact, the group would shun individuals who behaved this way. Practical behavior is related to

- efficacy,

- efficiency, and

- accuracy.

Primitive people also believe in traditions and ancestors. Ties to the family, sobriety, and honesty are approved by primitive societies because they are practical – not because they please a supernatural being. Some believe the spirits of dead ancestors have an interest in current behavior, especially if it is related to the group.

Behavior that damages the group is considered very serious. For example, killing a member of the group is considered very serious, but killing a member of another group is not. Correspondingly, infanticide is often approved to relieve pressure on the group from inadequate resources. In primitive societies, the result of a behavior is more important than the motive of the behavior. This is contrary to the belief of most modern Western societies.

In light of these observations, primitive societies seem very practical.

3.3 Evidence that Morality is Inherited

Life has existed on Earth for nearly 4 billion years; humans (i.e., family: Hominidae) have existed for 15 million years; and modern humans (i.e., Subspecies *Homo sapiens sapiens*) have existed for 200,000 years. Among species, our behavior has been unusually successful.[53]

---

[52] Encyclopedia Britannica, William Benton, Publisher, Volume 15, Morality, Primitive.

[53] The unusually long period of human success has been studied extensively by the evolutionary biologist, Edward O. Wilson: *The Meaning of Human Existence*, Edward O. Wilson. He says that of the 8-10 million species, about 2 million have been documented and only 20 lines of species have persisted. He considers these species and societies to be eusocial: These are societies in which there are eggs, cooperative brood care (including brood care of offspring from

We know that physically and mentally, we are designed by natural selection. Behavior that we consider "good" is also behavior that increases the probability of group success. Conversely, it also seems impossible to conjure behavior that we consider "bad" that does not also decrease the probability of group success.

Natural selection shows that behavior that does not enhance the probability of group success is unnecessary and tends to be selected with indifference; conversely, behavior that increases the probability of group success tends to be selected - because individuals exhibiting it are more likely to be selected and are, thus, more likely to pass their successful genotype to their offspring.

In this book, *behavior is moral behavior if and only if it increases the probability of freedom (including life).*

Early Theories of the Infant Mind

The following two theories were certainly logical, but they were based on a great lack of current knowledge.

Blank Slate Theory

Ancient philosophers, such as Aristotle, believed that babies are born with minds that are blank slates (i.e., in Latin, *tabula rasa*). Aristotle, wrote, "What it [the mind] thinks must be in it just as characters may be said to be on a writing-tablet on which as yet nothing stands written: This is exactly what happens with the mind."

At that time (c. 375 BC), the functions of the brain were relatively unknown, and evolution was merely a suspicion.

Amoral Slate Theory

Nearly twenty-three hundred years later, neurologists, including Sigmund Freud (1856-1939), theorized that humans begin life as amoral.

Evidence of Inherent Individual, Group, and/or Species Morality

The remainder of this section discusses a variety of evidence that morality is inherited:

3.3.1 Some Inherent Emotions are Consistent with Individual Morality

3.3.2 Infants' Inherent Behavior is Consistent with Group Morality

---

other individuals), overlapping generations within a colony of adults, and a division of labor in reproductive and non-reproductive groups.

3.3.3 Preference for Family and Friends is Consistent with Group Morality

3.3.4 Discouragement of Disadvantageous Mating is Consistent with Group Morality

3.3.5 Moral Characteristics of Individuals, Groups, and Species are Independent of the Environment that Designed Them

3.3.6 Levels of Moral Characteristics of Individuals, Groups, and Species are Dependent upon the Environment that Designed Them

3.3.1 Some Inherent Emotions are Consistent with Individual Morality

Emotions of fear and survival are located in the amygdala, and emotions of pleasure and disgust are located in the anterior insular cortex.[54] These two bodies communicate regularly (i.e., fear and disgust - including disgust from immorality - are complementary). Following are some emotions of pleasure (that encourage behavior that we must/should do) and emotions of disgust (that discourage behavior that we must not/should not do).

Pleasure Encourages Successful Behavior

The emotion of pleasure encourages behavior that would enhance the probability of individual success:[55]

- **Food.** We enjoy eating when we are hungry.
- **Water.** We enjoy drinking water when we are thirsty.
- **Minerals.** We crave food that contains minerals in which we are deficient.
- **Progeny**. We are generally attracted to individuals of the opposite sex because we need to procreate.[56]

Disgust Discourages Unsuccessful Behavior

Disgust is one of the oldest human emotions. It discourages behavior that would diminish our probability of individual success. Unpleasant odors/tastes can come from bodily excrements, including perspiration from stress.[57] It shouldn't be surprising that we have evolved to consider

---

[54] The anterior insular cortex processes the sense of disgust - from smells, taste, sights of contamination, and immoral acts.

[55] The emotion of pleasure that encourages the following four activities might be related to self-interest that necessarily coevolves with life.

[56] Many evolutionary biologists, such as Richard Dawkins, wonder if we (i.e., our phenotypes) are simply vehicles or agents for our genotypes - so they may persist.

[57] Cells and organisms communicate by molecular signaling. Consequently, the sense of smell (i.e., distinguishing molecules) is our most primitive sense. The two amygdalae, components of

odors/tastes from matter that contains toxic bacteria to be unpleasant. Those who might have considered those odors/tastes to be pleasant would not have been "fit" - and their genes would, therefore, no longer be with us.

The following are sources of pathogens:

- **Decomposing Organic Matter**. Decomposing organic matter can be human food (i.e., dead organisms) or other dead organisms.[58]

- **Persons Who Neglect Hygiene**

- **Persons Who Have Contagious Illnesses**

Why do we universally agree that spoiling/decomposing organic matter smells "bad" rather than "good?" We haven't been taught that by our parents, teachers, religions, etc. Rather, I suspect we don't like the smell of spoiling organic matter (i.e., molecules or pathogens) because of natural selection acting on the individual. Simply, those individuals who did not reject the odor of decomposing organic matter were, themselves, more likely to be rejected by natural selection; their genes were less likely to persist: Natural selection must be the reason our minds *universally* reject this odor.[59]

Near the beginning of Section 3.1, moral is defined in a dictionary as right and wrong. (But what does right and wrong mean?) Now, odors are defined in terms of pleasant or unpleasant. Behavior is wrong (i.e., immoral) because it decreases our probability of success, and an odor is unpleasant because those molecules and pathogens that emit the odor also decrease our probability of success. Natural selection has designed us to dislike behavior and odors from dangerous and unsuccessful situations. It is simple because it is logical.

---

the limbic brain that are concerned with survival, developed from the sense of smell. The amygdala provides an emotional component to decisions, including moral decisions.

[58] Conversely and undoubtedly, decomposers consider the smell of decomposing organic matter to be pleasant.

[59] The following two diseases do not warn our senses, and their causes have apparently been misunderstood: Trichinosis is a parasitic disease (from a roundworm) that can result if humans eat undercooked pork. We are vulnerable because the worm doesn't warn our senses, and since the cause of trichinosis was unknown, a religion teaches that God wants its adherents to avoid eating pork. Similarly, venereal disease can occur from contact during sexual intercourse. We are vulnerable because the cause usually doesn't warn our senses, and since the cause was unknown, a religion teaches that God wants adolescents to be circumcised.

3.3.2 Infants' Inherent Behavior is Consistent with Group Morality

Recent experiments using infants reveal that their minds are neither blank nor amoral as Aristotle and Freud theorized, but they *inherently* prefer behavior that adult humans consider moral.

Psychology professors, Karen Wynn and Paul Bloom, from the Yale Infant Cognition Center authored a number of publications on the subject of inherent morality, including a 2007 article in *Nature* and in a book by Paul Bloom.[60] (Their experiments have also been featured on *CBS's 60 Minutes* and on CNN.)

They found that infants

- judge actions,

- prefer both fairness and kindness,

- are distressed by strangers, and

- are prone toward provincialism and bigotry.

These results would be consistent with group morality of humans who evolved only in small groups until approximately 5,000 BC.

Infants Prefer the Morality of Adults

Infants between 3-5 months of age viewed puppet shows in which one puppet exhibited what *adults consider* bad behavior (i.e., a "bad" puppet) and another puppet exhibited what *adults consider* good behavior (i.e., a "good" puppet). The infants preferred

- the good puppet constantly (while also holding a gaze at the good puppet for 33 seconds and at the bad puppet for 5 seconds),

- the puppet that showed vengeance toward the bad puppet. (Surprisingly, infants showed the most approval when puppets took the initiative to *reward* good behavior and *punish* bad behavior.), and

- the puppet that, physically, more closely resembled themselves (by 87%).

Infants and Young Children Prefer Individuals Similar to Themselves

Generally, infants prefer individuals similar to themselves: Specifically, they prefer individuals who have the same

- race (tested at 3 months old),

---

[60] Paul Bloom, *Just Babies: The Origin of Good and Evil*

- food (tested at 11 months old),

- language (tested at 12 months old), and

- clothes (tested with young children).

Since humans traveled solely in groups for 15 million years and in larger societies for only the last 7,000 years (i.e., only 0.0047% of the period during which humans have existed), group morality was necessarily "provincial" and individuals of groups were necessarily apprehensive of strangers and strange "things." (The functions of the amygdala explain such apprehensions.)

3.3.3 Preference for Family and Friends is Consistent with Group Morality

Empathy and group morality seem to exist in humans and in other eusocial species. Group morality, in particular, would probably not exist unless group selection existed - with its judicious mixture of competition and cooperation within the group. Recently, evolutionary biologists have conducted experiments whose results support the existence of empathy and group morality.[61]

Since natural selection exists, at least, at the individual and group level, it is logical that kindness within the group is instinctive; the success of the group increases the probability that the individual will succeed, and its genes will persist. These data are reasons to consider the inherent nature of individual and group morality. As stated in Section 2.3.4, evidence of group morality has also been located in the dorsomedial prefrontal cortex (dlPFC).

3.3.4 Discouragement of Disadvantageous Mating is Consistent with Group Morality

We avoid incest and unwanted sexual advances. The Westermarck effect (i.e., reverse sexual imprinting) is a hypothetical effect in which individuals who live in close domestic proximity during the first few years of their lives become desensitized to later sexual attraction between each other. If true, this effect could be evolution's way to discourage incest. (The incest taboo is

---

[61] The British biologist, Richard Dawkins, argues against group selection and supports the "selfish gene" theory of natural selection. He builds on the theory posed by George C. Williams. It is a gene-level view of natural selection rather than a group-level view of natural selection: This theory also explains pseudo-altruism because individuals with similar genes would act "selflessly" toward each other. It seems that Richard Dawkins doesn't argue against the results of group selection as much as against the motive for it. Whereas most evolutionary biologists believe the motive for group selection is success of the group or species (phenotypes), he and some other evolutionary biologists believe the motive is supplied by the genes that want success for themselves (genotypes). Perhaps, the gene simply has self-interest rather than acts "selfishly."

a widespread cultural taboo because incest increases the probability of mutations - which decreases the probability of group success.)[62]

3.3.5 Moral Characteristics of Individuals, Groups, and Species are *Independent* of the Environment that Designed Them

Humans seem to have the same basic sense of right and wrong (i.e., universally). They

- possess notions of compassion and group morality,

- value loyalty and kindness,

- perceive motive in behavior, and hence, distinguish between intentional bad behavior and unintentional bad behavior (i.e., a mistake), and

- categorize people as either good or bad.

Even though moral characteristics seem to be universal, *levels* of moral characteristics vary among environments. (See Section 2.5.5, *Group Morality*.)

3.3.6 Levels of Moral Characteristics of Individuals, Groups, and Species are *Dependent* upon the Environment that Designed Them[63]

Characteristics are Universal, but Their Levels are Local (i.e., Environmental)

Environments vary widely. Natural selection designs individuals from species to be compatible with their environments. Therefore, individuals and species vary widely, and success in these different environments requires different strategies, tactics, and abilities. Successful implementation of strategies, tactics, and abilities is moral behavior. It is doubtful that the *characteristics* of species morality (such as trust) vary among societies from different

---

[62] There is a large and interesting exception to the incest taboo: Arab countries of the Middle-East and North Africa. Judaism and Christianity discourage inbreeding for the reasons given above. However, Mohammed practiced in-breeding, and the Qur'an does not discourage it. Muslims in these regions practice inbreeding widely (i.e., as many as 25-30% of all marriages are with first cousins), even with the knowledge of the frequent mutations it can cause - which is reported to be very significant. Possible reasons for inbreeding are thought to be tribalism, fear and distrust of strangers, a desire to keep wealth in a family, culture, geographic isolation, and socioeconomic class. *Tadmouri, Ghazi O.; Nair, Pratibha; Obeid, Tasneem; Ali, Mahmoud T. Al; Khaja, Najib Al; Hamamy, Hanan A. (2009-10-08). "Consanguinity and reproductive health among Arabs". Reproductive Health. 6 (1): 17. doi:10.1186/1742-4755-6-17. ISSN 1742-4755. PMC 2765422.PMID 19811666*

[63] Re. *Eye color* is a characteristic, and the color, blue, is a level of the characteristic.

environments, but it should be expected that the *levels* of these characteristics vary. There is considerable evidence that this is true - because individuals in societies are being designed or fashioned by natural selection to fit their environments. [64]

Rates of Merging Groups

Even though almost all groups in the "developing" world merged into tribes approximately 7,000 years ago, there is probably a very large range about this date. Correspondingly, humans have different levels of acceptance of and cooperation with strangers. We see this today.

Generally, individuals from more (technologically) developed societies have evolved with strangers over a longer period than have those from lesser developed societies (i.e., mingling is dangerous, difficult, and costly).

---

[64] Joseph Henrich, et al, Cambridge University Press, Behavioral and Brain Sciences, Volume 28, Issue 06, December 2005, pp 795- 815 *"Economic man" in cross-cultural perspective: Behavioral experiments in 15 small-scale societies*

Part II
Morality and Freedom

Chapter 4 Moral Propensities

The primary purpose of the three chapters of Part I is to describe who we are and to show that morality is innate.

The purpose of Chapter 4 is to discuss the properties of innate moral propensities. A propensity is an inherent tendency to behave in a particular way. (Behavior is the manifestation of one or more propensities.) We have many propensities. Moral propensities are in the limbic brain and the neocortex (i.e., the amygdala, dorsolateral prefrontal cortex, ventromedial prefrontal cortex, orbitofrontal cortex, insular cortex, and anterior cingulate cortex). Morality is a *system* of moral propensities that evaluates situations and encourages us to behave in a manner that increases the probability of freedom.

The following sections of this chapter discuss the characteristics of moral propensities:

> *4.1 Structure of Moral Propensities*
>
> *4.2 Logic of the Moral Propensity System*
>
> *4.3 Levels of Moral Propensities are Designed by Environments*
>
> *4.4 Moral Propensity Space*
>
> *4.5 Traditional Classification of Innate Morality*

4.1 Structure of Moral Propensities

Although Charles Darwin perceived natural selection as benefiting the individual, he soon suspected it as also benefiting the group. It is now seen as possibly benefiting other biological levels as well.[65]

Natural selection must act on the individual, but it can also act for the benefit of others. If all traits of an individual are adequate for a level of selection, the individual can be selected at that level.

The belief that natural selection may act on one or more biological levels is relatively new; the idea is still being developed and debated. [66] I believe multi-level selection is an important

---

[65] Natural selection *benefits* individuals because it designs future generations of individuals to be increasingly compatible with their environment.

[66] Multi-level natural selection should appeal to those interested in the Holistic hypothesis, such as the Gaia hypothesis.

concept. Moreover, it provides a *logical structure* from which to discuss the evolution of human morality and, consequently, social, political, and economic behavior.

Figure 4.1-1 is a diagram that covers periods from the beginning of the Earth to the present. The period is divided into 10 cycles of a logarithmic scale. Each cycle is a period between consecutive powers of 10 (i.e., a cycle is from 1 to 10, from 10 to 100, from 100 to 1,000, etc.). The figure uses bar graphs to depict two eras of capital development (i.e., primitive and modern) and four levels of moral propensities (i.e., individual and group morality have moral propensities, but species and ecosystem morality may not yet). Colors of the bars indicate the difference of moral propensities. Orange for individual and group morality indicates that moral propensities exist, and blue for species and ecosystem morality indicates that few or no moral propensities exist yet.

Figure 4.1-1 two estimated eras of capital development and periods of four levels of morality

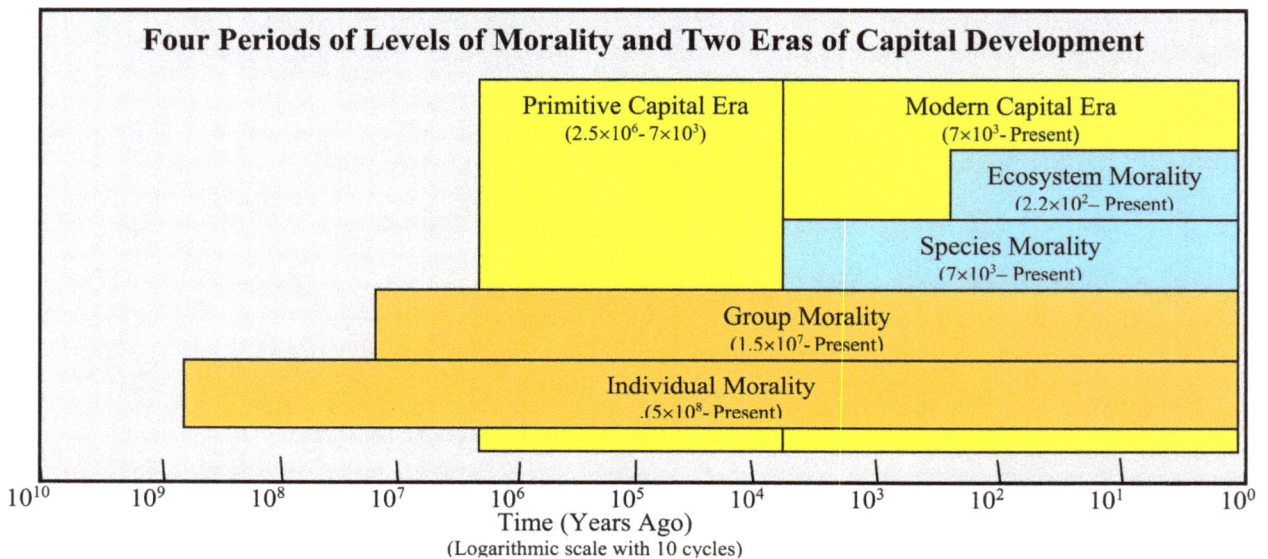

Four Periods of Levels of Morality and Two Eras of Capital Development

Primitive Capital Era ($2.5×10^6$- $7×10^3$)

Modern Capital Era ($7×10^3$- Present)

Ecosystem Morality ($2.2×10^2$– Present)

Species Morality ($7×10^3$– Present)

Group Morality ($1.5×10^7$- Present)

Individual Morality ($5×10^8$-Present)

Time (Years Ago)
(Logarithmic scale with 10 cycles)

Two Capital Eras

We divide the period of capital development into two eras, depending upon its effects on human history: the primitive capital era and the modern capital era:

- **Primitive Capital Era (2.5 Million BC – 5,000 BC).** Tools (i.e., stones fashioned for scraping flesh and possibly killing) were created 2.5 million years ago. However, capital (e.g., knowledge and its manifestations) was not sufficiently developed to enable groups to easily migrate and interact with strangers until about 5,000 BC.

- **Modern Capital Era (5,000 BC – Present).** Capital was sufficiently developed to allow groups to migrate and interact with strangers, but it was not sufficiently developed until 200 years ago (i.e., the Industrial Revolution) for it to cause noticeable damage to the ecosystem.

Four Levels of Morality

All four levels of morality exist, but their times of origin differ greatly:

- **Individual Morality (0.5 Billion BC-Present).** Approximately 0.5 billion years ago, the first "brain-like" structure appeared. Consequently, we assume that some individual moral propensities existed as early as 0.5-1.0 billion years ago.

- **Group Morality (15 Million BC–Present).** Approximately 15 million years ago family Hominidae appeared, so we assume that group moral propensities began to develop then.

- **Species Morality (5,000 BC–Present).** Much later (i.e., 7,000 years ago), species moral propensities could have begun to develop because groups were able to migrate and mingle more easily.

- **Ecosystem Morality (1,800 AD-Present).** Even later (220 years ago), ecosystem moral propensities also could have begun to develop because of the Industrial Revolution (1760-1840).

Of course, the moral propensities of the first two levels of morality are vastly more developed than those of the last two levels of morality.

We believe that the degree of empathy between individuals of any two moral levels diminishes as the genetic distance between them increases.

Table 4.1-2 lists examples of moral characteristics of an individual (for itself) and between individuals, within groups, within species, and within the ecosystem.

Table 4.1-2 examples of moral characteristics of individuals and toward individuals of higher levels

Individual Morality			
Personal Moral Characteristics That Apply to the Individual Only			
Acceptance	Discipline	Intuition	Remembrance
Accuracy	Effectiveness	Joy	Resilience
Ambition	Efficiency	Knowledge	Responsibility
Assertiveness	Eloquence	Liberality	Restraint
Attention	Endurance	Logic	Self-interest
Awareness	Enthusiasm	Majesty	Sensitivity
Balance	Excellence	Meekness	Simplicity
Bravery	Faith	Mindfulness	Sobriety
Caution	Flexibility	Moderation	Spirituality
Chastity	Focus	Modesty	Spontaneity
Cleanliness	Forbearance	Objectivity	Stability
Commitment	Foresight	Order	Steadfastness
Confidence	Fortitude	Peace	Strength
Conscientiousness	Frugality	Perseverance	Temperance
Constancy	Grace	Piety	Tenacity
Contentment	Health	Potential	Thrift
Courage	Honor	Prudence	Toughness
Creativity	Hope	Punctuality	Vigilance
Curiosity	Humor	Purity	Vitality
Determination	Idealism	Purpose	Wisdom
Diligence	Industry	Reason	Wonder
Discernment	Intelligence	Reliability	Zeal

Group Morality		Species Morality		Ecosystem Morality
Cooperative Moral Characteristics That Intentionally Apply to Others		**Neutral Moral Characteristics That Incidentally Apply to Others**		**Necessary Moral Characteristics That Apply to All Individuals,**
Altruism	Goodness	Accountability		Respect (i.e., do not unnecessarily
Benevolence	Helpfulness	Candor		• abuse,
Caring	Honesty	Courtesy	-	• contaminate,
Charity	Kindness	Dependability		• deplete,
Compassion	Love	Fairness		• erode,
Consideration	Loyalty	Faithfulness		• harm,
Cooperation	Mercy	Fidelity		• manage, or
Empathy	Self-sacrifice	Gratitude		• modify
Fairness	Selflessness	Honesty		resources or individuals of
Favoritism	Thoughtfulness	Hospitality		any species in this level).
Friendliness	Trust	Humility		
Generosity	Unity	Impartiality		
Gentleness				

60

4.1.1 Individual Selection and Individual Morality

Since the earliest evidence of a brain structure dates to 0.5 billion years ago, we assume that some individual morality existed as early as 0.5 billion years ago. [67]

Individual Selection

If an individual is selected without the aid of others, it is selected at the individual level. This individual is probably more fit than is an individual that is selected because it is aided by others.

Individual Morality

Individual morality is a system of moral propensities that increases the individual's probability of freedom. Individuals must compete for resources. If their resources are inadequate, they are not selected. Personal character is often not considered a moral trait because it does not necessarily involve others. However, admirable personal traits constitute a type of morality, called individual morality, because these traits can increase the individual's probability of selection (i.e., freedom). Examples of personal traits are self-interest, constancy, courage, health, strength, intelligence, wisdom, etc.

4.1.2 Group Selection and Group Morality

Humans began 15 million years ago (i.e., the family Hominidae). We assume some group morality began then.

Even though Darwin perceived natural selection as selection of the individual, he suspected natural selection might also operate at the group level. It is reasonable (and observable) that a group may have a greater probability of freedom if individuals in the group cooperate rather than if they act either independently or competitively. Individuals that are considered more desirable are also more likely to receive cooperation from others in the group than are individuals that are considered less desirable.

Group Selection

Natural selection selects an individual or a group with respect to its traits. Even if one or more traits are inadequate for selection, the individual can be selected if other members of the group effectively supplement its necessary, but deficient, traits by sharing resources (or by providing activities according to ability or need - called division of labor).

---

[67] In a sense, any behavior, even non-conscious behavior is moral if it increases the probability of freedom.

Group selection is the selection of an individual whose traits are expected to benefit the group. An individual can be selected at the group level in either of two ways:

- **Inherent Traits**. An individual i can be selected at the group level if its traits are expected to benefit the group.

- **Shared Resources**. If individual g is selected only with the aid of members of its group, individual g is selected at the group level. Because aid is necessary, individual g is probably less fit than is a similar individual i.

Group Morality

Group morality is a system of moral propensities that increases the group's probability of being selected. Evidence of the evolution of group morality comes from observation, simulation, and the human brain.

Evidence from Observation and Simulations

The eminent Harvard evolutionary biologist, E. O. Wilson, notes that of the millions of species that have been observed, only 19-20 "lines" of species have persisted (for an extraordinary period). They include ants, bees, wasps, termites, naked mole-rats, and humans. Their common characteristics are eggs, parents that nurture their offspring into maturity, etc. Wilson believes that existence of these species supports the group selection hypothesis, and he calls these species *eusocial*.[68]

The success of group selection has been confirmed by observing cooperation and using computer simulations. [69, 70] (Interestingly, simulations have not only revealed cooperation within the group, but they have also revealed unexpected hostility toward individuals not in the group!)

Evidence from the Dorsolateral Prefrontal Cortex (dlPFC)

An individual continues to exist only because it possesses traits that are adequate for its environment. (Consequently, its genotype becomes highly represented in the population.) These traits include appropriate physical ability, intellectual ability, and moral behavior. It is moral behavior that is implemented as judicious combinations of cooperation and competition among

---

[68] Eusocial species are characterized by a cooperative family group, overlapping generations, and a division of labor between reproductive and non-reproductive groups. The division of labor creates types of behavior, called castes.

[69] T.R. Shultz, M. Hartshorn, and A. Kaznatcheev. *Why is ethnocentrism more common than humanitarianism?* Proceedings of the 31st annual conference of the cognitive science society, 2009.

[70] Kaznatcheev, A. (2010, March). *Robustness of ethnocentrism to changes in inter-personal interactions. Complex Adaptive Systems–AAAI Fall Symposium.*

individuals of the group: The dlPFC in the human brain is known to decide in favor of fair distributions of scarce resources and to discourage greed. That is, this *inherited* function of the dlPFC implies the existence of group morality.

Individuals within groups are more likely to cooperate than compete. When they cooperate, morality is called cooperative morality (or magnanimous morality). Figure 4.1.2-1 is a structured diagram of group morality between two individuals of the same group.

Figure 4.1.2-1 structured diagram that depicts group morality for two individuals within a group of a species and the ecosystem

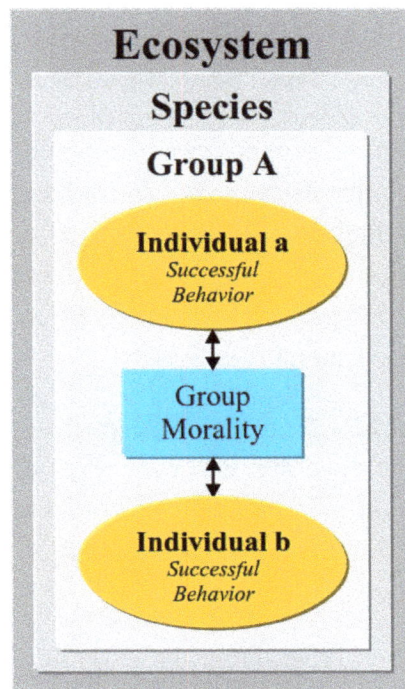

4.1.3 Species Selection and Species Morality

Since capital allowed groups to mingle with strangers 7,000 years ago, we assume this is the beginning of species morality.

Biologists generally concur that individuals belong to the same species if mating individuals can procreate. [71]

---

[71] Ecological theory also suggests that a species can exist in a niche only if it differs fundamentally from other species in its niche.

Species Selection

Species selection is selection of an individual whose traits are expected to benefit the species. Individuals can cooperate to benefit their group - so too, individuals and groups can cooperate to benefit their species. An individual can be selected at the species level in either of two ways:

- **Inherent Traits.** An individual can be considered to be selected at the species level if its traits can benefit the species.

- **Shared Resources.** If individual s is selected only with the aid of members of another group, but within its species, individual s is selected at the species level.[72] Because aid is necessary, individual i is probably more fit than is a similar individual s.

Species Morality

Species morality is a system of moral propensities that increases the species' probability of being selected. Groups of a species compete for resources. In the case of humans, groups were small groups (i.e., perhaps 100-150 individuals) until approximately 5,000 BC, when tools (i.e., capital) allowed smaller societies to merge into larger societies such as tribes, chiefdoms, etc. History shows that groups within species are more likely to compete than to cooperate. When they cooperate, morality is called mundane morality. [73]

Economists Dwight R. Lee and J.R. Clark describe species morality as a morality in which the donor respects the recipients, and the donor is neutral. Figure 4.1.3-1 is a structured diagram that depicts species morality of individuals between two groups within a species.

---

[72] If the individual were aided by an individual of the same group, selection would be group selection, and if the individual were aided by an individual of another group, selection would be species selection. Judging the likelihood of the level by its proximity to the individual level renders it more likely that the selection is group selection than species selection.

[73] An example of the difference between group morality and species morality is this rather common saying among political scientists: "Individuals have friends, and countries have interests."

Figure 4.1.3-1 structured diagram that depicts species morality for two groups within a species

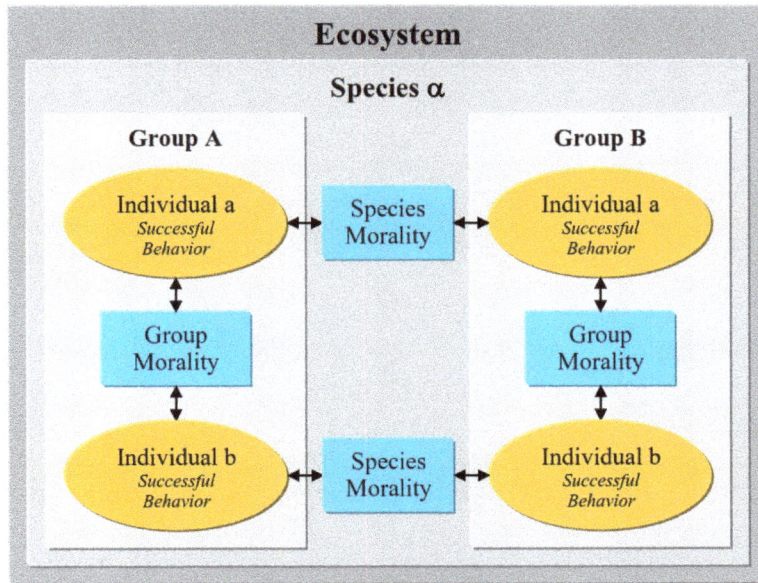

4.1.4 Ecosystem Selection and Ecosystem Morality

The Industrial Revolution began about 260 years ago. Since pollution began to increase greatly then, we assume this is the effective beginning of ecosystem morality.[74]

Even though the ecosystem has approximately 10 million species, and only one of these is the human species, it is important to seriously discuss ecosystem selection and ecosystem morality.

Ecosystem Characteristics

Ecosystem selection necessarily involves different species. Even though competition between species is common, individuals of any species can cooperate with individuals of another species for the benefit of the ecosystem.

The ecosystem is a widely dependent, diverse, robust, and sustainable system.[75] There are at least two types of interspecies dependencies in the ecosystem: the food cycle and symbiosis.

---

[74] It is true that tools allowed humans to alter the food cycle (2.5 million years ago), domesticate animals (17,000 years ago), and domesticate agriculture (10,000 years ago).

[75] In this case, *dependent* means *need* rather than statistical dependence from activities such as competition and cooperation.

The Food Cycle

The food cycle is depicted in Figure 8.3.4-1. All heterotrophic individuals in the ecosystem need to consume individuals of other species as nutrient resources. The first unnatural break in the food cycle occurred when capital allowed humans to move higher in the food cycle (except for the final type of consumer, the decomposers – that consists of bacteria and fungi). [76]

In at least one environment, the lynx (predator) and hare (prey) are approximately equally capable as predator and prey, respectively - otherwise, *neither* could easily persist.

Symbiosis

Symbiosis is a relationship between two dissimilar individuals, usually of different species. There are four types of symbiosis:

- **Amensalism.** Amensalism is a type of symbiosis in which one individual is harmed or inhibited, and the other is unaffected;

- **Commensalism.** Commensalism is a type of symbiosis that is beneficial for one individual but is neutral for the other;

- **Mutualism.** Mutualism (i.e., cooperation) is a type of symbiosis that is beneficial for both individuals; [77] and

- **Parasitism.** Parasitism is a non-mutual type of symbiosis between species, in which one species, the parasite, benefits at the expense of the other species, the host.

Ecosystem Selection

Ecosystem selection is the selection of an individual whose traits are expected to benefit the ecosystem. An individual can be selected at the ecosystem level in either of two ways:

- **Inherent Traits.** An individual can be considered to be selected at the ecosystem level if its traits can benefit the ecosystem. As an example of ecosystem selection, suppose there is a surplus of lynx. Then ecosystem selection might compensate by selecting, say, lynx that are less capable.

---

[76] Naturally opposing binary states are overlooked but fascinating situations that are discussed in Section 8.3 Part B.

[77] Coevolved obligate mutualism exists when two species co evolve; they are inextricably bound through mutual dependence (mutualism); and they need each other to survive (obligate).

- **Shared Resources.** If individual e is selected only with the aid of members of another species, individual e is selected at the ecosystem level. [78] Because aid is necessary, individual i is probably more fit than is a similar individual e.

The great degree of dependence within the ecosystem suggests the importance of balance among species in each environment.

Ecosystem Morality

Ecosystem morality is a system of moral propensities that increases the probability that the ecosystem is selected.[79] Figure 4.1.4-1 depicts the relationships among the four highest biological levels.

Unlike lower-level genetic organisms, the ecosystem does not need to conform to an environment – it must be internally compatible.

Additionally, some religions exacerbate the damage to the ecosystem by teaching "speciesism," the superiority of one species (humans) relative to other species (i.e., disrespect, as if the only value of other species is their value to humans).[80] It is clear that most humans today do not possess ecosystem morality.

We can't easily know the regard that species feel for each other. Because of capital, we are the only species capable of (unnatural) ecosystem abuse. Clearly, ecosystem morality is a large and extremely important subject, but it is also addressed by many others. Because of capital, humans are a robust species: To some degree, we can protect ourselves from the ecosystem damage that we have caused - other species cannot.

---

[78] If the individual were aided by an individual of the same group in the same species, selection would be group selection, and if the individual were aided by an individual of another group in the same species, selection would be species selection. If the likelihood of the selection of levels is correlated with their proximity to the selected individual, it is most likely that the selection is group selection, less likely that the selection is species selection, and least likely that the selection is ecosystem selection.

[79] And, what would we do if the ecosystem, itself, were not selected?

[80] Species extinction is accelerated by the widespread human disregard for other species (i.e., "speciesism"). Disregard could result from the belief that God granted a license to human animals to treat nonhuman animals merely as a means to human ends. The license is expressed in this statement from Genesis (the first book of the Hebrew Bible and the Christian Old Testament): God gave humans "dominion over the fish of the sea, and over the fowl of the air, and over the cattle, and over all the Earth, and over every creeping thing that creepeth upon the Earth."

Figure 4.1.4-1 is a structured diagram that depicts ecosystem morality.

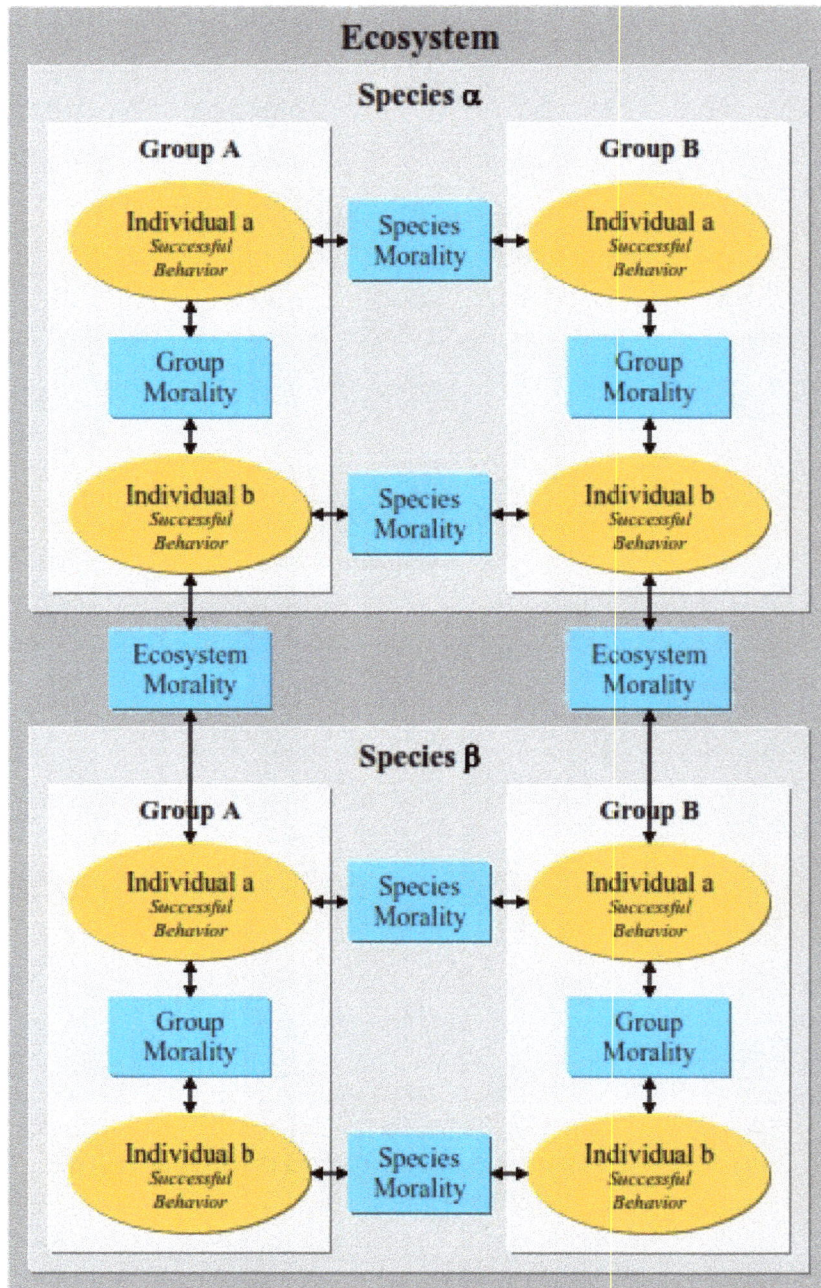

4.2 Logic of the Moral Propensity System

Because our system of moral propensities must be a logical system, we should compare its properties to the properties of a logical system – such as the axiom system that defines Euclid's geometry.

Axioms are simple statements that define relationships between objects or entities (e.g., two points define a line). In fact, axioms are so simple that they can't be proved.[81] Moral propensities also define relationships between objects or entities (e.g., don't steal from another). Probably the system of moral propensities should have the same logical properties as a system of axioms. Specifically, within each individual, the moral propensities should be independent, consistent, and complete.

Family Hominidae is estimated to have existed for 15 million years and individuals during this time have lived an average of 15 years. Therefore, humans have existed in groups for approximately one million *generations* – an incredible number of trials and errors.

Conversely, capital is an exponentially developing force that changes some environments much more rapidly than sporadic evolution changes inhabitants. This can introduce some inconsistencies and incompleteness that remain until evolution can "catch up" and somewhat restore the logical system.

4.2.1 Independent

To determine if moral propensities are independent within an individual, we can apply the following practical test: A moral propensity is independent of a second moral propensity if our knowledge of the second moral propensity does not influence our opinion of the first moral propensity. Also, an independent set of moral propensities should not contain a superfluous moral propensity. If it does, a moral propensity and the superfluous moral propensity could be contradictory. (Evolution is so efficient that superfluous moral propensities would be rare and unexpected.) Except for sporadic genetic mutations in individuals, there are virtually no species whose phenotypes contain persistent redundancies.

---

[81] Because Euclid's fifth axiom (i.e., defining parallel lines) was not simple enough for many mathematicians (i.e., it consists of 43 words) – after 2,100 years of discombobulating – some mathematicians (i.e., Bolyai in Hungary and Lobachevsky in Russia) finally replaced it, creating an alternative geometry that fortunately enabled Einstein's theory of general relativity to make greater sense. I think this is a most interesting example of two things: 2,100 years of human indecisions and a beautiful application of a mathematical model. It also lets us realize that there can be more than one type of geometry! It was so fortuitous. We discuss mathematical models in subsequent chapters.

4.2.2 Consistent

Consistency within an individual requires that no two moral propensities are contradictory. If the moral propensities are consistent, they can support each other, allowing the system to be robust. In a mature system an inconsistency should never happen without a genetic mutation or capital-induced changes in environments. All moral propensities should work toward their common purpose of behavior that increases the probability of freedom.

4.2.3 Complete

Since individuals and their environments are evolving systems (unlike Euclid's system of axioms), it is theoretically impossible for our set of moral propensities to be complete - even though the relatively slow rate of *environmental evolution* allows it to be practically complete. There is a more formidable hindrance to completeness than the rate of evolution: The rate of *capital development* is changing our environments so fast that the system of evolving moral propensities is always lagging badly. In fact, moral propensities are missing for almost all types of situations that have been allowed to happen by employing "tools" – and causing many of our current situations to be confusing for us and for the remainder of the ecosystem. Clearly, the first tools allowed us to defend ourselves from predators and, consequently, allowed many humans to move higher in the food cycle. This was probably the first noticeable change from tools. It must have caused great consternation among other members of the food cycle and the environment. The most consequential incompleteness occurred when groups were able to more easily migrate. These migrations were the beginning of species morality. They created novel types of situations for which we still have no propensities (i.e., uncharted territory).

The important property of incompleteness is characterized by moral dilemmas. It is examined in Sections 4.3-4.4 and discussed throughout the remainder of this book.

4.3 Levels of Moral Propensities are Designed by Environments

4.3.1 Humans Migrated from Sub-Saharan Africa and to Environments throughout the Earth

The motivations for the early human migrations from Sub-Saharan Africa are not known, but the usual cause of migrations is survival.[82] Survival becomes an issue when the availability of necessary resources and the population density are unbalanced. Consider supply and demand:

- **Supply.** Some climate scientists believe the original migration of *Homo sapiens* from Sub-Saharan Africa 100,000 years ago was caused by droughts that occurred roughly every 20,000 years. Of course, draughts would cause decreased supplies of necessary resources.

- **Demand.** Population density that exceeds the "carrying capacity" of the local environment could also cause excessive demand for necessary resources.

Some earlier humans migrated from Sub-Saharan Africa, but they became extinct. Figure 2.2.4-1 depicts the migrations of *Homo sapiens* from Sub-Saharan Africa over the last 100,000 years.[83] Most humans remained in Sub-Saharan Africa and are now called Negroids.[84] The primary migration of *Homo sapiens* from Sub-Saharan Africa was to the Middle-East. After approximately 30,000 years in the Middle-East, some *Homo sapiens* also migrated east. They evolved in Asia as Mongoloids. Then after 30,000 more years, there was another migration from the Middle-East. This time, it was to the west. They passed through the Caucuses (between the Caspian Sea and the Black Sea) and evolved in Europe as Caucasoids.

Secondary migrations of *Homo sapiens* occurred about 7,000 years ago. See Figure 2.2.4-1. These migrations to other environments created further human evolution and diversity. Because these migrations occurred relatively recently, they are discussed extensively in subsequent chapters.

---

[82] https://www.pnas.org/content/106/38/16007

[83] https://www.worldhistory.org/image/6605/map-of-homo-sapiens-migration/

[84] We use the forensic archaeology terms of Negroid, Caucasoid, and Mongoloid to indicate the three races.

Figure 2.2.4-1 where and when *Homo sapiens* migrated during the last 100,000 years

- Most *Homo sapiens* remained in Africa and continued to evolve as Negroids during this 100,000 period.
- In this primary migration, *Homo sapiens* migrated from Sub-Saharan Africa approximately 100,000 years ago to the Middle-East. Approximately 70,000 years ago some moved east to Asia and evolved as Mongoloids, and approximately 40,000 years ago, some of those migrants moved west to Europe and evolved as Caucasoids. Some Middle-Eastern people remained.
- In many secondary migrations, approximately 7,000 years ago, groups dispersed and caused many strangers to interact – causing human conflicts to begin evolving propensities for species morality.
- From 200-400 years ago, the slave trade brought some Sub-Saharan Africans to the Americas. (This forced migration is depicted by the very, very short line segment, resembling a dot, on the right side.)

Legend

Era of Evolution due to Physical Environments (i.e., Group Era) (100,000-7,000 years ago)

Era of Evolution due to Physical Environments & Conflicts with Strangers (i.e., Species Era) (7,000-0 years ago) (See Section 8.3.2.)

Environments in which *Homo sapiens* have evolved over the Last 100,000 Years

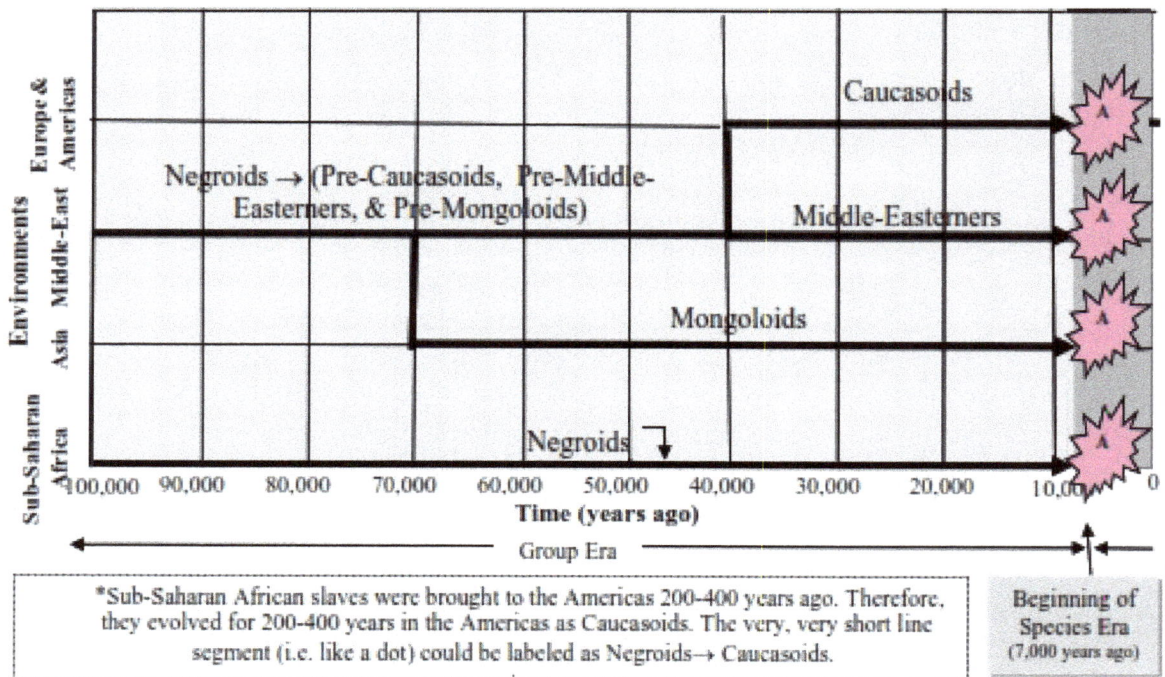

*Sub-Saharan African slaves were brought to the Americas 200-400 years ago. Therefore, they evolved for 200-400 years in the Americas as Caucasoids. The very, very short line segment (i.e. like a dot) could be labeled as Negroids→ Caucasoids.

Beginning of Species Era (7,000 years ago)

4.3.2 Human Evolution

Evolution is caused by any of the following four phenomena:

- random genetic drift,

- migration,

- mutation, and

- natural selection.

Section 1.3 discusses how characteristics of individuals of a species are identical, but the levels of the characteristics vary among those individuals.[85] That is, levels of characteristics of individuals tend to evolve in the following ways:

- *Within a group* they evolve due to random genetic drift and mutation.

- *Among groups* they evolve due to random genetic drift, mutation, and migration.

- *Within species* they evolve due to any of the four phenomena but – most significantly - natural selection.

Because natural selection is its own standard, it is unbiased, and we can say with confidence that the optimum environment for an individual is the environment that designed it.

4.3.3 Diverse Moral Behaviors and their Interactions

As we have seen, 100,000 years ago, *Homo sapiens* migrated from Sub-Saharan Africa to the Middle-East. Then many migrated to Europe (where they evolved as Caucasoids) and to Asia (where they evolved as Mongoloids) – and into the Pacific and the Americas.[86] Since they were the first humans outside of Sub-Saharan Africa, they did not encounter other humans. (This important observation could explain significant moral conflicts in the Americas (i.e., Section 8.3.3)).

Migrations and other causes of evolution have created great diversity among humans. Most significantly, because morality is innate, moral behavior is greatly diverse! The diversity of moral behavior has created an enormous potential problem that became obvious 7,000 years ago when capital enabled increased migrations and interactions of diverse moral behavior around the World.

---

[85] The color of the iris of the eye is a characteristic. Blue is a level of that characteristic.

[86] Anthropologists believe that the Caucasoids and the Mongoloids are more similar to each other than either is similar to the Negroids.

Our essential innate fear of strange situations and strangers warns us that we have great potential problems with interactions with strangers, but we are not armed with moral propensities that can help us deal with these problems. If you believe that we currently have moral propensities for species morality, consider how seamless group morality is compared to the frequent inconsistencies and conflicts in species morality.

We are describing what might be *the most serious unrealized problem now facing humanity*. The following section defines the extent of this unrealized problem.

4.4 Moral Propensity Space

Innate morality can be defined as an abstract space of moral propensities whose dimensions are defined by the six interrogatives in Table 4.4-1.

Table 4.4-1 six dimensions of the moral propensity space as defined by the interrogatives

		Dimensions of the Moral Propensity Space	
Interrogatives	Why	The purpose of moral propensities is to increase the probability of freedom.	
	How	An individual's moral propensities may be manifested and augmented by multi-level moral behavior.	
	What	Moral propensities are manifested by the constancy of acquiring necessary resources for the individual. (See Section 5.3.3 or Section 6.1.2.)	3-dimensions of Figure 4.4-1
	When	Moral propensities are available for all types of situations that have existed for at least 7,000 years.	
	Where	Moral propensities are available for all types of situations that have existed for at least 7,000 years in environments that have designed individuals.	
	Who	Moral propensities are available to all individuals for all types of situations that have existed for at least 7,000 years in the environment that designed them.	

All environmental changes require appropriate adjustments by its inhabitants, but capital has accelerated the normal rate of change of human environments.

Adjustments of individuals can be accomplished by their genes. Genes require thousands of years of trial and error (i.e., over many generations) to adjust to environmental changes. Interactions with strangers increased dramatically 7,000 years ago. But even then, many individuals either did not experience strangers or had only casual interactions with them. That is, not all interactions with strangers caused genetic replacements, and most genetic replacements could have occurred later than 7,000 years ago.

With the exception of mutations in a few individuals, we have no issue with group morality. That is, group morality is firmly in our genes and there are relatively few problems. However, we have enormous problems with species morality. We believe that species morality hasn't had enough time to become a significant part of our genome.

Figure 4.4-1 is a 3-dimensional schematic diagram that depicts the moral propensity space. Moral propensities are a function of environments and time. The three components of the figure (i.e., the moral propensity space, the moral dilemma space, and the four levels of morality) are depicted here:

- **Moral Propensity Space (What).** The interrogative dimension, what, is the system of moral propensities. Since we are concerned only whether moral propensities exist or not, the figure depicts all propensities as having the same value. They are all depicted as the rectangular cuboid labeled Moral Propensity Space.

  - **Time (When).** The interrogative dimension, when, begins with the evolution of the human brain (i.e., 0.5 billion years ago) and continues to the present. However, the period of the moral propensity space terminated 7,000 years ago. This is because we assume that moral propensities cannot exist until 7,000 years after the initial occurrence of a novel type of situation (e.g., interactions with strangers).

  - **Environments (Where).** The interrogative dimension, where, includes all human-inhabited environments. Humans inhabit almost all land environments. (The boundaries needn't be specified.)

- **Moral Dilemma Space.** Only moral dilemmas exist for types of situations that initially occurred more recently than 7,000 years ago; this is too recent to have developed moral propensities. Moral dilemmas are depicted in the plane and have zero value. They are labeled Moral Dilemma Space.

- **Four Levels of Morality.** The four horizontal bars, one for each level of morality, are depicted in the vertical plane defined by the interrogative dimensions, when and what:

  - **Individual and Group Morality.** Moral propensities exist for the moral levels of individuals and groups.

  - **Species and Ecosystem Morality.** Only moral dilemmas exist for the moral levels of species and the ecosystem (because they both occurred too recently).

Figure 4.4-1 a 3-dimensional schematic depiction of the moral propensity space for novel types of situations that first occurred prior to 7,000 years ago, the moral dilemma space for novel types of situations that first occurred more recently than 7,000 years ago, and the four levels of morality

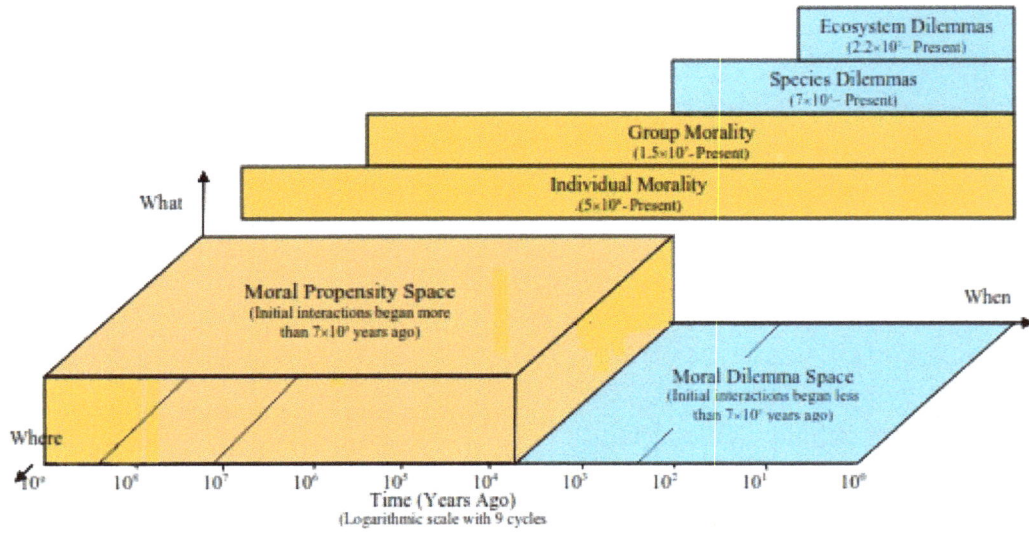

Ecosystem Dilemmas
(2.2×10⁻² – Present)

Species Dilemmas
(7×10⁻² – Present)

Group Morality
(1.5×10⁻² – Present)

Individual Morality
(5×10⁰ – Present)

What

Moral Propensity Space
(Initial interactions began more
than 7×10⁹ years ago)

When

Moral Dilemma Space
(Initial interactions began less
than 7×10⁰ years ago)

Where

10^9 10^8 10^7 10^6 10^5 10^4 10^3 10^2 10^1 10^0

Time (Years Ago)
(Logarithmic scale with 9 cycles

4.5 Traditional Classification of Innate Morality

We are not advocating the traditional classification, but we are including it as a courtesy to readers who might use it to classify morality. The traditional classification of morality is described further in Appendix C. The classification consists of three types of definitions, two types of senses, and two types of standards.

4.5.1 Definition

The three types of definitions are deontology, consequentialism, and virtue ethics. Innate morality (i.e., the subject of this book) seems to be defined as *consequentialism* because we consider behavior to be moral if and only if it can increase the probability of freedom.

4.5.2 Sense

The two types of sense are descriptive and normative. Innate morality might be morality in the *descriptive* sense because there are countless implicit moral codes. Each moral code is designed by the environment in which the group evolved. However, since each individual in an environment can vary, each environment also has a *normative* sense of morality.

4.5.3 Standard

The two types of standard morality are objective and subjective. I believe that innate morality might be considered *objective* for the following reason: Innate morality is an implicit code "written" as the genetic code of each individual. It is a set of moral propensities within each individual of a group that evolved in the environment. Each moral propensity could be represented by a probability distribution composed of moral propensities from all individuals of the group. The central tendency (e.g., mean, median, etc.) of the distribution for each moral propensity would be considered normative for that group, and the laws for the group could define acceptable values with respect to the means or medians.

4.5.4 Classification

Therefore, in terms of the traditional moral classification, *innate morality can be defined as consequential, but the sense and the standard do not clearly apply to innate morality.*

Chapter 5 Moral Behavior

Behavior is a sequence of actions that is the manifestation of one or more moral propensities. Moral behavior is behavior that increases the probability of freedom. The purpose of this chapter is to investigate moral behavior and then summarize it by creating the table in Section 5.5 that applies moral behavior to the three criteria of natural selection.

The sections of this chapter are

5.1 Proponents of Moral Behavior

5.2 Levels of Moral Behavior are Designed by Environments

5.3 Documentation of Moral Behavior

5.4 Types of Dependent Behavior

5.5 Moral Behavior Applied to the Criteria of Natural Selection

5.1 Proponents of Moral Behavior

Table 5.1-1 lists four proponents of morality: innate morality, and three observed behaviors (i.e., natural law, religious, and governmental).

Table 5.1-1 four proponents of moral behavior and five purposes

Legend				Innate Moral Behavior	Observed Moral Behavior (e.g., Natural Law)	Religious Moral Behavior	Governmental Moral Behavior
	Applicable		√				
	Not Applicable		-				
	Unknown Applicability		?				
Purpose of Moral Behavior	Freedom			√	-	-	-
	Miscellaneous			-	√	-	-
	General Well-Being (i.e., health/wealth)			-	-	√	-
	Everlasting Life / Intimidation of Strangers			-	-	√	-
	Control / Protect Citizens			-	-	-	√

5.1.1 Innate Moral Behavior

The purpose of innate group morality is to increase the probability of freedom. Individual and group behaviors that facilitate this purpose are manifestations of the propensities of these behaviors.

5.1.2 Observed Moral Behavior (e.g., Natural Law)

Natural law is derived from observations of the ethical and moral beliefs and practices of humans.

Natural law includes observations over, perhaps, twenty-five hundred years – and the conclusions of many philosophers. It was documented and proposed by the Ancient Greeks (e.g., Aristotle) and Romans (e.g., Cicero). It is mentioned in the Old and New Testaments of the Bible. It includes contributions from the Age of Enlightenment (i.e., the great intellectual and philosophical achievements that occurred during the 18th and 19th century in Europe). Natural law has also been used to challenge the Divine Right of Kings (i.e., the belief that a monarch is preordained by God to inherit the crown).

The concept of natural law is considered to be similar to the concept of natural rights – assumed rights that are manifested as freedom. Natural law is believed and practiced. However, natural rights are believed but often not practiced when they are forcibly denied by others (i.e., restrained) or when an individual has inadequate resources (i.e., constrained). Perhaps the rights are denied by others because species morality is very immature. Denial of rights seems to occur almost without exception in socialist governments. Life and freedom must coexist; both can be lost from the absence of responsible (i.e., moral) behavior. See Section 8.3.5.

Natural law is considered to be universal. That is, it is moral behavior that is considered to be normative among all humans. Apparently advocates of natural law do not believe that morality is innate. Much of natural law was proffered before genetics was known. We believe that morality cannot be universal. Section 5.2 shows that morality is designed by environments.

5.1.3 Religious Moral Behavior

The purpose of religions is to teach adherents what is "good" behavior and to encourage their adherents to be "good." Abrahamic religions also teach how to achieve an everlasting life. However, some scholars wonder if the extreme characteristics of God proffered by the Abrahamic religions (i.e., all powerful, all knowing, all present, etc.) were intended to intimidate strangers – encouraging them to behave morally with regard to the natives.

Religious moralities seem to be a subset of group morality. Both seek to maintain group harmony - which would increase the probability of freedom for the group.

Whereas the purpose of religious *moral behavior* might increase the probability of *natural* selection and freedom, the purpose of *faith* (i.e., a component of Abrahamic religions) is to increase the probability of *supernatural* selection. See Table 5.3.1-1.

5.1.4 Governmental Moral Behavior

The minimal purpose of a government is to perpetuate itself by controlling its citizens and by protecting them from outside forces.

In history, many governments have been associated with a specific religion. Currently, fewer of these associations remain. In any case, many governments create laws that codify the normative morality of their citizens. If they were not normative, there would be broad disobedience and cognitive dissonance. Non-native citizens generally have more difficulty complying with some laws than native citizens do.

5.2 Levels of Moral Behavior are Designed by Environments

Humans appeared 15 million years ago as family Hominidae in either Africa or Eurasia. *Homo sapiens* appeared 200,000 years ago in east Africa. Some migrated 100,000 years ago from Sub-Saharan Africa to the Middle-East in what we call the primary migration of *Homo sapiens*. The following figure, Figure 2.2.4-1, depicts where and for how long they have evolved. The figure also indicates the beginning of the Species Era about 7,000 years ago when secondary migrations began worldwide.

Because we believe that morality is innate, both *where and for how long* we evolved are important to our discussion of the morality designed by environments. For example, some *Homo sapiens* from the primary migration moved east after 30,000 years and evolved in Asia as Mongoloids and others moved west after 60,000 years and evolved in Europe as Caucasoids. Genetic data show that Caucasoids and Mongoloids are closer to each other than either is to Negroids.[87] The asterisk on the right side of the figure is intended to draw attention to the very, very short line segment that indicates that some Negroids were brought to the Americas in the slave trades about 400 years ago. Whereas Negroids that migrated to Europe have evolved in *Europe* toward Caucasoids for 40,000 years, those that were brought to the Americas as slaves have evolved in the *Americas* towards Caucasoids for 400 years (i.e., only 0.004% as long as those that migrated to the Middle-East and then to Europe).

Since the environments in which we evolved designed us, we repeat our belief that the optimum environment for an individual is the environment that designed it. We will discuss a few

---

[87] https://pubmed.ncbi.nlm.nih.gov/7163193/

examples of behavioral data from different environments that demonstrate the variations in humans created by environments.

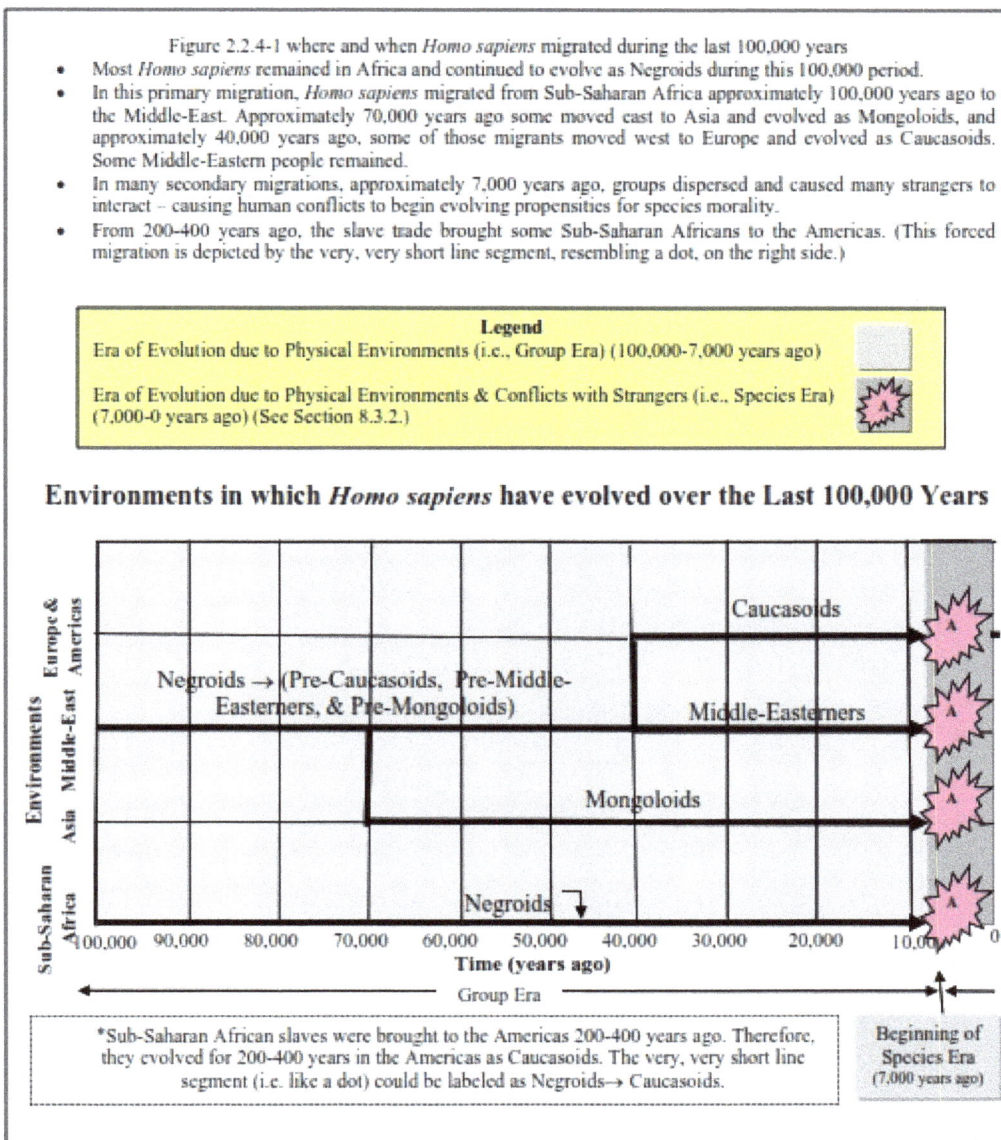

Figure 2.2.4-1 where and when *Homo sapiens* migrated during the last 100,000 years
- Most *Homo sapiens* remained in Africa and continued to evolve as Negroids during this 100,000 period.
- In this primary migration, *Homo sapiens* migrated from Sub-Saharan Africa approximately 100,000 years ago to the Middle-East. Approximately 70,000 years ago some moved east to Asia and evolved as Mongoloids, and approximately 40,000 years ago, some of those migrants moved west to Europe and evolved as Caucasoids. Some Middle-Eastern people remained.
- In many secondary migrations, approximately 7,000 years ago, groups dispersed and caused many strangers to interact – causing human conflicts to begin evolving propensities for species morality.
- From 200-400 years ago, the slave trade brought some Sub-Saharan Africans to the Americas. (This forced migration is depicted by the very, very short line segment, resembling a dot, on the right side.)

Legend
Era of Evolution due to Physical Environments (i.e., Group Era) (100,000-7,000 years ago)

Era of Evolution due to Physical Environments & Conflicts with Strangers (i.e., Species Era) (7,000-0 years ago) (See Section 8.3.2.)

Environments in which *Homo sapiens* have evolved over the Last 100,000 Years

*Sub-Saharan African slaves were brought to the Americas 200-400 years ago. Therefore, they evolved for 200-400 years in the Americas as Caucasoids. The very, very short line segment (i.e. like a dot) could be labeled as Negroids→ Caucasoids.

Beginning of Species Era (7,000 years ago)

The subsections of this section are

5.2.1 Homicide and Incarceration Rates of Two Races from Two Environments

5.2.2 Homicide Rates of All Races and Ethnic Groups from Most Environments

5.2.3 Political Freedom from Most Environments

5.2.4 Economic Freedom from Most Environments

81

It is difficult to obtain comprehensive and accurate data that include different behaviors, races, ethnic groups, and their environments. That is, some governments do not collect data about behaviors unless laws are violated; they classify data in different ways; and their accuracy is often uncertain because governments may manipulate data to protect their reputation or favor certain groups of citizens. Additionally, human migrations from other environments have contaminated the purity of some ethnic or racial populations.

However, because homicides and incarcerations (for any purpose) are such extreme and universal moral behaviors, they are reported by virtually all countries. [88]

Following are two examples that depict some homicide rates and incarceration rates from races in different environments.

5.2.1 Homicide and Incarceration Rates of Two Races from Two Environments

To illustrate this example, we have selected the USA whose population is 13.4% Black and 60% White and whose total population is 328 million. Then we have selected 14 Sub-Saharan African countries whose populations are 99-100% Black and whose total population is 355 million.[89] Because there are very few Whites in Sub-Saharan African countries, their governments do not collect much data for Whites or other races.

USA Populations

Even though the USA has a mixed racial population, data are collected separately for the races. We compare the homicide rates and the incarceration rates for Blacks in those environments, and we compare those rates with Blacks and Whites in the USA.

---

[88] Other universal illegal behaviors are assault, theft, robbery, etc.

[89] The 14 African countries are: Central African Republic, Democratic Republic of Congo, Gabon, Ghana, Lesotho, Liberia, Malawi, Namibia, Niger, Nigeria, Rwanda, Togo, Zambia, and Zimbabwe.

https://en.wikipedia.org/wiki/List_of_countries_by_intentional_homicide_rate

Sub-Saharan African Populations

Of the 14 Sub-Saharan African countries, Nigeria has the largest population (i.e., 196 million), and Namibia and Rwanda have the smallest populations (i.e., 2 million and 12 million, respectively). Because of the disproportionate populations in these countries, we compute the weighted average of the homicide rates and the incarceration rates over the 14 Sub-Saharan African countries.

Figure 5.2.1-1 is two sets of bar graphs for homicide rates and two sets of bar graphs for incarceration rates.

Homicide Rates

The bar graphs on the left side of the page depict homicide rates.

- **Top Bar Graph**. The top bar graph is the White-on-White homicide rate in the USA (1.07).[90][91] (We cannot compare the White-on-White homicide rate in these Sub-Saharan African countries because there are so few Whites in the selected countries.)

- **Bottom Bar Graphs.** The bottom two bar graphs depict the Black-on-Black homicide rates in the USA and in the Sub-Saharan African countries.
    - The Black-on-Black homicide rate in the USA (5.94) is more than five times that of White-on-White (1.07). (Given an equal number of each race in the USA, the Black homicide rate of Whites is more than 12.57 times the White homicide rate of Blacks.)[92]
    - The Black-on-Black homicide rate in the USA (5.94) is 0.728 that of the Black-on-Black homicide rate in the selected African countries (8.16).

Incarceration Rates

The bar graphs on the right depict incarcerations. Incarcerations occur from homicides as well as many other types of illegal behaviors - such as assault, theft, and robbery. The bar graph at the top is the incarceration rate of Whites in the USA (394). (We cannot compare Whites in these Sub-Saharan African countries because there are so few Whites in the selected countries.) The two bar graphs at the bottom show that the incarceration rate of Blacks in the USA is high (1989)

---

[90] https://ucr.fbi.gov/crime-in-the-u.s/2018/crime-in-the-u.s.-2018/tables/expanded-homicide-data-table-6.xls

[91] The number 1.07 indicates 1.07/100,000.

[92] This rate is discussed in depth in Section 8.3.3.

– more than five times that of Whites in the USA and nearly 30 times that of Blacks in Sub-Saharan Africa (67).

Does the relatively high incarceration rate in the USA deter Blacks in the USA from having a higher homicide rate? The homicide rate of Blacks in Africa is 37.4% higher than in the USA - 8.16 instead of 5.94.

Why is the incarceration rate so low in Sub-Saharan Africa (i.e., 67 instead of 1989)?[93] Customary law is the term that refers to traditional legal rules and ideas of indigenous populations; they are almost never documented. Before colonial times, most Sub-Saharan African societies consisted of small groups based on families. Economic and social relations were administered by the native society and by its elders. In customary law, punishment usually depends on the situation rather than on a set of rules. The flexibility of customary law could explain some of the relatively small incarceration rates in these Sub-Saharan African countries. (The colonialists usually allowed customary law to rule unless it conflicted with their laws.)

---

[93] The following information is not directly about incarceration, but it demonstrates permissiveness that would be rare in most other cultures: In approximately 2015, in Kenya, the government received nearly 10,000 complaints of abuse by the police, and only three policemen were convicted. (The Economist, August 18th, 2018. page 39)

Figure 5.2.1-1 same-race homicide rates and incarceration rates for two races and two types of environments: USA and 14 countries from Sub-Saharan Africa. Homicide rates are on the left side, and incarceration rates are on the right side

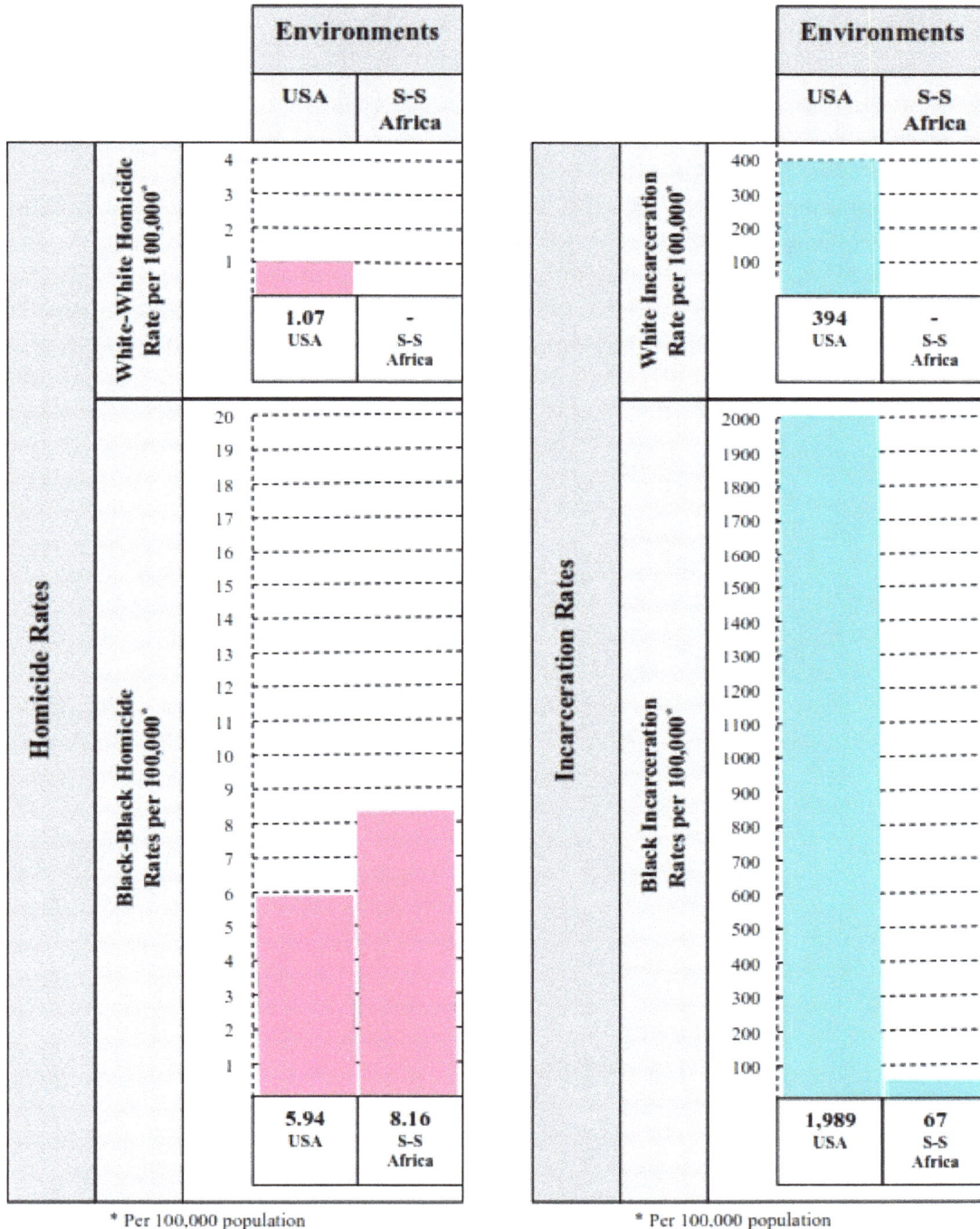

* Per 100,000 population

* Per 100,000 population

5.2.2 Homicide Rates of All Races and Ethnic Groups in Most Environments[94]

Figure 5.2.2-1 depicts bar graphs of homicide rates for 18 regions in four continents around the world: Africa, the Americas, Asia, and Europe. Australia and New Zealand are not included. China is omitted because it is a dictatorship whose homicide rate is not considered reliable. Table 5.2.2-1 lists the number of countries in each region – a total of 195 countries.

The purpose of this figure is to support our belief that humans and their moralities are designed by their environments. The range of homicide rates is between 0.94 in Western Europe and 26.12 in Central America - a ratio that is nearly 28 times!

The regions of Africa and the Americas that are near the Equator have strikingly high homicide rates, and those that are not near the Equator have more moderate homicide rates.

---

[94] https://en.wikipedia.org/wiki/List_of_countries_by_intentional_homicide_rate

Figure 5.2.2-1 homicide rates within countries in all regions of the Earth except Australia New Zealand and China

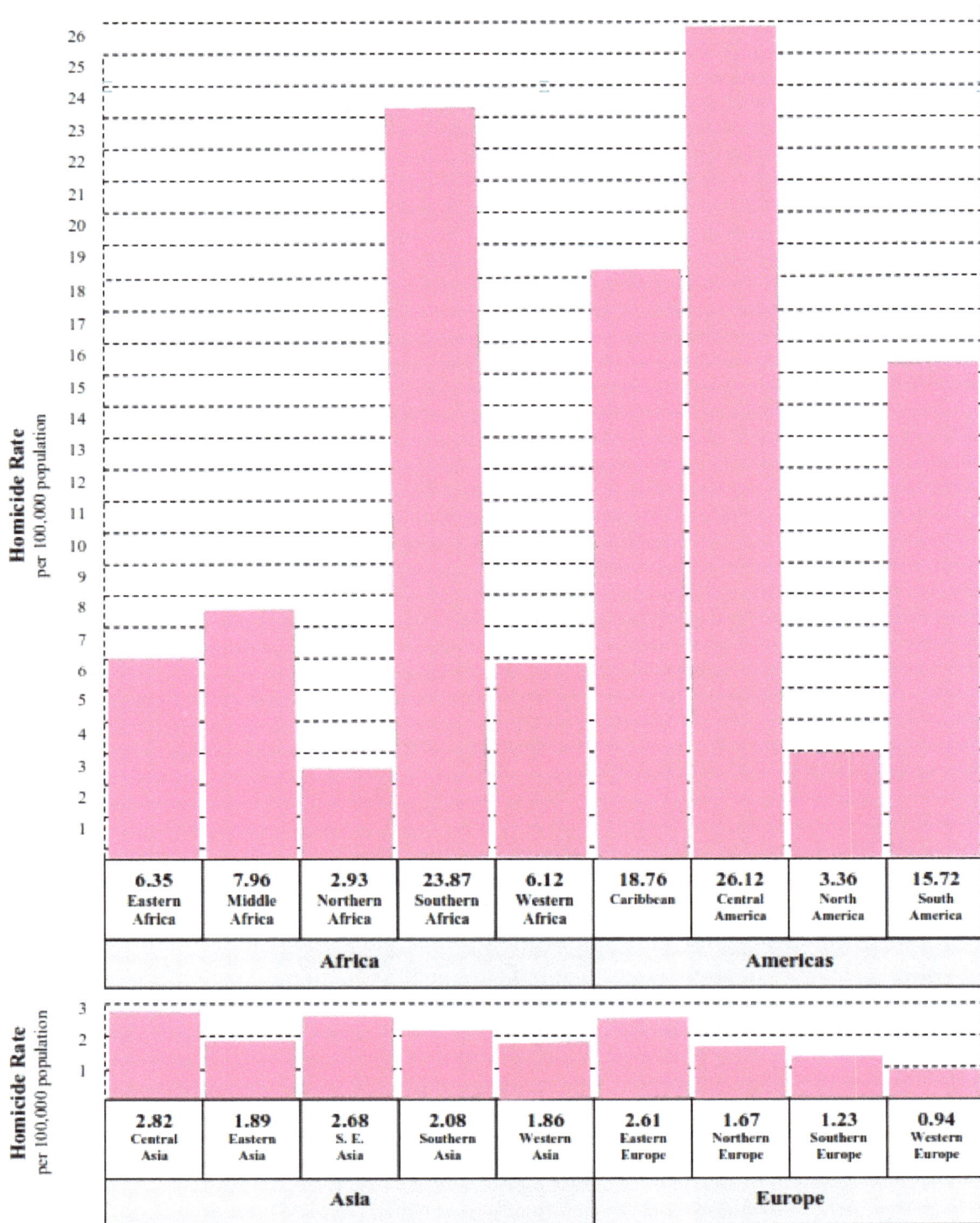

6.35 Eastern Africa	7.96 Middle Africa	2.93 Northern Africa	23.87 Southern Africa	6.12 Western Africa	18.76 Caribbean	26.12 Central America	3.36 North America	15.72 South America
Africa					Americas			

2.82 Central Asia	1.89 Eastern Asia	2.68 S. E. Asia	2.08 Southern Asia	1.86 Western Asia	2.61 Eastern Europe	1.67 Northern Europe	1.23 Southern Europe	0.94 Western Europe
Asia					Europe			

Table 5.2.2-1 number of countries in each region of Figure 5.2.2-1

Region			Number of Countries	Homicide Rate
Africa		Eastern Africa	20	6.36
		Middle Africa	9	7.96
		Northern Africa	5	2.93
		Southern Africa	5	23.87
		Western Africa	16	6.12
America		Caribbean	24	18.76
		Central America	8	26.12
		North America	2	3.36
		South America	13	15.71
Asia		Central Asia	5	2.82
		Eastern Asia (excluding China)	7	1.89
		South Eastern Asia	11	2.68
		Southern Asia	9	2.08
		Western Asia	18	1.86
Europe		Eastern Europe	11	2.61
		Northern Europe	13	1.67
		Southern Europe	13	1.23
		Western Europe	6	0.94
			195	

5.2.3 Political Freedom in Most Environments

Political freedom is monitored and measured by the Freedom House.[95] It evaluates and judges the political freedom of each country around the world as being free, partly free, or not free. We convert their judgment for each country into a number by assigning 1 for free, 0.5 for partly free, and 0 for not free. We divide countries of the world into 18 regions. In each region we average the political freedom numbers from those countries. Then we express the average number for each region as a percentage (i.e., from 0% to 100%).

Figure 5.2.3-1 depicts the average political freedom for countries in each of the 18 regions as a bar graph.

The bar graphs show clearly the variation among regions. *Except for the region of Central America, all five regions of Africa and all five regions of Asia are less politically free than the four regions of the Americas and the four regions of Europe.* The Asian region is the least free politically. The regions of North America, Northern Europe, and Western Europe are 100% free politically.

5.2.4 Economic Freedom in Most Environments

Economic freedom is monitored and measured by the Index of Economic Freedom. It is from an annual report compiled by the Heritage Foundation and The Wall Street Journal.[96]

Economic freedom of countries is judged as belonging to one of seven probability intervals.[97] The report judges 178 countries and ranks them from 1 (the freest) to 178 (the least free). We average the ranks of the countries in each of 18 regions in the world. The average rank in each region is

- subtracted from 178,

- that number is divided by 178, and

- that number is multiplied by 100 to provide the percentage of economic freedom for each region. [98]

---

[95]https://web.archive.org/web/20201003133208/https://freedomhouse.org/countries/freedom-world/scores

[96] https://en.wikipedia.org/wiki/List_of_countries_by_economic_freedom

[97] free (80–100), mostly free (70–79.9), moderately free (65–69.9), moderately not free (60–64.9), mostly not free (55–59.9), mostly not free (50–54.9), and repressed (0–49.9)

[98] That is, if A is the average rank of countries in a region, the economic freedom percentage is $100 \times [(178-A)/178]\%$.

Figure 5.2.4-1 depicts the average economic freedom of countries in each region as a bar graph. The economically freest continents are North America (i.e., Canada and the U.S.), and the four regions of Europe. Again, the Asian regions are the least economically free.

Figure 5.2.3-1 average political freedom of countries in 18 major regions of the world depicted as bar graphs

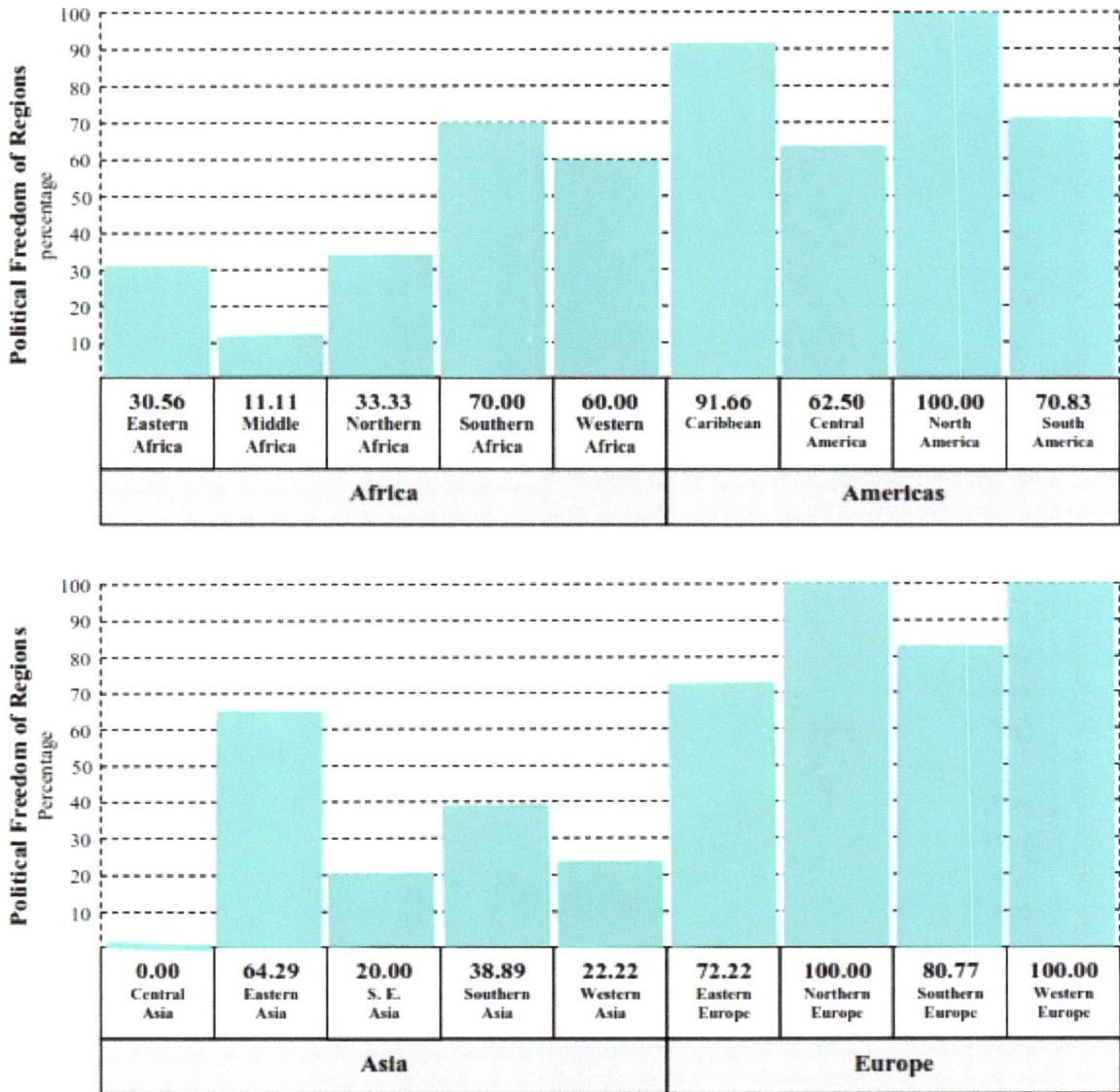

Figure 5.2.4-1 average of economic freedom of countries in 18 major regions of the world. Economic freedom varies considerably with environments

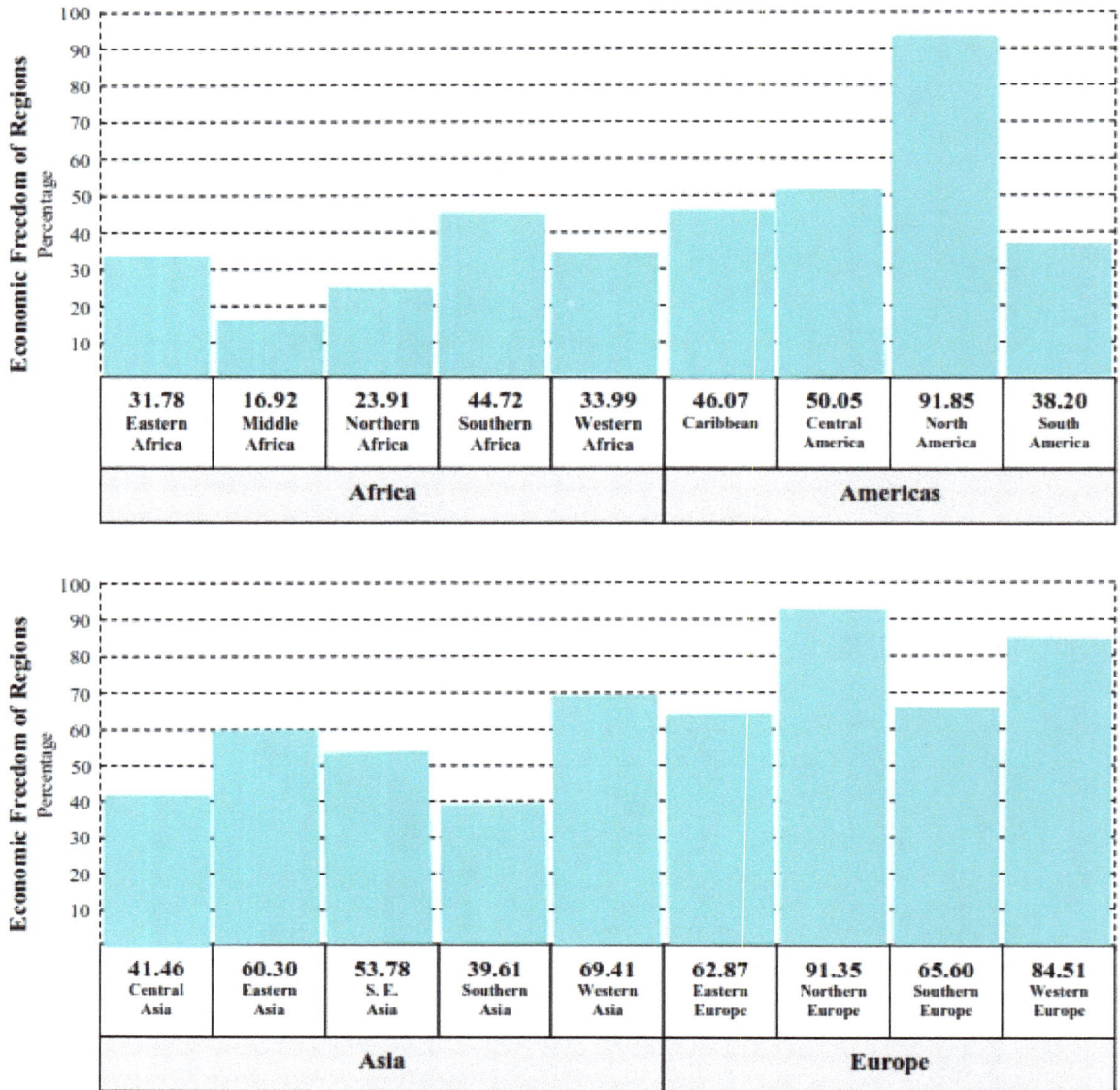

31.78 Eastern Africa	16.92 Middle Africa	23.91 Northern Africa	44.72 Southern Africa	33.99 Western Africa	46.07 Caribbean	50.05 Central America	91.85 North America	38.20 South America
Africa					Americas			

41.46 Central Asia	60.30 Eastern Asia	53.78 S. E. Asia	39.61 Southern Asia	69.41 Western Asia	62.87 Eastern Europe	91.35 Northern Europe	65.60 Southern Europe	84.51 Western Europe
Asia					Europe			

5.3 Documentation of Moral Behavior

Since morality is innate, it is implicit. Documentation is a conversion of the implicit to the explicit. If morality is documented, we can compare individual behaviors over different environments, races, cultures, religions, governments, etc. We can document moral behavior with increasing accuracy by

- **Define.** defining moral behavior with words,

- **Model.** modeling moral behavior with a mathematical function, and

- **Measure.** measuring moral behavior using data in the mathematical function.

5.3.1 Defining Moral Behavior

A. Earliest Known Definitions of Moral Behavior

The earliest known definitions of moral behavior are the Ur-Nammu law code (2100-2050 BC) and the Code of Hammurabi (1760 BC). Both codes originated in or near the ancient city of Ur in Babylonia (present-day Iraq).

Following are several interesting and amusing (in our time) examples of the Code of Hammurabi:

- If a man wants to throw his son out of the house, he has to go before a judge and say, "I don't want my son to live in my house any more." The judge will find the reasons. If the reasons are not sufficient, the man can't throw his son out.

- If the son has done some great evil to his father, his father must forgive him the first time. But if he has done some great evil twice, his father can throw him out.

- If a thief steals a cow, a sheep, a donkey, a pig, or a goat, he will pay ten times what it is worth. If he cannot pay, he will be put to death.

- An eye for an eye, a tooth for a tooth:

    o If a man puts out the eye of another man, put out his eye.

    o If a man knocks out another man's tooth, knock out his tooth.

    o If a man breaks another man's bone, break his bone.

- If a doctor operates on a patient and the patient dies, the doctor's hand will be cut off.

- If a builder builds a house and that house collapses and kills the owner's son, the builder's son will be put to death.

- If a robber is caught breaking a hole into the house so that he can enter and steal, he will be put to death in front of that hole.

- If someone cuts down a tree on someone else's land, he will pay for it.

- If someone is careless when watering his fields, and he floods someone else's field by accident, he will pay for the grain he has ruined.

Other ancient definitions of moral behavior are the Ten Commandments, which are said to have been revealed to Moses by God on Mt. Sinai (1300-1600 BC). The commandments have also been adopted by Christians.

It is interesting that early moral codes ignored the concept of freedom. Life is clearly the most important freedom; however, freedom is often associated with decreased security.[99]

Freedom is now considered to be a human right in more countries. As capital has gradually replaced labor, there has been a growing interest in freedom and in other conceivable human rights. (See Chapter 6.)

B. Early Religious Definitions of Faith and Moral Behavior

Table 5.3.1-1 lists important principles of the five largest religions. They are divided according to faith or morals. The three Abrahamic religions (i.e., Christianity, Judaism, and Islam) believe faith will aid *supernatural* selection (by God), and morals (proposed by all five religions) will aid *natural* selection (by nature).

There is an interesting relationship between the two concepts, faith and morals, and the two concepts, emotion and logic, as depicted in Figure 2.3.4-1. That is, faith is emotional and morals are logical.

It is also very interesting that 24 religious precepts can be considered individual or group moralities. There seems to be no religious precepts that could be considered species morality and only one that could be considered ecosystem morality (i.e., the Buddhist precept, *do not harm living beings*).

The ancients knew almost nothing about biology, genetics, or evolution. They could not have known that morality is innate, and, as with many things that they could not have known, they linked morality to God/gods.

---

[99] Life is usually measured by the quantity of life, and freedom is usually measured by the quality or opportunities of life. The next chapter reveals the long-sought relationship between morality and freedom.

Table 5.3.1-1 early religious principles of faith (for supernatural selection) and morals (for natural selection)

Religions	Estimated Date of Origin
Judaism	1850-2000 BC
Christianity	0-3 AD
Islam	600 AD
Buddhism	540 AD
Hinduism	1500-2300 BC

			Five Largest Religions				Objects of Faith and Morals
			Christianity/Judaism (Ten Commandments)	Islam (Ten Moral Commandments)	Buddhism (Five Precepts)	Hinduism (Ten Yamas & Ten Niyamas)	
Two Types of Religious Principles: Faith and Morals	Principles of Faith to Achieve Supernatural Selection	Have No Other Gods before Me.	√	-	-	-	God
		Have No Graven Images.	√	-	-	-	
		Do Not Take the Lord's Name in Vain.	√	-	-	-	
		Remember the Sabbath Day.	√	-	-	-	
		Hajj - Lifetime Pilgrimage to Mecca	-	√	-	-	
		Salat - Worship as in Prayer	-	√	-	-	
		Sawm - Fast during Ramadan.	-	√	-	-	
		Shahadah - Profession of Faith	-	√	-	-	
		Trustful Surrender to God/Thought	-	-	-	√	
	Principles of Morality to Achieve Natural Selection	Do Not Become Intoxicated.	-	-	√	√	Individual
		Do Not Eat Unhealthfully.	-	-	-	√	
		Do Not be Arrogant.	-	√	-	-	
		Honor Thy Father and Mother.	√	√	-	-	Group
		Care for Orphaned Children.	-	√	-	-	
		Be Generous.	-	-	-	√	
		Tzedakah - Jewish Charity.	√	-	-	-	
		Zakat - Muslim Charity.	-	√	-	-	
		Dāna - Buddhist-Hindu Charity.	-	-	√	√	
		Do Not Commit Adultery.	√	√	√	√	
		Do Not Steal.	√	√	√	√	
		Do Not Lie.	√	√	√	√	
		Do Not Kill.	√	-	√	√	
		Do Not Mercy Kill (i.e., Starvation).	-	√	-	-	
		Do Not Covet.	√	-	-	√	
		Do Not be Cruel.	-	-	√	√	
		Do Not be Indecent.	-	√	-	√	
		Do Not be Dishonest.	-	√	-	√	
		Do Not be Impatient.	-	-	-	√	
		Do Not be Wasteful.	-	√	-	-	
		Do Not Have Non-marital Sex.	-	-	√	√	

C. Definition of Innate Moral Behavior for which Life is the Basic Freedom

Our definition of innate moral behavior states that moral behavior increases the probability of freedom, of which life is the basic freedom. Whereas early moral definitions listed specific behaviors (e.g., the Ten Commandments) and possible supernatural rewards (e.g., heaven) for good behavior, our definition of moral behavior does not specify the means - only the desired outcome (i.e., increased freedom for the individual and its group).

5.3.2 Modeling Moral Behavior

We have been modeling the behavior of the physical system for some time (e.g., Newton's Law of Gravity) - and with great success. Initially, physical behavior is described by written text. Then, if possible, it is modeled mathematically – otherwise it cannot be measured. On the other hand, because life and freedom are inseparable, the biological system is usually more complex to model mathematically. Fortunately, in this text, we have also been able to model and measure moral behavior and related concepts, such as freedom and market freedom.

A. Modeling Physical Behavior

In 1939, my dear friend and mentor, Dr. Aubrey Kempner, was president of the American Mathematical Association. He was invited to address the student body of the University of Colorado to answer the questions, *What is the Nature of Mathematics, and in What Sense Does Mathematics Explain a Science?*[100] (These important questions arise so frequently regarding mathematical models, possibly because others did not explain them as succinctly as I think he did.) He said, "When mathematics is applied, for example, to physics, a mathematician will attempt to construct a mathematics which is *isomorphic* to the physical behavior."[101] That is, the

---

[100] Rene Descartes (1596-1650) combined algebra and geometry to create the coordinate system (so we can draw graphs). Although primitive mathematical models have been used for centuries (i.e., even a map is a model), they were used extensively beginning in the late eighteen hundreds, particularly by Hermann Minkowski, and David Hilbert who were Aubrey Kempner's professors and mentors at the famous University *in* Göttingen, Germany (officially, Georg-August University). At that time, they were also working at the university with Albert Einstein to create the theory of general relativity. It is interesting that Hermann Minkowski also conceived the idea of combining the dimension of time with the dimensions of space – creating an invaluable tool for applied mathematical models. The newly developed projective geometry also provided a model that helped Einstein prove his General Theory of Relativity (i.e., the way it treated the concept of infinity).

[101] isomorphic: identical or similar form, shape, or structure.

mathematical formulas that model the physical behavior define the same shape as the behavior.[102] Mathematical formulas provide the *most accurate definition* of the physical law.

We mention this clear explanation of natural behavior only because the isomorphic explanation is analogous to the isomorphic explanation we need to model moral behavior, freedom, accuracy, and market freedom.

B. Modeling Moral Behavior

We can model moral behavior by specifying the following parameters:

1. **Purpose.** This is increasing the probability of freedom,

2. **Means.** This is the constancy of necessary behavior, and

3. **Model.** This is the moral behavior function (i.e., the autocorrelation coefficient of lag 1).

1. Purpose: Increase the Probability of Freedom

Let f represent the unknown probability of freedom for an individual. The morality of the individual's behavior depends upon its effect on f:[103]

- **Moral Behavior.** Behavior is moral if and only if it increases the probability of f.

- **Amoral Behavior.** Behavior is amoral if and only if it does not affect the probability of f.

- **Immoral Behavior.** Behavior is immoral if and only if it decreases the probability of f

---

[102] Consider Newton's law of universal gravitation. The law was observed by empirical observations (i.e., information obtained by the senses, observed patterns of behavior, and experiments). The law states that every point-mass attracts every other point-mass by force acting along the line that intersects the two points. The force is proportional to the product of the two masses, and inversely proportional to the square of the distance between them. The law was formalized when mathematicians constructed an isomorph of the observed behavior of masses. That is, when they constructed the equation that explains the law:

$$F = Gm_1m_2/r$$

where

F = Newton's law of universal gravitation (i.e., gravitational force acting between the masses of two objects).

G = gravitational constant.

m_1 and m_2 = masses of the two objects.

r = distance between the centers of the masses of the two objects.

[103] It is probably a matter of opinion whether to be moral, the behavior must *actually* increase the probability or *be expected to* increase the probability. This is discussed in Section 3.2

2. Means: Constancy of Necessary Behavior[104]

Some types of behavior are necessary for freedom, and some types are relatively unnecessary. Capital (alone) can increase productivity (i.e., Section 7.1.2). Now that productivity is driving many of us past *need* and into *want*, the fraction of our behaviors that is necessary is increasingly less.

Once life is lost, it is lost forever. The duration of an individual's phenotype is its lifetime, but the duration of an individual's genotype is, actually, any number of lifetimes – depending on its descendants.[105] To achieve natural selection, life must be continuous for a period that is long enough for the individual to procreate (i.e., to pass its genotype – just as passing a baton in a relay race).

Achieving natural selection allows our genes at least one more lifetime. For selection, we need constant protection from the physical environment (Criterion #1). Because of entropy (i.e., the continuous loss of energy to regions of lesser energy), we constantly need protection from large predators and pathogens because they constantly need nutritional resources (i.e., us) (Criterion #2). Also, because of entropy, we need constant nutrition (Criterion #3). A lapse in the constancy of any one of these three criteria can end life prematurely - and often deny natural selection. See Section 1.4.3.

3. Model: The Moral Behavior Function

Morality can be modeled on a scale from 1 to -1. That is, totally moral (constant) behavior is 1, amoral behavior is 0, and totally immoral (inconstant) behavior is -1. Moral behavior can be modeled "isomorphically" by either of the following two types of correlation functions: the cross-correlation function or the autocorrelation function of lag 1.[106]

- **Cross-Correlation Function of Variables x and y**. The cross-correlation, r_{xy}, is a function of

  o two sequences of behavior for cooperation, competition, or any other purpose or

  o a single sequence of behavior that can be cross-correlated with another (pacer) sequence of behavior that is believed to be moral, (e.g., normative, etc.).

---

[104] Consistency implies with harmony or without contradiction. Constancy implies steadfastness. Constancy is marked by steadfast resolution or faithfulness.

[105] The individual's phenotype is the individual. The individual is a manifestation of its genotype.

[106] Autocorrelation of lag 1 compares the single sequence with itself by comparing each observation of the sequence with the immediately following observation (i.e., lag 1). If we were to use lag 2, we would compare each observation of the sequence with the observation two behind it. Autocorrelation with a lag is also called Markov correlation.

The value of the cross-correlation function is in the interval [-1, 1], and the behavior of multiple acts is moral if $r_{xy}>0$. This function is defined in Section 6.1.1.

- **Autocorrelation Function of Lag 1.** The autocorrelation of lag 1, r_1, a function of the single sequence created by the multiple acts of an individual is a model of moral behavior.

  The value of the autocorrelation function of lag 1 is in the interval [-1, 1], and the behavior of multiple acts of an individual is moral if $r_1>0$. This function is defined in Section 6.1.2.

Even though this book discusses both types of correlation, our goals can usually be achieved by the autocorrelation of lag 1.

In summary, either of these two types of correlation can be *isomorphic* to moral behavior.[107]

5.3.3 Measuring Moral Behavior

Constancy of behavior is a necessary characteristic of moral behavior. Morality can be measured by either of the two correlation functions:[108] This is done in Section 6.1.

5.4 Types of Dependent Behavior

If behavior consists of multiple actions, any of the following types of behavior can create a sequence of dependent (e.g., constant) observations. Four important types of dependent behavior are from the individual, cooperation, competition, and force.

Cooperation bears a similarity to group morality and socialism, and competition bears a similarity to species morality and capitalism.

5.4.1 Individual

Individuals often act independently - in their self-interest. Even though they act alone, their multiple acts over time are serially dependent. Individual behavior creates a sequence of observations that can be measured by the autocorrelation function. The sequence can be relatively constant or inconstant.

---

[107] Physical behavior is usually modeled by a simple formula because, except for some parameters, the formula doesn't change with time or individuals. However, behavior of a living individual is often modeled by a formula from probability and statistics (i.e., because of freedom, the values change with individuals and time).

[108] Types of activities that can be moral are seeking nourishment, seeking shelter, defending ones-self, etc.

5.4.2 Cooperation

Almost always, individuals prefer to act independently rather than to cooperate because cooperation requires sacrificing some freedom and then sharing the benefits. Cooperation is often a "fallback" option when competition is not expected to be successful.

Cooperation is more likely to occur within a group than between groups. Cooperation can exist when two or more individuals seek the same goal and believe it is more likely achieved by cooperation than otherwise. To achieve this goal, their behaviors are probably similar – which would cause the cross-correlation coefficient of a pair of participants to be relatively constant and, therefore, positively correlated.

Cooperation is similar to group morality:

- it allows less freedom of behavior than competition;
- it is usually more risk-avoidant than competition;
- it is related to lesser motivation and lesser productivity; and
- it is sometimes responsible for the same biased markets as are monopolies and unions.

5.4.3 Competition

Competition is dependent behavior between individuals, groups, or species who seek the same goal. Attempting to achieve the same goal causes the participants to behave similarly – which would cause the cross-correlation coefficient of the pair of sequences to be relatively constant and, therefore, positively correlated.

In nature, populations of a species often shrink when individuals compete intensely for resources (i.e., a biological phenomenon called density dependence). Competition is usually intense if resources are insufficient. In free markets, prices rise when *consumers* compete to purchase a resource, and prices fall when *producers* compete to sell a resource.[109]

It is difficult to envision life without competition - because efficiency of production is less important without competition. Without competition there probably would be little or no progress. Cooperation might help us get *along*, but competition helps us get *ahead*. (Competition, like efficiency, gravity, or magnetism, tends to increase order.)[110]

---

[109] It seems that a result of competition depends upon how it is solved: If capital is employed to solve competition, capital becomes more competitive, and if humans are employed to solve it the human becomes more competitive.

[110] Marx and Engles' comments about competition (from Section 9.7.3, *The Nature of Economics*, Martin J. Miles). Charles Darwin published *On the Origin of Species* in 1859. This

Competition exists more frequently between groups than within groups. Research of primitive societies has shown that competition within a group is almost always confined to seeking a mate.

Competition is similar to individual morality:

- it allows freedom of behavior;

- it is relatively risk-acceptant;

- it is related to greater motivation and greater productivity; and

- it causes lower and more accurate market prices.

Competition and cooperation are usually considered opposite behaviors, but they have some similar behaviors: If two or more parties seek the same resource, they compete if each considers it individually obtainable, and they cooperate if each considers it unlikely to be individually obtainable.

Natural selection or freedom may be more likely if individuals in a group employ a judicious combination of competition and cooperation.

5.4.4 Force

If an individual feels that a behavior is in his/her interest, it needn't be forced. Our definition of moral behavior is that the individual expects the behavior to increase his/her probability of freedom. If behavior is forced, it is the behavior of a commanding authority by restraint rather than the behavior of the subject individual.

Governments are our representatives. If governments do what citizens want, such as in a democratic government, they are more likely to behave morally. However, the more diverse is the citizenry, the less the democratic government is able to do what the citizens want.

---

was 11 years after Marx and Engels published *Communist Manifesto* and 35 years before they published *Das Kapital.*
Engels ridiculed Darwin:

- He wrote in 1872 that "*Darwin did not know what a bitter satire he wrote on mankind when he showed that free competition, the struggle for existence, which the economists celebrate as the highest historical achievement, is the normal state of the animal kingdom*".

- He ridiculed Darwin for theorizing that free competition is normal animal behavior. Engels believed competition was not normal human behavior.

Karl Marx abhorred competition; he believed it was wasteful. Even though he abhorred competition, shockingly, he contradicted himself when he said, *"It is absolutely impossible to transcend the laws of nature."*

A common purpose of forced behavior is the involuntary redistribution of income or wealth to another individual or group – beyond the natural group. It is immoral because it is forced giving to strangers. It causes the taxpayer, whose wealth is being redistributed to strangers, to have less freedom, and it is intended to give the recipient more freedom – but this result is usually effective only in the near term: Receiving unearned benefits encourages hubris, sloth, irresponsibility, and unsuccessful behavior. This behavior is contrary to individual and group morality.

Section 5.2.3 introduces the concept of political freedom. Freedom exists inherently in life forms, but it can be denied or diminished by other individuals and groups, particularly by governments after they assume the responsibilities of individuals. Almost invariably, governments require forced cooperation.

When an amount is extracted from the taxpayer by the government, it creates one or more intervening negative events in the taxpayer's sequence of events whose moral behavior could be measured by the autocorrelation function. If these forced acts are inconsistent with the taxpayer's self-interest, the value of the autocorrelation function will be reduced, and it will possibly be negative.

5.4.5 Summary of Types of Dependent Behavior

Table 5.4.5-1 lists the expected fraction of a resource, q, sought by parties using each of the four types of dependent behavior.

Table 5.4.5-1 fraction, of a resource, q, acquired by each party using each of the four types of dependent behavior

		Method	Parties	Fraction of Resources Acquired by Each Party	
				Party 1	Party 2
Types of Dependent Behavior	Individual	Autocorrelation: $r_1 = \text{cov}(x_i, x_{i+1})/s_x^2$ $= [\Sigma(x_i - m_x)\cdot(x_{i+1} - m_x)] / [\Sigma(x_i - m_x)^2]$	Party 1 (i.e., Individual)	$[(1+r_1)/2]\cdot q$	-
	Cooperation	Cross-Correlation: $r_{xy} = \text{cov}(x, y)/(s_x\cdot s_y)$ $= [\Sigma(x_i - m_x) \cdot (y_i - m_y)] / [\Sigma(x_i - m_x)^2\cdot\Sigma(y_i - m_y)^2]^{1/2}$	Party 1 and Party 2	$[(1+r_{xy})/2]\cdot zq^*$	$[(1+r_{xy})/2]\cdot (1-z)\cdot q^{**}$
	Competition		Party 1 vs Party 2 (i.e., assuming Party 1 is the Winner of Competition)	$[(1+r_{xy})/2]\cdot q$	0
	Force	Confiscation	Party 1 vs Party 2 (i.e., assuming Party 1 is the Authority)	q	0

*z = agreed fraction of a resource, q, to party 1
**1-z = agreed fraction of a resource, q, to party 2

5.5 Moral Behavior Applied to the Criteria of Natural Selection

The individual is always the object of natural selection, but individuals are often more likely to be selected if they judiciously compete and cooperate with other individuals from their group, species, or the ecosystem.

Table 5.5-1 is a convenient summary of the system of four dependent behaviors that can occur to achieve natural selection (i.e., freedom) from the three criteria. It also lists the probability of rejection from each of the three criteria and the resulting probability of natural selection from all three criteria.

Table 5.5-1 dependent moral behaviors matched with the criteria of natural selection

			Natural Selection Criteria		
			Physical Environment Criteria	Biological Environment Criteria (Entropy Designs the Predator-Pathogen-Prey Food Cycle)	
			1 Environment Protection Criteria	2 Predator-Pathogen Protection Criteria	3 Prey Acquisition Criteria
Moral Behavior (Behavior that Increases the Probability of Freedom and, S_r of Natural Selection)	Dependent Behavior ($0 < r$)	Individual — Constant Resource Acquisition	Inherent or Constant Acquisition of Necessary Resources to Protect from the Physical Environment Including the Immune System's Ability to Repair Injury	Inherent or Constant Acquisition of Necessary Resources to Protect from Predators Including the Immune System's Ability to Protect from Pathogens	Constant Acquisition of Necessary Prey
		Cooperation — Resource Acquisition in an Idealized Fair Society	Cooperation to Acquire Necessary Protection from the Physical Environment	Cooperation to Acquire Necessary Protection from Large Predators Including Humans	Cooperation to Acquire Necessary Prey
		Competition — Resource Acquisition in an Idealized Free Market	Competition to Acquire Necessary Protection from the Physical Environment	————	Competition to Acquire Necessary Prey
Immoral Behavior (Behavior that Decreases the Probability, S_r of Natural Selection)	Dependent Behavior ($r < 0$)	Force and/or Individual — Inconstant Resource Acquisition (e.g., Force and/or Inconstant Individual Behavior)	Inconstant Acquisition of Necessary Protection from the Physical Environment or Forced Redistribution	Inconstant Acquisition of Necessary Protection from Large Predators Including Humans or Forced Redistribution	Inconstant Acquisition of Necessary Prey or Forced Redistribution
Probabilities of Rejection			R_1	R_2	R_3
Probability of Selection			$S = 1 - \{(R_1 + R_2 + R_3) - [(R_1 \cdot R_2) + (R_1 \cdot R_3) + (R_2 \cdot R_3)] + (R_1 \cdot R_2 \cdot R_3)\}$		

Chapter 6 Measure Moral Behavior, Freedom, Accuracy, and Market Freedom

This chapter has the following sections:

---

[111] We shall use the theories of probability and statistics to analyze the behavior of one or more individuals. It is conventional in statistics to use Greek letters for parameters that represent the *population* of observations (e.g., rho (ρ) for the correlation coefficient, mu (μ) for the mean, and sigma (σ) for the standard deviation), and it is convenient to use Roman letters to represent a *sample* of observations taken from the population of observations (e.g., r for the correlation coefficient, m for the mean, and s for the standard deviation).

As discussed in the previous chapter, a process can be increasingly well-defined in three steps: described with words, modeled with a mathematical formula that is isomorphic to the process behavior, and measured with the mathematical model.

Measurement is the most precise step of the definition. The purpose of this chapter is to measure four very important parameters:

- moral behavior (i.e., Moral Behavior function),
- freedom (i.e., Freedom function),
- accuracy (i.e., Accuracy function), and
- market freedom (i.e., Market Freedom function).

Constancy of behavior produces the same remarkable results for both moral behavior and accuracy:

- Constancy of moral behavior is consistent with freedom.
- Constancy of accuracy is consistent with a free market because accuracy is a function of the variance and constancy is consistent with a small variance.

It is common to measure physical phenomena (i.e., from mathematical models). They are isomorphic to known physical laws. It is, however, uncommon to measure social parameters (because life is freedom). However, we are able to do it here and answer a few questions, some of which have been sought for centuries.

We begin with a set of four structured diagrams to show how the four measured parameters relate to each other. Figure 6-1 consists of four structured diagrams that depict the relationships among these four important parameters. If you do not care about the logical *relationships*, you can skip Figure 6-1 and simply concentrate on the logic of *each* formula.

Figure 6-1 Formulas measure the Moral Behavior function, the Freedom function, the Accuracy function, and the Market Freedom function: They are depicted by four structured diagrams: (a) the expected value of an interval estimator, cov(x^, y^), of the covariance; (b) the expected value of a point estimator, θ^, of the mean; (c) formulas for the Moral behavior function; and the Freedom function, and (d) formulas for the Accuracy function and the Market Freedom function. (See Appendix A.)

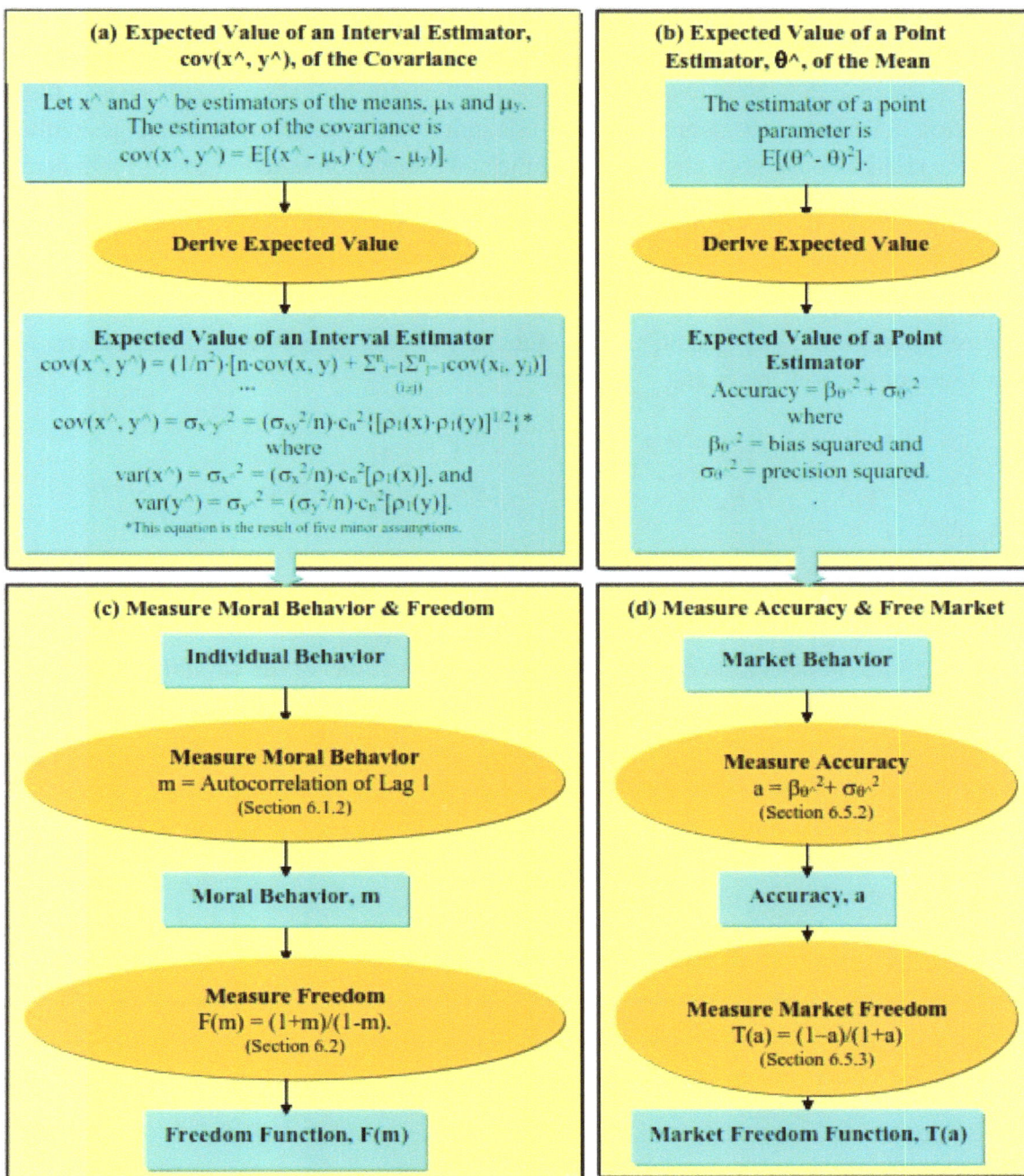

6.1 Correlation Functions Measure Moral Behavior

Moral behavior can be modeled on a scale from 1 to -1. That is, totally moral (constant) behavior is 1, amoral behavior is 0, and totally immoral (inconstant) behavior is -1. Then, moral behavior can be modeled "isomorphically" by either of the following two types of correlation functions: the cross-correlation function or the autocorrelation function of lag 1.

Estimating correlation is the first step in accounting for dependence. The correlation function is a formula that measures the correlation of one or two sequences of observations. It measures either the degree to which two individuals or phenomena change together (i.e., the cross-correlation function) or the degree to which one individual or phenomenon changes within itself over time relative to the previous value (i.e., the autocorrelation function of lag 1). In both cases, the range of values for the correlation coefficient is the interval, [-1, 1].[112]

6.1.1 Cross-Correlation Function

The cross-correlation coefficient, r_{xy}, is a function of two sequences of observations *between* individuals or phenomena, x and y. That is,

$$r_{xy} = \text{cov}(x, y)/(s_x \cdot s_y)$$

$$= [(1/k) \cdot \Sigma(x_i - m_x) \cdot (y_i - m_y)] / \{[(1/k) \cdot \Sigma(x_i - m_x)^2]^{1/2} \cdot [(1/k) \cdot \Sigma(y_i - m_y)^2]^{1/2}\}$$

$$= [\Sigma(x_i - m_x) \cdot (y_i - m_y)] / [\Sigma(x_i - m_x)^2 \cdot \Sigma(y_i - m_y)^2]^{1/2} \quad [113]$$

where

- r_{xy} = cross-correlation of the sequences of observations of the variables, x and y.

- k = number of observations (i.e., the sample size) in each sequence.

- x_i = i[th] observation in the sequence of k observations of the x phenomenon.

- y_i = i[th] observation in the sequence of k observations of the y phenomenon.

- Σ denotes the sum of the k terms.

- m_x = mean of the observations, x_i.

- m_y = mean of the observations, y_i.

---

[112] It is common to hear that "correlation is not necessarily causation." This is true, but causation is not an issue here.

[113] The number of observations, k, is omitted from this expression of the equation only because entries in the numerator and the denominator of this term of the equation cancel each other.

- $cov(x, y) = [(1/k) \cdot \Sigma(x_i - m_x) \cdot (y_i - m_y)]$ = covariance of x and y.

- $s_x = [(1/k) \cdot \Sigma(x_i - m_x)^2]^{1/2}$ = standard deviation of x (i.e., positive square root of the variance of x).

- $s_y = [(1/k) \cdot \Sigma(y_i - m_y)^2]^{1/2}$ = standard deviation of y (i.e., positive square root of the variance of y).

Two common examples of positively correlated random variables for individuals are height and weight and also income and education.

Figure 6.1.1-1 is two graphs of cross-correlation. The upper graph depicts positive cross-correlation between the sequence, X (e.g., a zigzag) and the sequence, A (e.g., a straight diagonal line). The correlation is $r_{xy} = 0.830$. The lower graph depicts negative cross-correlation between the sequence, Y (another zigzag) and A (the same straight diagonal line). The correlation is $r_{ay} = -0.946$. The straight diagonal line, A, could be considered a normative, constant, or moral sequence.

Following are two types of cross-correlation (that are not depicted).

Cross-Correlation between Two Sequences: Individual Behavior and Normative (i.e., Group) Behavior

Since group morality is the normative morality within a group's native environment, cross-correlation can compare a sequence of normative moral behavior to a sequence of individual behavior. In this case the closer the cross-correlation coefficient is to 1, the more normative is the individual's behavior.

Cross-Correlation between Two Sequences: Both Sequences from either Cooperation or Competition

Positive cross-correlation between two individuals or two phenomena is consistent with moral behavior. Two types of dependent behavior are cooperation and competition.

- **Cooperation.** If two individuals or two phenomena cooperate, their goal would be common (e.g., defending against the same threat) and their behaviors would probably be so similar as to mimic each other. This behavior would cause the cross-correlation coefficient to be positive and close to 1.

- **Competition.** If two individuals or two phenomena compete, their goal would be common (e.g., acquiring the same resource) and their behaviors would probably be similar. This behavior would cause the cross-correlation coefficient to be positive and close to 1.

These two types of behavior would be moral only if their purpose is moral.

Figure 6.1.1-1. The cross-correlation coefficient for two different sequences is shown as dashed lines, relative to the diagonal straight line. The upper graph depicts integer values of a sequence, X, whose correlation coefficient with the integer values of the diagonal straight line, A, is r_{ax} = 0.830. The lower graph depicts integer values of a sequence, Y, whose correlation coefficient with the integer values of the diagonal straight line, A, is r_{ay} = -0.946.

$$r_{ax} = [\Sigma(a_i-m_a)(x_i-m_x)] / [\Sigma(a_i-m_a)^2 \cdot \Sigma(x_i-m_x)^2]^{1/2} = 17/(42 \times 10)^{1/2} = 0.830$$

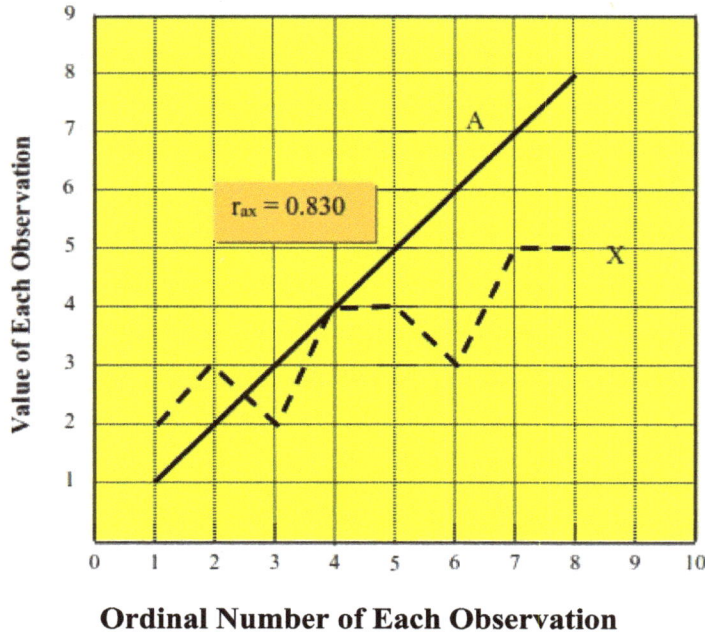

$$r_{ay} = [\Sigma(a_i-m_a)(y_i-m_y)] / [\Sigma(a_i-m_a)^2 \cdot \Sigma(y_i-m_y)^2]^{1/2} = -26/(42 \times 18)^{1/2} = -0.946$$

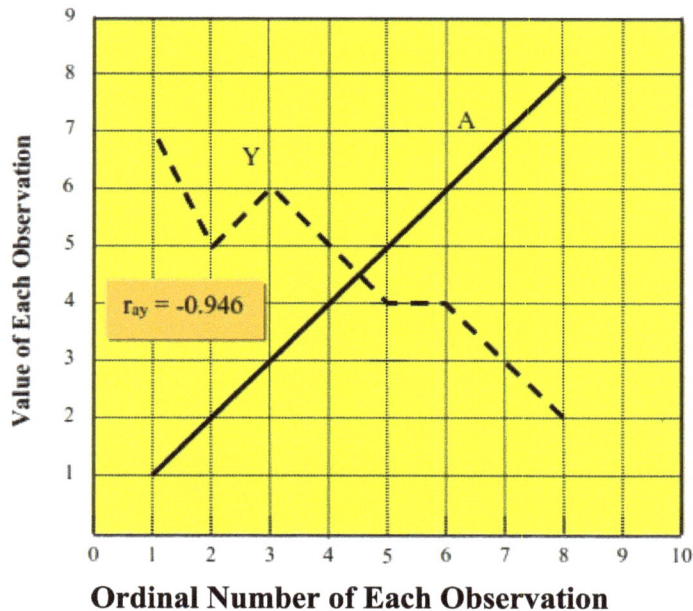

110

6.1.2 Autocorrelation Function of Lag 1

Observations that occur close in time or space are more likely to be similar than observations that are not. Hence, if dependence exists, it most likely exists between consecutive observations (i.e., observations of lag 1). This view of dependence measures constancy. It is called first-order Markov dependence. The estimate of the autocorrelation of lag 1 for a single sequence of the variable, x, is

$$r_1 = cov(x_i, x_{i+1})/s_x^2$$

$$= [(1/k) \cdot \Sigma(x_i - m_x) \cdot (x_{i+1} - m_x)] / [(1/k) \cdot \Sigma(x_i - m_x)^2]$$

$$= [\Sigma(x_i - m_x) \cdot (x_{i+1} - m_x)] / [\Sigma(x_i - m_x)^2] \quad [114] [115]$$

where

- r_1 = estimate of the autocorrelation of lag 1 of the sequence of observations of a variable, x.

- k = number of observations (i.e., the sample size).

- x_i = ith observation in the sequence of k observations.

- x_{i+1} = (i+1)th observation (i.e., lag 1) in the sequence of k observations.

- Σ denotes the sum of the k terms.

- $m_x = (1/k) \cdot \Sigma_1^k x_i$ = mean of the observations, x_i.

- $cov(x_i, x_{i+1}) = [(1/k) \cdot \Sigma(x_i - m_x) \cdot (x_{i+1} - m_x)]$ = covariance of observations, x_i and x_{i+1}.

- $s_x^2 = (1/k) \cdot \Sigma(x_i - m_x)^2$ = variance of observations, x_i.

Figure 6.1.2-1 depicts the autocorrelation of three sequences of observations. They show why the constancy of E and F each tend to be positively correlated and why the inconstancy of P tends to be negatively correlated.

---

[114] The number of observations, k, is omitted from this expression of the equation only because entries in the numerator and the denominator of the same term of the above equation cancel each other.

[115] This estimate of the autocorrelation of lag 1 is a desirable estimate because it is unbiased, consistent, and efficient. See Appendix A.

Figure 6.1.2-1 The graph of the sequence, P, is an example of negative autocorrelation, $r_{1p} = -1.0$. The two graphs of the sequences E and F, are examples of positive autocorrelation, $r_{1e} = 0.7021$ and $r_{1f} = 0.7021$, that illustrate that the autocorrelation is independent of the slope.

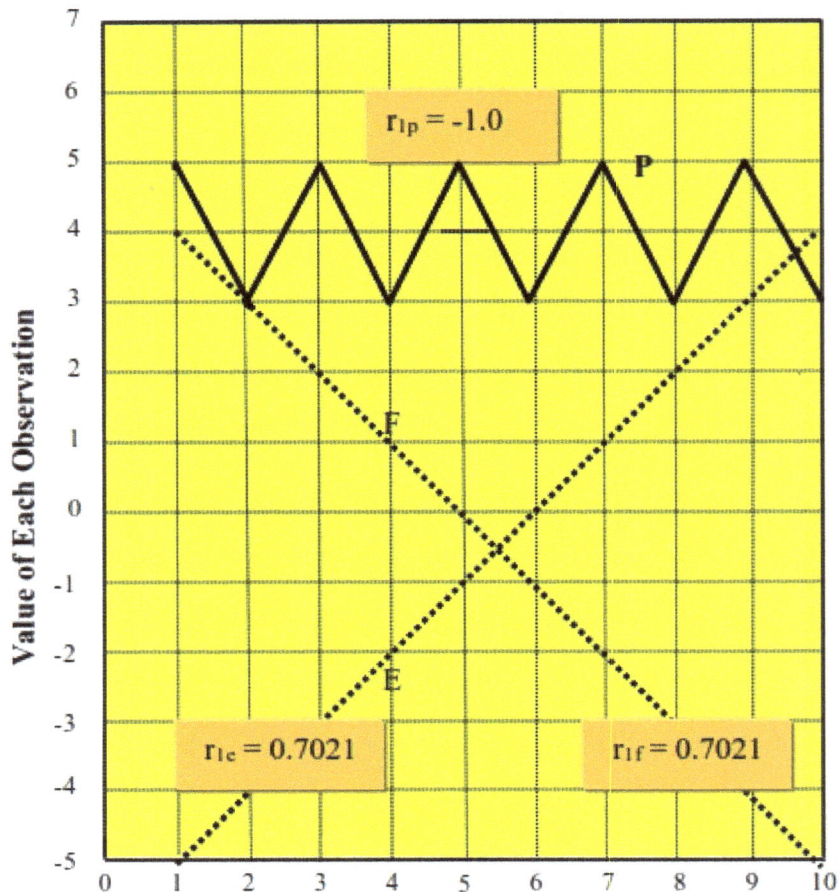

Dependent Behavior *within* a Sequence

Because a constant sequence of obtaining a necessary resource is essential for life (i.e., freedom), a constant sequence represents successful (and moral) behavior. Immoral behavior would be created by one or more inconstant aberrations, such as would be created by force (e.g., redistribution by a government). Autocorrelation measures the constancy of behavior. The more constant, the more positive is the correlation, and the less constant, the more negative is the correlation. This relationship is discussed in Section 6.2.

Measuring the Morality of Individual Behavior

The autocorrelation coefficient of lag 1 is ideal for measuring the constancy of moral behavior: Hence, the correlation of moral behavior is in the interval [-1, 1] where totally moral behavior is 1, amoral behavior is 0, and totally immoral behavior is -1.

More Examples of Autocorrelation

Appendix B shows many graphs of autocorrelation of lag 1 to illustrate the effects, if any, of

- orientation,
- number of observations,
- constancy (i.e., shape), and
- slope.

This appendix also shows how constancy can be measured, and it discusses the conditions that cause the autocorrelation to be negative.

Because we shall use the autocorrelation coefficient as the mathematical model to measure moral behavior, we shall label it the Moral Behavior function.

6.2 Freedom and the Freedom Function

Ideally, freedom is the ability to behave morally. Freedom can be viewed as a collection of rights which probably include human rights and legal rights. Freedom can be denied in at least three ways:

- **Death.**
- **Restraint.** Freedom can be denied (actively) by the restraint of an authority.
- **Constraint.** Freedom can be denied (passively) by the constraint of insufficient capital or natural and acquired resources – including knowledge.

Table 6.2-1 ways in which freedom can be increased

		Method to Increase Freedom
Type of Freedom Denial	Death	Moral Behavior
	Restraint (Physical)	
	Constraint (Insufficient Resources)	

In Section 6.2, we measure freedom as a function of moral behavior, and in Sections 6.5.2 and 6.5.3, we measure a specific type of freedom – freedom of markets as a function of accuracy. (The same method used here might also apply to other types of freedom.)

6.2.1 Network Performance and the Freedom Function

Americans were so shocked in 1957 when the USSR launched its Sputnik satellite that, in 1958, President Eisenhower created an agency to study and develop emerging technologies. That agency is the Department of Defense's Advanced Research Projects Agency (ARPA). Among its projects in 1969, ARPA created a primitive network of a few computers, called the ARPANET. In 1974 the Office of Telecommunications of the Department of Commerce in Boulder, Colorado joined that primitive network as its 23rd computer, called a terminal interface processor (TIP).[116] At that time, this author and his late colleague, Dr. Edwin L. Crow generated and analyzed digital communication data from this TIP of the ARPANET to develop network performance standards. These standards were published as the *American National Standard X3.141,* which became the de facto World standard.[117] The ARPANET became the Internet in 1991 with government approval of the High-Performance Computing Act (HPCA).

---

[116] Two events were particularly noteworthy for the development of the Internet: Networks could *communicate* with other networks after 1983 when the Transmission Control Protocol and Internet Protocol (TCP/IP) were developed and implemented. Then, the ARPANET evolved quickly into the Internet after 1991 when the High-Performance Computing Act (HPCA) provided more funding. (In 2020 the Internet had more than 4.3 billion Internet Protocol addresses worldwide!)

[117] *Performance Evaluation of Data Communication Services: NTIA Implementation of American National Standard X3.141*, NTIA Report 95-319, *Volume 5 Data Analysis*, Martin J. Miles. In that publication, the function that we now call the Freedom function was known as the Dependence factor. It was defined in *Appendix A: Formulas for Analysis of a Single Test,*

As mentioned earlier, statistical dependence is almost always ignored by analysts (by merely assuming that observations are independent). To analyze dependent behavior, we derived a function that we called the Dependence factor.[118] Its purpose is to correct the degrees of freedom so that the autocorrelation of lag 1 can be estimated more precisely when the observations are dependent. Beginning with the covariance, we derived the Dependence factor to accurately estimate the autocorrelation of lag 1.

Specifically, the Dependence factor is multiplied by the confidence limits – to make them appropriately smaller or larger, depending upon whether the dependence causes negative or positive autocorrelation, respectively.

6.2.2 Derivation of the Freedom Function

Appendix A lists the derivation of the Dependence factor.[119] However, we summarize it here: It is likely that some serial statistical dependence exists among the trials in a sample. Dependence among trials in a sample can be expressed by the second-order moments of the mean of a sampling distribution. Specifically, if $x^\wedge$ is the estimate of the mean of the sample of size n, where the trials are $x_1, \dots, x_n$, and if μ is the population mean, it can be shown that the expected value of the variance of $x^\wedge$ is

$$E[(x^\wedge - \mu_x)^2] \equiv \sigma^2_{x^\wedge} = (\sigma^2_x/n) \cdot c^2_n(P)^{120}$$

---

equation A-1, and it was used in *Appendix E: Formulas for Analysis of Multiple Tests* in equations E-7, E-12, E-13, E-17, E-19, E-22, E-46, and E-51 of the *American National Standard X3.141*.

[118] The Dependence factor corrects the *degree of freedom* because of dependence in the F statistic (i.e., for the F test in the analysis of variance) that determines if multiple means can be considered to come from the same statistical population.

[119] The derivation in Appendix A uses five reasonable and inconsequential assumptions. (1) It is assumed that the observations deviate randomly. (2) It is assumed that dependence depends upon the relative order of the observations. (This assumption of dependence causes cross-correlation to become autocorrelation.) (3) It is then assumed that dependence between observations of the single sequence decreases monotonically with respect to the order within the sequence. (4) It is then assumed that, because of dependence, the covariance converges to zero. (5) Finally, it is assumed that dependences between all consecutive observations are equal (i.e., called first-order Markov dependence).

[120] This is equation A-12. As discussed in Appendix A, five desirable types of statistical estimators are unbiased, consistent, efficient, Best Asymptotic Normal (BAN), and Maximum Likelihood (ML). BAN estimators have many desirable properties, but ML estimators have the most desirable properties.

where σ^2 is the population variance, and $c^2_n(P)$ is the Dependence factor for ρ_1. The Dependence factor for ρ_1 is

$$c^2_n(P) = 1 + (1/n)\cdot(\Sigma^n_{i=1} \Sigma_{=1} \rho_{ij})$$
$$i \neq j$$

where ρ_{ij} is the population correlation between the trials, x_i, and, x_j, and, P, (i.e., upper case ρ) indicates that c_n is a function of the set of ρ_{ij}'s. If the trials are independent, each $\rho_{ij} = 0$, and $c^2_n(0) = 1$.

A. Assumptions about the Dependence Factor

This subsection shows how the Dependence factor for ρ_1, $c^2_n(P)$, can be reduced to

$$(1+ \rho_1)/(1- \rho_1).$$

If it is assumed that dependence between pairs of trials is a function of the lag between them, let $k = |i - j|$, and $\rho_{ij} \equiv \rho_k$. Then

$$c^2_n(P) = 1+ 2\cdot\Sigma^{n-1}_{k=1} (1- k/n)\cdot\rho_k.$$

Trials that occur close in time or space are more likely to be similar than are trials that are not close. Hence, if serial dependence exists, it is likely to occur between adjacent trials (i.e., trials of lag 1). If it is further assumed that dependence is exponential with respect to the lag, then $\rho_k = \rho^k$. Although it is unnecessary, this relationship can be viewed as the product of k correlations, each of lag 1 (i.e., $\rho_k = \rho_i^k$). This view of dependence is called Markov dependence, and

$$c^2_n(\rho_1) = 1 + [2\rho_1 /(1 - \rho_1)]\cdot \{1- (1/n)\cdot[(1-\rho_1^n)/(1-\rho_1)]\}.$$

Notice that

$$c^2_n(1) = n,$$
$$c^2_n(0) = 1,$$
$$c^2_n(-1) = \begin{cases} 0 \text{ for n even} \\ 1/n \text{ for n odd,} \end{cases}$$

and

$$\text{as } n \to\infty, c^2_n(\rho_1) \equiv c^2(\rho_1) = (1+ \rho_1)/(1- \rho_1). [121]$$

---

[121] $(1+ \underline{\rho_1})/(1- \rho_1)$ is also the hyperbolic cotangent, $ctnh[ln(\rho_1)]$. However, it can evaluate this expression only when $0< \rho_1 <1$.

116

B. The Dependance Factor is a Function of the Confidence Interval for the Estimate of the Autocorrelation Coefficient

This subsection shows the unnecessary but fortuitous relationship between the Dependence factor for ρ_1 and the confidence interval for the estimate of the autocorrelation coefficient of lag 1, ρ_1. This is an interval that we can be $\alpha100\%$ confident contains the estimate, where $0 \leq \alpha \leq 1$.

As mentioned in a previous footnote (i.e., Section A.1.1 of Appendix A in NTIA Report 95-319 of the American National Standard X3.141), the confidence interval for ρ_1 is the product of the following three values:

- The percentage point, t, from the Student t distribution corresponding to $\alpha100\%$ and n-1

- The standard deviation, σ, of ρ_1, divided by $n^{1/2}$

- Two times the square root of the Dependence factor, $c^2_n(\rho_1)$.

That is,

$$\text{(Confidence interval for } \rho_1) = 2t \cdot (\sigma/n^{1/2}) \cdot c_n(\rho_1).$$

Therefore,

$$\text{(Dependence Factor for } \rho_1) = \text{(Confidence interval for } \rho_1)^2 \cdot [n/(2t \cdot \sigma)^2].$$

C. The Dependence Factor Can be Relabeled as the Freedom Function

We introduce the Freedom function in Figure 6.2.2-1. This figure shows the same graph twice:
- The top graph is the Dependence factor, $c^2_n(r_1)$, as a function of the autocorrelation coefficient of lag 1 (including the formula depicted as a function of r_1).
- The bottom graph is the Freedom function, $F_n(m)$, as a function of moral behavior (including the formula depicted as a function of m).

The values in the two graphs are the same - only the purpose and the labels are different. Both graphs include, n, the number of observations. Both are a function of the autocorrelation coefficient of lag 1. When we use the function as the Freedom function, we use the single curve corresponding to $n \to \infty$. (That is, for greater precision we let the number of observations approach infinity.) Now, the formula for the Freedom function becomes extremely simple: That is,

$$F_n(m) = 1 + [2m/(1 - m)] \cdot \{1 - (1/n) \cdot [(1 - m^n)/(1 - m)]\},$$

reduces to

$$F(m) = (1 + m)/(1 - m),$$

as $n \to \infty$.[122]

Figure 6.2.2-2 depicts the Freedom function as a function of moral behavior. It notes that the late economist, Walter Williams, and others wanted to see a function such as this.

Of course, as $m \to 1$, freedom $\to \infty$. Infinite freedom could be considered a necessary characteristic for an afterlife.

---

[122] Specifically, when we want to estimate a value, we obtain a large random sample of values and determine its mean value, but that is not enough. We can determine an interval about the mean value within which we can be, for example, 95% confident that it contains the true value. However, the length of the interval varies if the samples are dependent. The Dependence factor (our Freedom function) corrects the end-points of the interval to correct them for the dependence.

Figure 6.2.2-1 curves for values of n for the dependence factor and the freedom function

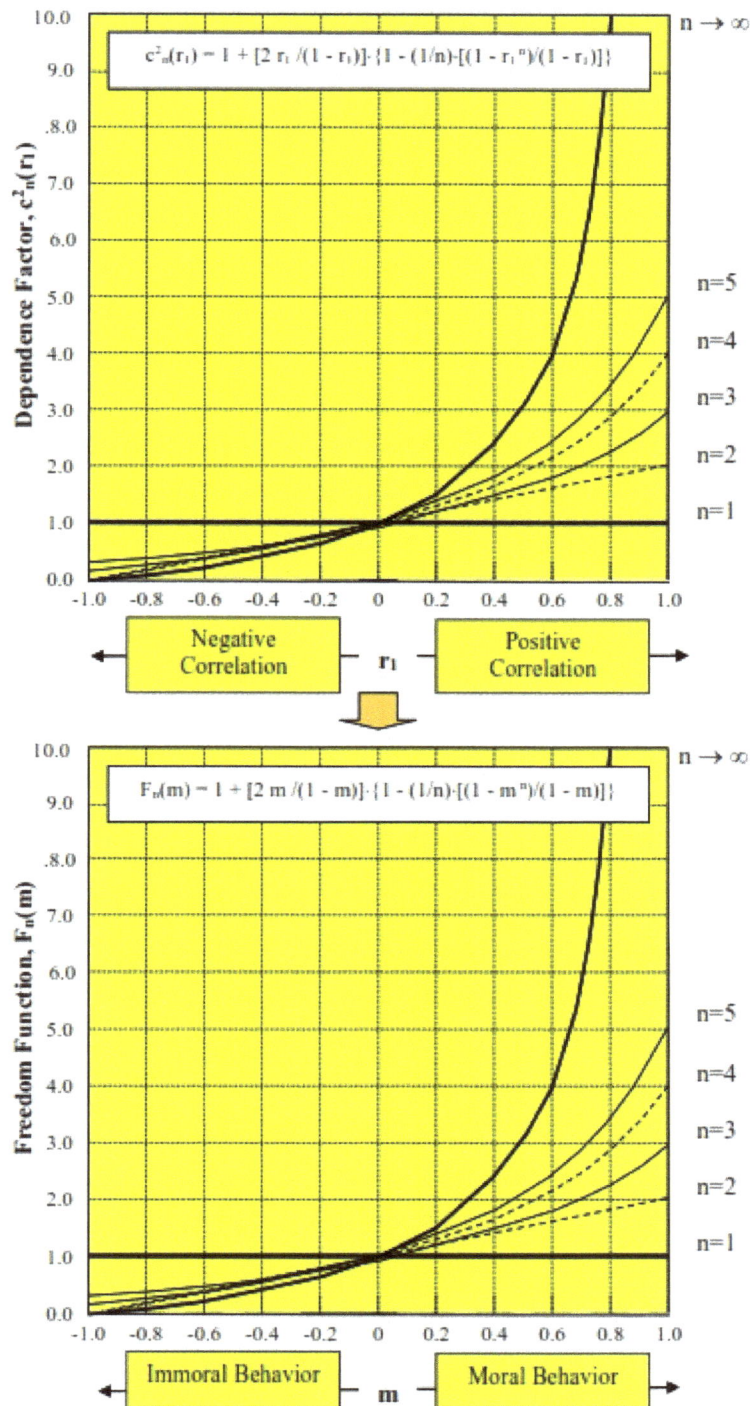

$$c^2_n(r_1) = 1 + [2 r_1 /(1 - r_1)] \cdot \{1 - (1/n) \cdot [(1 - r_1{}^n)/(1 - r_1)]\}$$

$n \to \infty$

Dependence Factor, $c^2_n(r_1)$

n=5
n=4
n=3
n=2
n=1

Negative Correlation r_1 Positive Correlation

$$F_n(m) = 1 + [2 m /(1 - m)] \cdot \{1 - (1/n) \cdot [(1 - m^n)/(1 - m)]\}$$

$n \to \infty$

Freedom Function, $F_n(m)$

n=5
n=4
n=3
n=2
n=1

Immoral Behavior m Moral Behavior

Figure 6.2.2-2 The Freedom function, F(m), is a function of moral behavior, m. It is defined over the interval -1≤ m < 1.

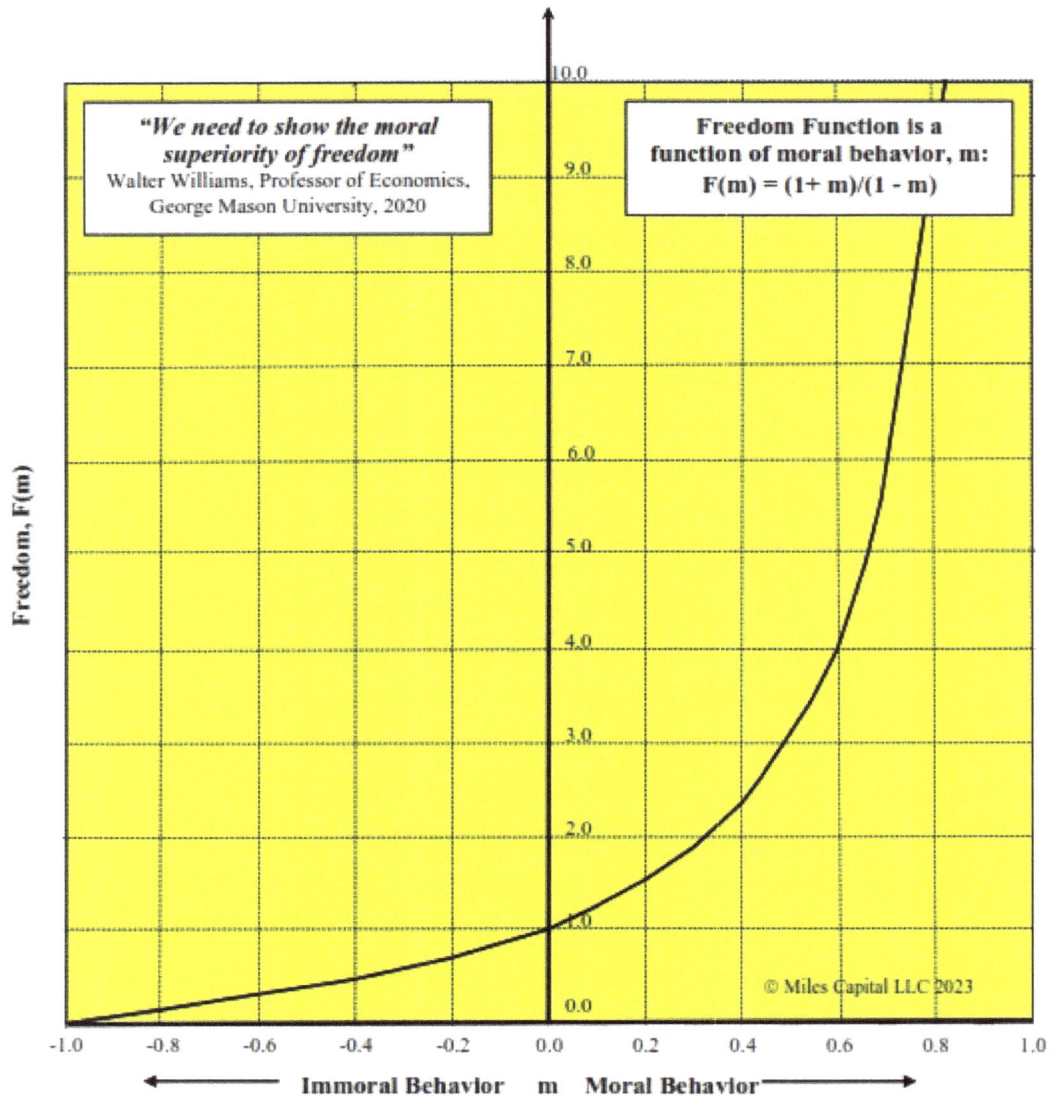

"*We need to show the moral superiority of freedom*"
Walter Williams, Professor of Economics, George Mason University, 2020

Freedom Function is a function of moral behavior, m:
$$F(m) = (1+ m)/(1 - m)$$

© Miles Capital LLC 2023

Immoral Behavior   m   Moral Behavior

6.2.3 Relationships between Moral Behavior and Freedom

Figure 6.2.2-2 depicts the Freedom function as a function of moral behavior. It notes that the late economist, Walter Williams, and others wanted a function such as this. Even though the Freedom function seems to be a perfect model for freedom, following are

A. criteria for a Freedom function,

B. freedom and moral behavior are naturally opposing binary states,

C. the three concepts of this book can increase exponentially if and only if they employ capital, and

D. the loss of thermal energy, the loss of life/freedom, and the loss of moral behavior.

A. Criteria for a Freedom Function

Any function that models freedom must be isomorphic to freedom, and it must satisfy the following criteria:

- It must be continuous.

- It must be non-negative.

- It must change monotonically with moral behavior.[123]

- When a Freedom function equals 0, moral behavior must equal -1 (i.e., totally *immoral* behavior).

- When a Freedom function approaches infinity, moral behavior must approach 1 (i.e., totally *moral* behavior).

B. Freedom and Moral Behavior are Naturally Opposing Binary States

For thousands of years, philosophers have been intrigued by the concept of duality in nature. In the East, duality is called Yin-yang, and in the West, it is often called naturally opposing binary states.[124] Generally, duality maintains balance between two opposing binary (and, sometimes,

---

[123] The closest tangent to the Freedom function is at the midpoint of the interval. This is true for any curve that doesn't have an inflection point in the interval. *An Extremum Property of Convex Functions*, M. J. Miles, Environmental Science Services Administration, Boulder, Colorado, American Mathematical Monthly, Vol. 76, No. 8, October 1969

[124] Projective (i.e., non-Euclidian) geometry has no parallel lines or planes. Since lines and planes intersect, it also is a system of duality:

- In two dimensions, two points define a line and two lines define a point.

- In three dimensions, two lines define a plane and two planes define a line; three points define a plane, and three planes define a point.

complementary) states. Some states are discrete and others are continuous. Our pairs are continuous. Sometimes one state is active, and the other is passive. The concept of duality is important to moral behavior and freedom.

Four Types of Naturally Opposing Binary States

We consider the following intriguing types of naturally opposing binary states: Table 6.2.3-1 lists common naturally occurring binary states as well as the naturally opposing binary states, moral behavior, and freedom. Responsibilities are a subset of moral behavior, and rights are a subset of freedom.

Table 6.2.3-1 This table is a list of common naturally opposing binary states. Responsibilities are a subset of moral behavior, and rights are a subset of freedom. All states are listed as either those that tend to give or those that tend to receive.

Naturally Opposing Binary States	
States that Give	**States that Receive**
Produce	Consume
Risk	Reward
Moral Behavior (e.g., Responsibilities)	Freedom (e.g., Rights)
Supply	Demand

To maintain balance, the states must remain as a pair. For example, we can't consume unless we produce; we shouldn't risk unless success is expected to provide an acceptable reward; and the supply of a good or service should equal the expected demand; etc.

States are Functions of Each Other

Each state can be considered to be a function of the other. That is, each state can be the independent variable, while the other state would be the dependent variable.

The types of dualities that are of special interest for this book are moral behavior and freedom and rights and responsibilities: Rights are specific freedoms, and responsibilities are specific moral behaviors. Therefore, rights are a subset of freedom and responsibilities are a subset of moral behaviors. That is, freedom and moral behavior are also naturally opposing binary states.

Table 6.2.3-2 is two tables that show that each state can be either the dependent variable or the independent variable when one variable is a function of the other.

Table 6.2.3-2 Each of the two tables lists both pairs of naturally opposing binary states. The table on the left lists the states that give as the independent variable and the states that receive as the dependent variable. The table on the right lists the states that receive as the independent variable and the states that give as the dependent variable.

States that Give	States that Receive	States that Receive	States that Give
Independent Variable	Dependent Variable	Independent Variable	Dependent Variable
Produce	Consume	Consume	Produce
Risk	Reward	Reward	Risk
Moral Behavior (e.g., Responsibilities)	Freedom (e.g., Rights)	Freedom (e.g., Rights)	Moral Behavior (e.g., Responsibilities)
Supply	Demand	Demand	Supply

Figure 6.2.2-2 and Figure 6.2.3-1 depict the conclusions of the above two tables. That is, Figure 6.2.2-2 depicts freedom as a function of moral behavior, and Figure 6.2.3-1 depicts moral behavior as a function of freedom!

Figure 6.2.3-1 Moral Behavior function, M(f), is a function of freedom, f.
It is defined over the interval $0 \leq f < \infty$.

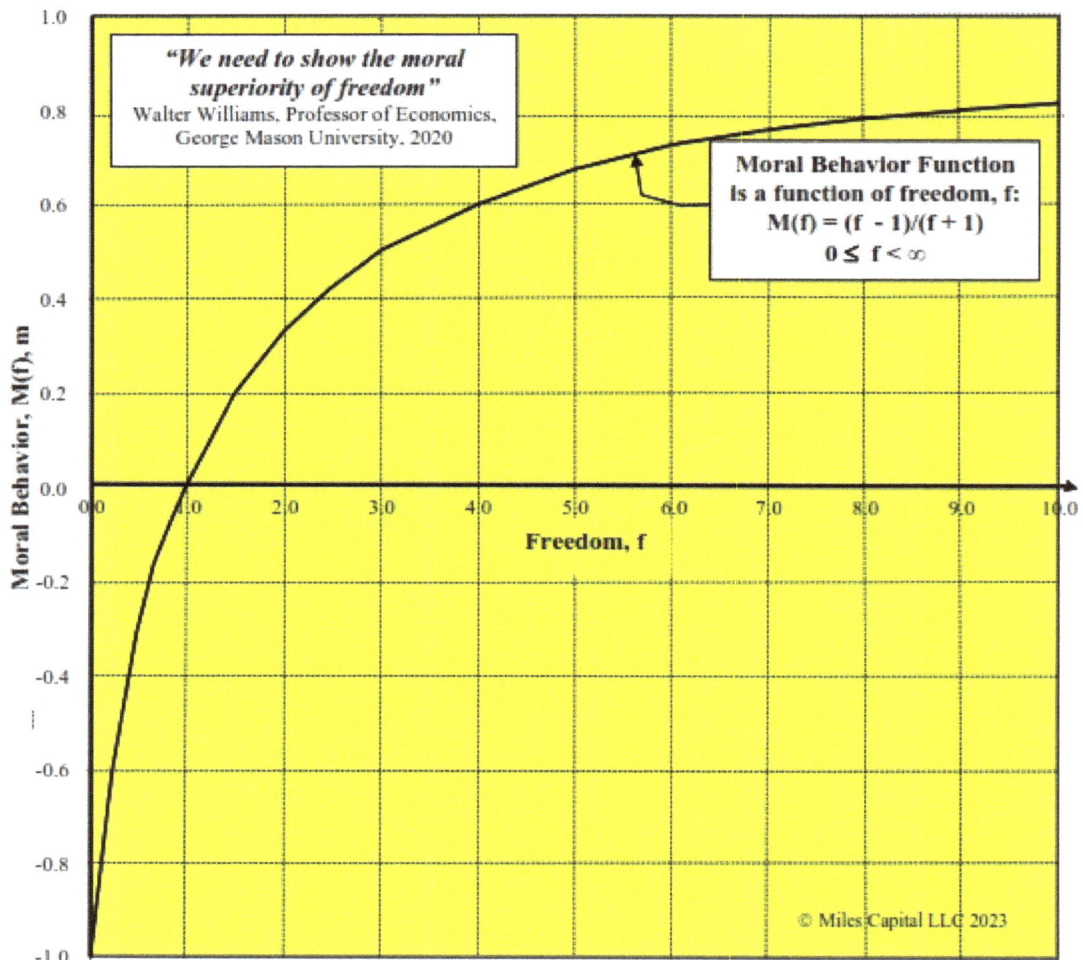

C. The Three Concepts in the Title of this Book can Increase Exponentially if and only if they Employ Capital

Capital consists of knowledge and its manifestations:
- Knowledge increases exponentially (i.e., in proportion to the amount present).
- Manifestations of knowledge require freedom (i.e., means and opportunity).

Productivity is the efficiency of production. It can regularly exceed the unity of the food cycle (i.e., production = consumption) if and only if capital is employed.

Life is the basic freedom. Practically, the human economy and human freedom cannot increase unless capital is employed. However, if it is, they can increase exponentially. That is,
- Moral behavior can beget moral behavior. It can increase exponentially.
- Except for restraint, freedom can beget freedom. It can increase exponentially.

124

- Capital can beget capital. It can increase exponentially.

All three concepts are depicted in the structured diagram of Figure 7-1.

D. The Loss of Thermal Energy, the Loss of Life/Freedom, and the Loss of Moral Behavior

Table 6.2.3-3 is a list of three mutually analogous causes and effects of loss: the loss of thermal energy in the thermodynamic system, the loss of life/freedom in the moral behavior system, and the loss of moral behavior in the freedom system.

Table 6.2.3-3 mutually analogous causes and effects among the thermodynamic system, the moral behavior system, and the freedom system

		Cause of Loss	Effect of Loss
Type of System	Thermodynamic System	(A) Disorder of the Microstates*	(A') Loss of Thermal Energy (i.e., Entropy)
	Moral Behavior System	(B) Inconstancy of Moral Behavior	(B') Loss of Freedom (i.e., life)
	Freedom System	(C) Loss of Freedom	(C') Loss of Moral Behavior

* Note that the order of the microstates is the momentum and location of its particles.

The sequence of activities in the three systems has the same two types of results: That is, if there is loss, the sequence of observations is relatively disordered, inconstant, or loss, and the effects (i.e., observations of the sequence) are loss, loss, and loss: All three sequences are

- negatively correlated, and
- have a large variance.

6.3 The Freedom Function Measures the Results of Dependent Behavior

6.3.1 Moral Behavior is Consistent with Greater Freedom

Ideally, freedom is the ability to behave morally. Unless an individual is restrained, freedom is the individual's responsibility. It seems clear that constant moral behavior provides the best opportunity of freedom. A sequence of constant moral behavior results in positive autocorrelation, and positive autocorrelation is consistent with moral behavior.

125

In the absence of restraint (by others), an individual's resources can increase one's freedom (by lessening constraint). When, the Freedom function is at least equal to 1, behavior is moral. If moral behavior increases, freedom increases, and if moral behavior approaches 1, freedom approaches ∞. There are practical limits to freedom but no theoretical limit.

6.3.2 Immoral Behavior is Consistent with Lesser Freedom

Other individuals and governments can diminish an individual's freedom: The ultimate immorality is the denial of an individual to behave morally. All governments control some behavior of their citizens. As fewer resources are available, freedom decreases. Life and freedom must coexist. Both life and freedom can be lost without responsible individual behavior.

Following are two common ways in which governments reduce freedom in an attempt to create a uniform society. Section 1.3.4.A shows that uniformity is an unnatural goal whose quest will produce drastically reduced freedom throughout a society.

A. Equalized Income

A variety of incomes normally indicates a free and robust economy. Surprisingly, some don't view a large variance of incomes as moral - particularly, if they measure their financial success relative to that of others. Consequently, it is common to characterize the variance of incomes by the pejorative, "income inequality."

Inequality of incomes can "trigger" envy that can also become a political issue. (The variance measures dispersion of results - not inequality of results.) We know that all common probability distributions have two parameters, the mean and the variance, and *the mean is independent of the variance*. That is, the mean income can increase or decrease, regardless of whether the variance of incomes increases or decreases. It is a mathematical fact. Moreover, why should incomes for different types of jobs be equal?

A variety of incomes is considered immoral by some only because the incomes are not equal. It seems that an individual should be interested only in his/her income relative to the supply of and demand for his/her type of contribution. Supply and demand are naturally opposing binary states!

B. Forced Redistribution of Income

An innate right should never include receiving resources - because resources must be provided by others.

Socialism is a form of government-enforced sharing that includes identity-based selection. But, natural selection is merit-based selection! As such, socialism causes a loss of freedom for its citizens. Socialism also reaches beyond our group morality and into our undeveloped species morality. It rewards unsuccessful behavior and punishes successful behavior.

126

Forced redistribution of income by governments is immoral to the extent stated in Section 5.4.4. Citizens who believe that other citizens should be helped should contribute individually. That is, contributions should be voluntary – particularly since species morality is undeveloped. If citizens do not believe that a particular individual should be helped, their opinion should be respected by allowing their aid to be voluntary (i.e., charity).

Rights and responsibilities are examples of *naturally opposing binary states*. See Section 8.3.5. These two states reside in the individual to provide moral balance. Generally, we are responsible for ourselves. If we allow governments to assume responsibility for us, they can take our rights. Does this mean losing our rights to a government is inevitable? It seems to be. Most governments (including socialist governments) govern a citizenry of strangers, but species morality does not yet exist.

6.4 Political Freedom

The concept of political freedom apparently did not exist until much after strangers began to interact (i.e., the beginning of species morality). However, group morality is innate, and within a group there is no need to formalize freedom and specific rights.

The inspiration for this section is an excellent article by the late professor J. Rufus Fears for the Foreign Policy Research Institute.[125] He contrasts security and freedom. He raises the question, "Is freedom a universal value, which all people in all times and places desire?" He continues to write, "why, if freedom is a universal value, has the history of the world been one of tyranny, misery, and oppression. "

Even though his article contributes greatly to the concept of political freedom, I believe our book answers his questions with our definition of innate moral behavior as it relates to freedom. That is, moral behavior is behavior that increases the probability of freedom. Moral behavior would increase security (in the form of the *quantity of life*), and it would increase freedom (in the form of the *quality of life*): The quantity of life is more important to almost everybody than the quality of life.

Mr. Fears says that

> "*The very beginning of civilization in the Middle East around 3000 BCE and in China around 1700 BCE represented the choice of security over freedom. Civilizations began with the decision to give up freedom in order to have the security of a well-regulated*

---

[125] *Freedom: The history of an idea*, Foreign Policy Research Institute, J. Rufus Fears https://www.fpri.org/article/2007/06/freedom-the-history-of-an-idea/

economy under a king. Time and again throughout history people have chosen the perceived benefits of security over the awesome responsibilities of freedom."[126]

Security and political freedom are usually behaviors of the state, and it seems that they are inversely related; that is, the more highly the state regards security, the more it denies political freedom. Actually, Figure 8.3.2-1 might show why freedom is a relatively new concept: Governments have grown larger and more powerful.

The Concept of Security

The concept of security is as old as humans. After all, the three criteria of natural selection are embodied in the concept of security.[127] Moreover, our definition of moral behavior is behavior that increases the probability of freedom. Consequently, we believe that nothing is more important to humans than security (i.e., Criteria #1, Criteria #2, and possibly Criteria #3).

The Concept of Political Freedom

On the other hand, the concept of political freedom is relatively new – probably because governments are larger and can more easily limit freedom. The Freedom function is a function of moral behavior. There are many types and definitions of freedom. Saying that, ideally, freedom is the ability to behave morally seems to apply to all types of freedom.

6.4.1 History of the Concepts of Political Freedom

History of the Concept of Security

The heading of this paragraph is included simply for completeness because the history of security is the subject of thousands of books. As stated above, the concept of security has been firmly embedded in our morality from the beginning of humanity.

History of the Concept of Political Freedom

Consider a mosaic of brief bulleted historical facts concerning freedom:

---

[126] We appreciate Mr. Fears' statement, "the awesome responsibility of freedom" because responsibility is so often ignored in the naturally opposing binary pair, rights-responsibilities. Rights are types of freedom, and responsibilities are types of moral behavior. Those who assume our responsibilities (e.g., strangers) take our rights. (Doing so maintains the balance of binary states.)

[127] It is a matter of opinion whether the definition of security should include the acquisition of necessary nutritional resources. However, without nutritional resources, physical security would be unnecessary.

- Egypt had no word for freedom.

- Mesopotamia had a word for freedom, but only the king could give it and take it.

- Middle-Eastern societies have no real concept of freedom. The relatively high rate of inter-marriage in the Middle-East might be evidence of their fear of strangers and their unusually high regard for security.

- The Persian Empire seems to have the earliest evidence of the concept of freedom in ancient times. Citizens of the Persian Empire had some freedom of religion, and slavery was abolished about 500 BC.

- Sparta had almost no individual freedom, and Rome had extensive individual freedom.

- Since the ninth century, Russia has not had a clear idea of individual and political freedom. I was in the former Soviet Union shortly after it collapsed. Because I am American, I was sure that I would be told how wonderful freedom was. It did not happen. Conversely, on two occasions, elderly Soviet women, shook their fist in the air and vehemently said to me: "Stability! We need Stability!" I was also told by other Russians that, "We seem to like strong leaders."

- The Chinese philosopher, Confucius, who lived in approximately 550 BC frequently discussed order but almost never discussed freedom. Today, China is known as a country that has order but very little political, economic, or individual freedom.

- China, the Middle-East, and even Europe had kingdoms until the Middle Ages.

- England was far ahead of other countries with its appreciation of freedom, and its colonies had the good fortune of inheriting many of its ideas.

- Slavery is thought to have existed worldwide for at least 14,000 years – possibly between 12,000 BC and 1,950 AD. It essentially ended in the middle of the 1800s. Figure 8.3.1-1 is especially important to understanding slavery in the U.S.

6.4.2 Sources of the Concepts of Political Freedom

J. Rufus Fears describes the history of some concepts of political freedom. Table 6.4.2-1 lists the sources of the concepts of freedom from four societies and one type of environment – called human frontiers. Each source played a role in expanding the concepts of political freedom in the world, particularly in the U.S.

Table 6.4.2-1 sources and concepts of political freedom

		Concepts of Political Freedom
Sources of Concepts of Political Freedom	**Old Testament**	Ark of Liberty*
	Greece and Rome	• Self-Governance • Consent of the Governed
	Christianity	• Natural Law • All Men are Created Equal • Individual Rights
	England	Government is under the Law
	Human Frontiers	Equality of Opportunity

* J. Rufus Fears writes that the Jewish people believe that they were chosen by God to bear the "ark of liberties" to the World.

6.4.3 The United States has the Broadest Array of Political Freedoms

Additionally, J. Rufus Fears describes three types of freedom in an orderly way. Since there are many types of freedom, he distinguishes three types as a hierarchy that is progressively more inclusive: individual, political, and national freedom. He also shows that various countries have one or more of those components - but rarely all three. The founding fathers were careful to see that the U.S. had all three concepts.

The nested ovals in Figure 6.4.3-1 depict the hierarchy of concepts of freedom for two governmental situations: a typical nation and the U.S.

Figure 6.4.3-1 is two Venn-type diagrams. The set of nested ovals on the left lists *the level* of freedom in each oval. The set of nested ovals on the right lists *the document* that provides each level of freedom specific to the U.S.

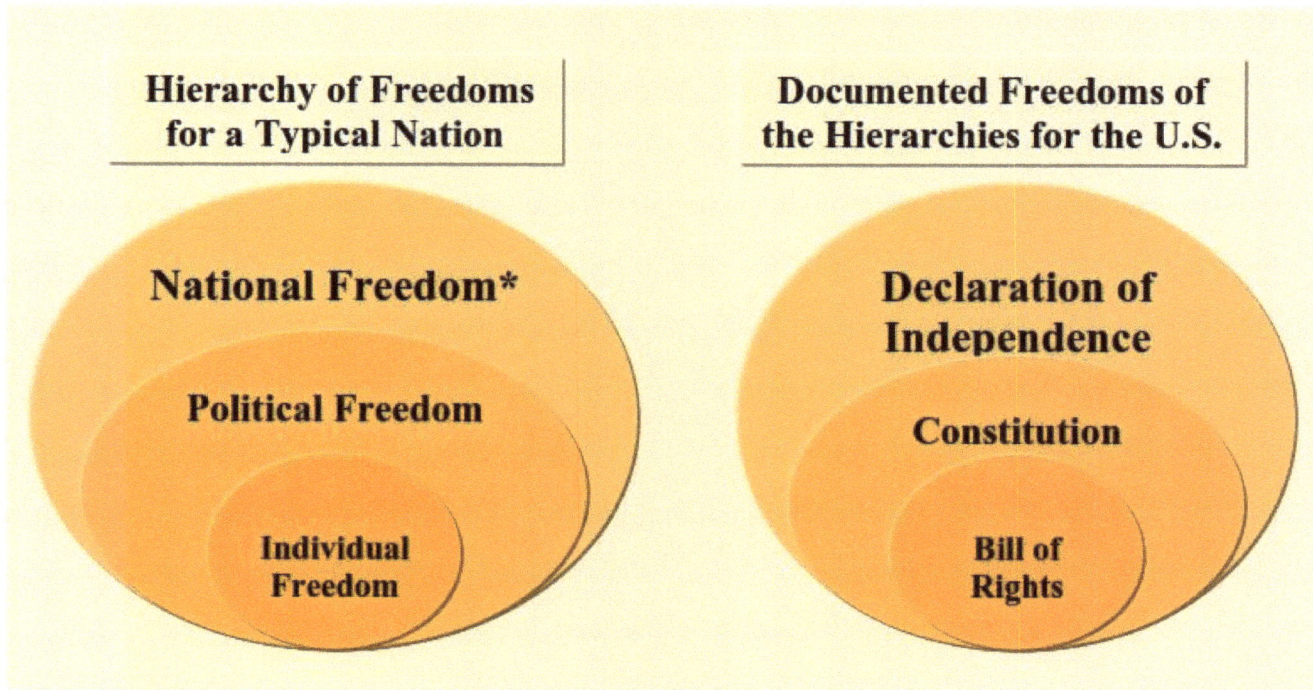

Hierarchy of Freedoms for a Typical Nation

National Freedom*

Political Freedom

Individual Freedom

Documented Freedoms of the Hierarchies for the U.S.

Declaration of Independence

Constitution

Bill of Rights

* National freedom is extremely important to all nations because citizens would rather be controlled by their leaders than by outside leaders (i.e., strangers). This is another example that morality is designed by environments.

Seeking security and seeking freedom are moral behaviors. However, many governments believe that strong security and strong freedom are incompatible. Certainly, the regard for both concepts varies greatly among societies from different environments.

Figure 5.2.3-1 illustrates the current degree of political freedom for most countries in the World. Countries in Asia and Africa have the least political freedom. Countries in North America, Northern Europe, and Western Europe have the most political freedom.

6.5 Economic Freedom

Generally, freedom is a function of moral behavior, and, specifically, economic freedom is a function of economic morality. A necessary characteristic of moral behavior is constancy. Constancy is also an important characteristic of economic freedom – and economic risk can be an enormous threat to economic constancy. (Risk is defined in Section 6.5.1, and accuracy is defined in Section 6.5.2.)

Economic Risk

Investments require exposure to many sources of risk. This fact has retarded economic progress throughout modern history. Two important ways to reduce risk are the rule of law and knowledge.

Rule of Law Reduces Economic Risk

The Industrial Revolution and the Age of Enlightenment were so significant to economic progress, partly because the introduction of the rule of law reduced economic risk significantly and enabled a great amount of investment.

Economic freedom and political freedom are mutually dependent, and there are several components of economic freedom – such as legal systems, property rights, contracts, accurate values, free markets, etc.

A secure system of property rights is essential to reducing economic risk. Included in this system are the rights to benefit from the control and transfer of property. Property rights must also prevent government interference, including arbitrary seizures of property.

Knowledge Reduces Economic Risk

Knowledge is a very important factor that can reduce economic risk: Historically, new governments immediately institute a bureau of weights and measures. Value is biased when markets are controlled. Free markets minimize bias. Investments propagate value through the financial system – magnifying the damage of the bias. Knowing bias allows investors to reduce risk and possibly eliminate it. Since controlled markets are biased markets, they are immoral.

Many authors can discuss the legal aspects of economic freedom as well or better than we can, but probably few can discuss knowledge and free markets as *accurately* as we can – so we will concentrate on accuracy and measuring the morality of a market.

Similarity of Morality and Economic Morality

As stated often, moral behavior is behavior that increases the probability of freedom. Similarly, we can state that moral economic behavior is behavior that increases the probability of *economic* freedom. Freedom is diminished if the economy is unnecessarily controlled or manipulated.

Current Economic Freedom of Countries

Figure 5.2.4-1 illustrates the current state of economic freedom for most countries in the world. We saw in the previous section that North America, Northern Europe, and Western Europe have the most political freedom. This is also true of economic freedom.

6.5.1 Importance of Knowing Value

In the 1900s, Friedrich Hayek realized a very important by-product of a free market - knowing the value of a resource allows associated resources to be applied properly! [128] Knowing value is as important as trust and stable prices.

Unless a trade occurs at its (true) value, the price is biased, and the bias from that trade is compounded as subsequently biased trades propagate through the economy. [129]

Knowing Value

Comments by Aristotle and Adam Smith refer to value as applied to an individual.

Aristotle

Aristotle (384-322 BC) believed that value is subjective.

Adam Smith

In *An Inquiry into the Nature and Causes of the Wealth of Nations*, Smith likened a free market to an "invisible hand" because consumers *independently and voluntarily subsume their desires into a value* - something that cannot be known or emulated by command or fiat. Section 6.5.2 shows how individual values are subsumed into a market value.

Its Importance

This section discusses comments by two prominent economists, many activities that benefit from knowing value, and the importance of knowing values so they can be applied properly to the concepts of risk and accuracy.

---

[128] In modern economies, it is difficult to know value because governments distort prices of resources by taxes, stimuli (e.g., subsidies, spending, borrowing, etc.), bailouts, wage and price controls, altered money supply, and unnecessary regulations (for other than the protection of property). Additionally, unions distort prices of resources by collective bargaining (i.e., enforced dependent behavior among individuals), strikes, identity selection, coercion, intimidation, etc. Note that these concepts usually refer to markets that deal in goods and services, rather than *matching markets* that match entities such as individuals for employment, marriage, organ donation and organ recipients, students for schools, equity, etc.

[129] Concerning the serious decline of the Chinese stock markets in June, 2015, Jason Zweig, *The Intelligent Investor*, *Wall Street Journal*, Saturday-Sunday, July 11-12, 2015, stated "The Chinese government regards markets as clay that can be molded. Instead, markets are like water. They always find their own level, no matter whom or what tries to control them."

Comments by Two Prominent Economists

Friedrich Hayek

In *The Pure Theory of Capital*, the Austrian-Hungarian economist, Friedrich A. Hayek (1899-1992), carried the free market concept to the next step. He made another simple, but fundamentally important, observation: If a market is not a free market, the price of a resource cannot be estimated without bias. Therefore, its value cannot be known accurately, and resources cannot be applied properly.[130]

Innovators, such as Hayek, learn that almost everything that is true is simple. (And, if we can't explain an idea simply, either we probably don't understand it or it probably isn't true.)[131] The reason that free markets work is so simple.

Milton Friedman

In *Free to Choose*, the American economist, Milton Friedman (1912-2006) stated that knowing the value of a resource allows

- resources to be applied properly,

- income from resources to be applied properly, and

- inefficiencies of resource production to be identified and reduced.

Some Economic Activities that Apply Resources

Ideally, value should be known accurately for many economic applications. Table 6.5.1-1 is a list of some common applications that depend upon value.

---

[130] Over time, the USSR knew the value of nothing. Also, shockingly, in a 2014 interview on the Charlie Rose Show on PBS, the president of Ecuador, Rafael Correa, stated (and with some bravado): "Men should control markets; markets should not control men."

[131] See Occam's razor: Generally, simplicity should be preferred as the solution to a problem because it has less probability of error.

Table 6.5.1-1 16 economic or financial applications that depend upon value

• acquire	• maintain
• allocate	• manage
• assess	• manufacture
• characterize	• optimize
• design	• risk
• dispose	• tax
• exchange	• trade
• insure	• etc.
• lease	

Definition of Risk

There is a reason that the senses for risk-taking, decision-making, and morality all reside as neighbors in the ventromedial prefrontal cortex (of the human brain): They are all important to the probability of success. Nearly every application of a resource involves risk. To emphasize the importance of knowing value - note that, the definition of risk requires knowing value:

$$\text{Risk} = (\text{Probability of Loss}) \times (\text{Value of Applied Resource}).[132]$$

(The probability of loss must be expressed as a fraction rather than a percent.) Knowing value is essential for our success. It is not a trivial feature of a free market. Consequently, any nonessential political control that reduces our ability to know value is immoral because it reduces our ability to make intelligent decisions and limits freedom.

6.5.2 Importance of Knowing Accuracy

Accuracy is not just a property of measurements; it is also a neighbor of truth. It is critical to morality, and it is important to making good decisions.[133] Following are a few steps that lead to accurate estimates – and creating a model to measure the degree to which a market is a free (moral) market.

---

[132] Of course, if the Value of Applied Resource is not accurately known, risk cannot be accurately known.

[133] The following definitions are unfortunately confusing: The *greater* the accuracy, the *smaller* the value of accuracy, and the *greater* the precision, the *smaller* the value of the variance.

135

Definition of Accuracy

Accuracy is a concept and a function that can estimate the true value from observations of a phenomenon. (Surprisingly, there are more than 20 definitions of accuracy.)[134]

We believe the following definition of accuracy is logical and best: Suppose $\theta^\wedge$ is an estimator of an arbitrary parameter, θ.[135] Then consider, $(\theta^\wedge - \theta)^2$, the random squared error. Accuracy is the *expected value* (denoted by E) of the random squared error:

$$\text{Accuracy} = E[(\theta^\wedge-\theta)^2] = [E(\theta^\wedge)-\theta]^2 + \sigma_{\theta^\wedge}^2. \ [136]$$

The quantity, $E[(\theta^\wedge)-\theta]^2$, is the square of the bias of the estimator, β^2, and the quantity, $\sigma_{\theta^\wedge}^2$, is the square of the precision (i.e., the variance) of the estimator.[137] Accuracy can usually be improved by obtaining a large number of independent observations of a value.

We define accuracy as the sum of two values: the square of the bias and the square of the precision (i.e., the variance). A great degree of accuracy can be achieved if and only if the estimate provides a small bias *and* a small variance (i.e., great precision):

- **Accuracy.** Accuracy of the parameter, $\theta = E[(\theta^\wedge-\theta)^2]$.

- **Bias.** Bias of the estimate, $\beta^2 = [E(\theta^\wedge)-\theta]^2$.

- **Precision.** Precision of the estimate, $\sigma^2 = (1/k) \cdot \Sigma(x_i - \mu)^2$ of observations, x_i, and μ is the mean of the k values.

---

[134] One morning about 40 years ago, my colleague, the late Dr. Edwin L. Crow, left our office to do research at the library on the concept of accuracy. That afternoon, he returned with a smile on his face. He was eager to tell me that he had found 23 definitions of accuracy! (This could only happen in a library such as ours - at the National Bureau of Standards.). We readily agreed to use the definition that is *the expected value of the random squared error*. This definition was also selected by the International Organization of Standardization (ISO).

[135] θ (i.e., the Greek letter, theta) is a parameter, and $\theta^\wedge$ is its estimator. Figure A-1 in Appendix A is a valuable Venn-type diagram that depicts the relationship among five desirable properties of a statistical estimator: consistent, efficient, unbiased, best asymptotic normal (BAN), and maximum likelihood.

[136] Notice that the random squared error does not explicitly refer to the mean or variance, but its expected value does.

[137] Many believe that accuracy and precision are synonymous, but precision is only one of the two components of accuracy: bias and precision. (Bias is sometimes called *trueness*.)

The Accuracy function is

$$\text{Accuracy} = (\text{Bias})^2 + (\text{Precision})^2$$

$$= \beta^2 + \sigma^2.$$

Bias

Bias is the difference between the mean of the observations and the unknowable true value. The true value is the value closest to the mean of the observations when the market is a free market.

Precision

The square of precision is the variance. The more constant is the sequence of observations, the smaller is the variance, and the more accurate is the market. Note the importance of constancy to both accuracy and moral behavior: The constancy of a sequence of observations in the precision of the *Accuracy function* is similar to the constancy of a sequence of observations of moral behavior in the *Moral behavior function.* See part (c) and part (d) of Figure 6-1.

Four Views of Accuracy

Figure 6.5.2-1 is a set of four targets depicting accuracy as it depends upon two extreme levels of bias and two extreme levels of precision. Hits (i.e., small black discs) in the targets represent sample observations of estimates.

Figure 6.5.2-1 schematic diagram of four targets that illustrate two extreme levels of the two components of accuracy, bias and precision, when accuracy is defined as the expected value of the random squared error. Accuracy exists only in the upper left target.

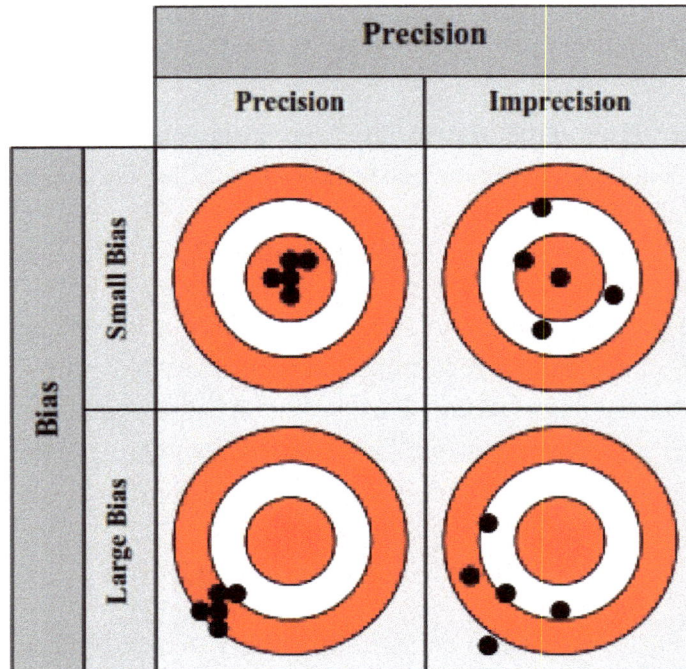

Figure 6.5.2-2 is a graph of accuracy over the domain $0 \leq \beta \leq 1$ and $0 \leq \sigma \leq 1$. The function of accuracy, the expected value of the mean squared error, is an elliptic paraboloid.

Figure 6.5.2-2 a graph of the Accuracy function (an elliptic paraboloid) over the domain $0 \leq \beta \leq 1$ and $0 \leq \sigma \leq 1$

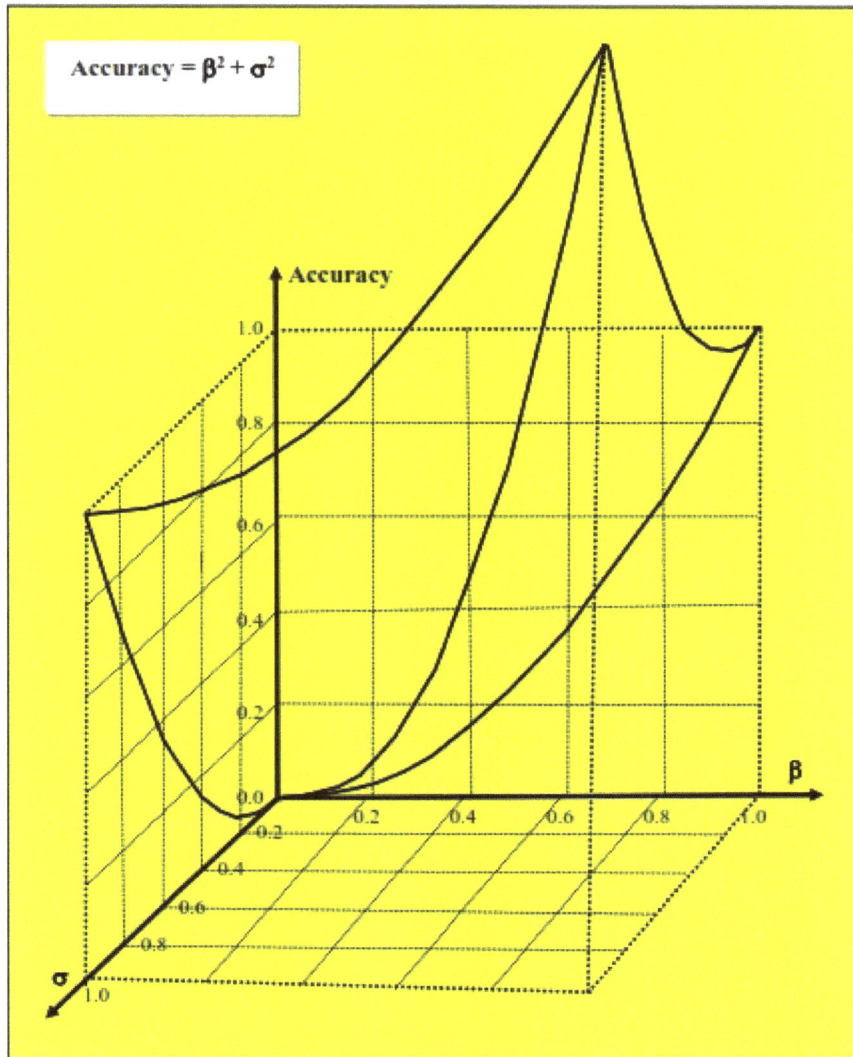

6.5.3 The Market Freedom Function

A Market is a Moral Market if and only if it is a Free Market

Two Types of Markets

We shall discuss two types of markets for which the Market Freedom function can apply: A. Markets of Goods and Services and B. Markets of Selection.

139

A. Markets of Goods and Services

Supply and Demand

The market value of a resource is the price that consumers will pay for the resource and the price that producers will accept for the resource. When these prices meet, the resource is exchanged, and a market is created in the resource. The law of supply and demand applies to all living entities; it is as fundamental to the biological system as the law of gravity is to the physical system.

A free market is a market for resources in which knowledgeable and free consumers and producers determine prices by choice or fair negotiation.

Manipulation

Markets of goods and services can be manipulated. Manipulation causes biased values to be created and propagated throughout the market - reducing the probability of success (i.e., freedom) for the participants.

Apply the Accuracy Function to Measure the Moral Behavior of a Market of Goods and Services

A free market is an important type of freedom. It is the freedom from manipulation of market prices. The degree of manipulation can be measured as the accuracy of non-free trades.

Consider the following four steps to determine the accuracy of market prices:

- **Two Populations of Prices.** If the Accuracy function of Section 6.5.2 is applied to a market, it becomes a function of its prices. If we suspect manipulation in a market, we can separate the market prices of a resource into two populations,

    o   one population of k free market prices and

    o   the other population of n non-free market prices (i.e., the suspected manipulated prices).[138]

Then we can compute the following values of the above two populations:

---

[138] Although it is not necessary to use here, the F test from the analysis of variance is a very handy tool for determining whether the difference between the means of two populations (e.g., free and non-free) is significant or not.

- **True Value of the Free Market Population.** We consider the mean of the k free market prices, μ_y, to be the true value (i.e., actually the best estimate of the unknowable true value).[139]

- **Square of the Bias of the Non-Free Market Population.** Then the square of the bias, β^2, is the square of the mean of the n differences between the non-free market prices and the best estimate of the true value.

- **Square of the Precision of the Non-Free Market Population.** Also, the square of the precision, (i.e., the variance) σ^2, is the mean of the square of the n differences between the non-free market prices and the best estimate of the true value.

Then, the accuracy, a, of a market is

$$a = \beta^2 + \sigma^2$$

$$= [(1/n)\cdot\Sigma(x_i - \mu_y)]^2 + [(1/n)\cdot\Sigma(x_i - \mu_y)^2]$$

where

- k = number of free market prices;

- y_i = the ith free market price, where i = 1, … , k;

- $\mu_y = (1/k)\cdot\Sigma y_i$, the best estimate of the true value;

- n = number of non-free market prices;

- x_i = the ith non-free market price, where i = 1, … , n;

- $\beta^2 = [(1/n)\cdot\Sigma(x_i - \mu_y)]^2$, the square of the bias; and

- $\sigma^2 = [(1/n)\cdot\Sigma(x_i - \mu_y)^2]$, the square of the precision.

---

[139] This is a reasonable and necessary assumption because the true value is unknowable, but this value is the best estimate of the true value.

The Market Freedom Function Measures the Moral Behavior of a Market of Goods and Services

The Accuracy function is applied to the free market population of a market and the non-free market population of a market. If trades are not accurate, the market is not moral. (Note that the moral behavior of both, the Freedom function and the Market Freedom function, are functions of the constancy of observations - which causes the variances to be small).

The Market Freedom function is

$$T(a) = (1-a)/(1+a)$$

where $a = \beta^2 + \sigma^2$.

Whereas Figure 6.2.2-2 depicts the Freedom function as a function of moral behavior, Figure 6.5.3-1 depicts the Market Freedom function as a function of a specific lack of freedom (i.e., accuracy). Even though accuracy can be infinitely large, it is depicted here in the interval $0 \leq a \leq 1.0$. The market is a free market if and only if $a = 0$.

Example of a Market of Goods and Services

Problem. Suppose a market of goods and services has k=4 trades of a resource that are thought to be free market trades (i.e., 3.7, 3.9, 3.2, and 4.0) and n = 5 trades of that resource that are suspected of being manipulated (i.e., 4.2, 4.0, 4.1, 4.2, and 4.0). Determine the moral behavior of the Market Freedom function.

Solution. To compute the Accuracy function, let

k= 4;

$i = 1, \ldots , 4$;

y_i = 3.7, 3.9, 3.2, and 4.0;

$\mu_y = (1/4) \cdot \Sigma y_i$

$\quad = (1/4) \cdot (3.7 + 3.9 + 3.2 + 4.0)$

$\quad = 14.8/4$

$\quad = 3.7.$

n= 5;

$j = 1, \ldots , 5$;

x_i = 4 .2, 4.0, 4.1, 4.2, and 4.0;

$\beta^2 = [(1/n) \cdot \Sigma(x_i - \mu_y)]^2$

$= (1/5)\cdot[(4.2\text{-}3.7) + (4.0\text{-}3.7) + (4.1\text{-}3.7) + (4.2\text{–}3.7) + (4.0\text{-}3.7)]^2$

$= [(0.5 + 0.3 + 0.4 + 0.5 + 0.3)/5]^2$

$= (2.0/5)^2$

$= 0.160;$

$\sigma^2 = [(1/n)\cdot\Sigma(x_i - \mu_y)^2]$

$= (1/5)\cdot[(4.2\text{-}3.7)^2 + (4.0\text{–}3.7)^2 + (4.1\text{-}3.7)^2 + (4.2\text{-}3.7)^2 + (4.0\text{-}3.7)^2]$

$= (1/5)\cdot(0.5^2 + 0.3^2 + 0.4^2 + 0.5^2 + 0.3^2)$

$= (1/5)\cdot(0.25 + 0.09 + 0.16 + 0.25 + 0.09)$

$= (1/5)\cdot0.84$

$= 0.168.$

Therefore, the accuracy is

$$a = 0.160 + 0.168$$
$$= 0.328.$$

Finally, the Market Freedom function is

$$T(a) = (1\text{-}a)/(1\text{+}a)$$
$$= (1\text{-}0.328)/(1\text{+}0.328)$$
$$= 0.506.$$

That is, the moral behavior, as measured by the Market Freedom function, is 0.506.

B. Markets of Selection

Markets of selection can be corrupted by selecting an entity for a position because of the entity's identity (rather than the entity's merit). It is immoral because it almost certainly *reduces the effectiveness* of the position and reduces the probability of success for all affected – including that of the entity selected for the position.[140] (Natural selection is merit-based; it works, and it cannot be repealed.)

Markets of selection apply to the six types of unearned benefits listed in Table 8.3.5-2.

---

[140] Affirmative Action is a long-standing example of identity selection and the abuse of merit selection.

Apply the Accuracy Function to Measure the Moral Behavior of a Market of Selection

A free market of selection is an important type of freedom. It is the freedom from manipulation of merit entities. The degree of manipulation can be measured as the accuracy of non-merit entities. An example of non-merit entities is identity entities.

Consider the following four steps to determine the accuracy of markets of selection:

- **Two Populations of Entities.** If the Accuracy function of Section 6.5.2 is applied to a market, it becomes a function of the values of the entities. The values of the market entities and non-merit entities must be estimated. If we suspect manipulation in a market, we can separate the values of the entities into two populations,

  o one population of k merit entities and

  o the other population of n other (i.e., non-merit) entities.[141]

  Then we can compute the following values of the above two populations:

- **True Value of the Merit Entities.** We consider the mean of the values of the k merit entities to be the true value (i.e., actually the best estimate of the unknowable true value).[142]

- **Square of the Bias of the Non-Free Population.** Then the square of the bias, β^2, is the square of the mean of the n differences between the values of non-merit entities and the mean values of the merit entities.

- **Square of the Precision of the Non-Free Population.** Also, the square of the precision, (i.e., the variance) σ^2, is the value of the mean of the square of the n differences between the values of the non-merit entities and the mean value of the merit entities.

Then, the accuracy, a, of a market is

$$a = \beta^2 + \sigma^2.$$

$$= [(1/n) \cdot \Sigma(x_i - \mu_y)]^2 + [(1/n) \cdot \Sigma(x_i - \mu_y)^2]$$

where

- k = number of merit entities;

---

[141] Although it is not necessary to use here, the F test from the analysis of variance is a very handy tool for determining whether the difference between the means of two populations (e.g., free and non-free) is significant or not.

[142] This is a reasonable and necessary assumption because the true value is unknowable, but this value is the best estimate of the true value.

- y_i = the ith value of the merit entities, where i = 1, ... , k;

- μ_y = (1/k)·Σy_i, the mean of the values of the merit entities:

- n = number of non-merit entities;

- x_i = the ith value of the non-merit entities, where i = 1, ... , n;

- β^2 = [(1/n)·$\Sigma(x_i - \mu_y)$]^2, the square of the bias; and

- σ^2 = [(1/n)·$\Sigma(x_i - \mu_y)^2$], the square of the precision.

The Market Freedom Function Measures the Moral Behavior of a Market of Selection

The Accuracy function is applied to the free-market population and the manipulated population of a market. If selection is not accurate (with respect to merit selection), the market is not moral. The morality of both, the Freedom function and the Market Freedom function, are functions of the constancy of observations (which cause the variances to be small).

The Market Freedom function is

$$T(a) = (1-a)/(1+a),$$

where a = $\beta^2 + \sigma^2$.

Whereas Figure 6.2.2-2 depicts the Freedom function as a function of moral behavior, Figure 6.5.3-1 depicts the Market Freedom function as a function of a specific lack of freedom (i.e., accuracy). Even though accuracy can be infinitely large, it is depicted in the interval $0 \le a \le 10$. The market is a free market if and only if a = 0.

Examples of Market of Selection

Even though the equations discussed here allow for multiple entities, some applications of selection involve only one pair of entities.

Problem 1. Consider a position for which a merit entity is rated as y_1 = 1.0 and for which an identity entity is rated as x_1 =0.5. What is the morality of choosing the identity entity instead of the merit entity?

Solution. To compute the accuracy function, let

k = 1;

y_1 = 1.0;

μ_y = (1/1)·Σy_i

$\quad$ = (1)·1.0

$= 1.0$;

$n = 1$;

$x_1 = 0.5$;

$\beta^2 = [(1/n) \cdot \Sigma(x_i - \mu_y)]^2$

$\quad = (1/1) \cdot (0.5 - 1.0)^2$

$\quad = (0.5)^2$

$\quad = 0.25$;

$\sigma^2 = (1/n) \cdot \Sigma(x_i - \mu_y)^2$

$\quad = (1/1) \cdot (0.5 - 1.0)^2$

$\quad = (0.5)^2$

$\quad = 0.25.$

Therefore, the accuracy is

$$a = 0.25 + 0.25$$
$$= 0.5.$$

Finally, the moral behavior, as measured by the Market Freedom function, is

$$T(a) = (1-a)/(1+a)$$
$$= (1-0.5)/(1+0.5)$$
$$= 0.3333.$$

Problem 2. Consider five positions for which five merit entities are rated as $y_1 = 1.0$ and five identity entities are rated as $x_i = 0.5$. What is the morality of choosing all five identity entities instead of the five merit entities?

Solution. To compute the accuracy function, let

$k = 5$;

each $y_i = 1.0$;

$\mu_y = (1/5) \cdot \Sigma y_i$

$\quad = (1/5) \cdot 5.0$

$\quad = 1.0$;

$n = 5$;

each $x_i = 0.5$;

$$\beta^2 = [(1/5) \cdot \Sigma(x_i - \mu_y)]^2$$

$$= (1/5)^2 \cdot [(0.5-1.0) + (0.5-1.0) + (0.5-1.0) + (0.5-1.0) + (0.5-1.0)]^2$$

$$= (1/5)^2 \cdot [(-2.5)]^2$$

$$= (0.5)^2$$

$$= 0.25;$$

$$\sigma^2 = (1/5) \cdot \Sigma(x_i - \mu_y)^2$$

$$= (1/5) \cdot [(0.5-1.0)^2 + (0.5-1.0)^2 + (0.5-1.0)^2 + (0.5-1.0)^2 + (0.5-1.0)^2]$$

$$= (0/5) \cdot (2.5)^2$$

$$= (0/5) \cdot (6.25)$$

$$= 1.25.$$

Therefore, the accuracy is

$$a = 0.25 + 1.25$$

$$= 1.50.$$

Finally, the moral behavior, as measured by the Market Freedom function, is

$$T(a) = (1-a)/(1+a)$$

$$= (1-1.5)/(1+1.5)$$

$$= -0.5/2.5$$

$$= -0.2.$$

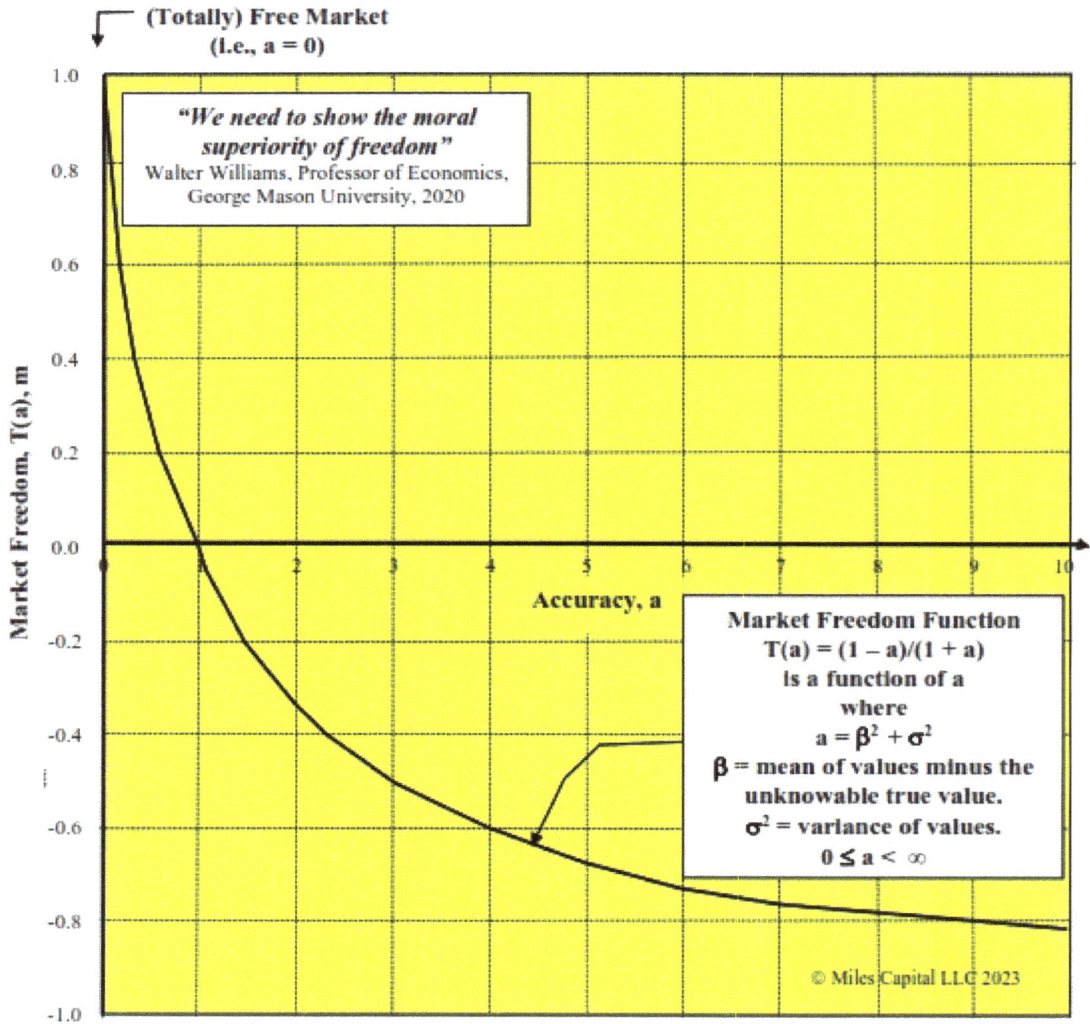

Figure 6.5.3-1

The Market Freedom Function, T(a), is a function of accuracy, a.
It is defined over the interval $0 \le a < \infty$

(Totally) Free Market
(I.e., a = 0)

"We need to show the moral superiority of freedom"
Walter Williams, Professor of Economics,
George Mason University, 2020

Accuracy, a

Market Freedom Function
$$T(a) = (1 - a)/(1 + a)$$
is a function of a
where
$$a = \beta^2 + \sigma^2$$
β = mean of values minus the
unknowable true value.
σ^2 = variance of values.
$$0 \le a < \infty$$

© Miles Capital LLC 2023

Market Freedom, T(a), m

148

Part III
Capital

Chapter 7 Capital Augments Moral Behavior and Freedom

Capital is unique to humans, it is uniquely productive, and it can be extraordinarily beneficial to human morality.

The sections of this chapter are

Figure 7-1 This structured diagram depicts the process of moral behavior and its relationships with the three inputs of capital, necessary resources, and morality and the output of freedom.

A structured diagram contains ovals that depict processes and rectangles that depict input and output to processes.
- **Capital.** Capital is knowledge and its manifestations.
- **Necessary Resources**. Necessary resources are water, nutrients, and shelter.
- **Morality.** Morality is a set of moral propensities within an individual that also applies to its group, its species, and the ecosystem.
- **Moral Behavior.** Moral behavior is behavior that increases the probability of freedom.
- **Freedom.** Freedom is the ability to behave morally.

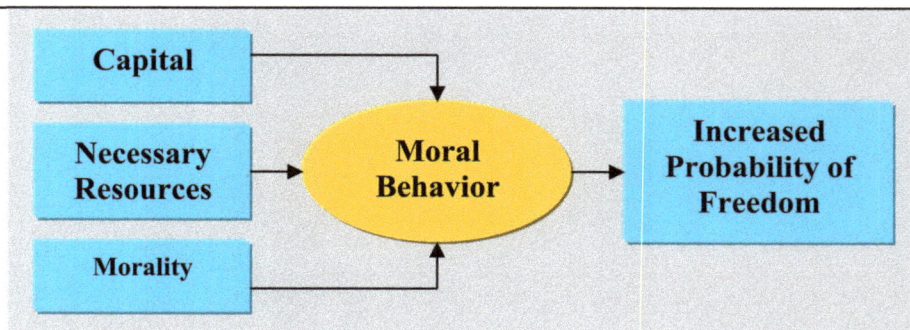

7.1 Capital

Roughly 160 years ago, the economists, Adam Smith, David Ricardo, etc. identified three factors of production: land, labor, and capital. However, as ownership, economic freedom, the rule of law, and the sophistication of capital increased, the role of the entrepreneur in production became more robust and important. Now, many economists believe that the factors of production were not complete because it must have a "head" who provides motivations and unique responsibilities such as coordination, management, risk assessment, and strategy. Hence, economists now define four factors of production:

- **Land**. Land is the physical system and its improbable parasite, the nonhuman biological system. They are the sources of all natural resources.

- **Labor**. We consider labor to be human *physical* activity that contributes to the production of goods and services - but not to knowledge. (We consider the human quest for knowledge to be capital.)

- **Capital**. Capital is knowledge and the manifestations of knowledge. Some capital produces goods and services for consumption, and some capital produces goods and services for further production. Capital consists of four types of the following manifestations (i.e., assets):

    o **Physical Capital** (i.e., chemicals, machines, buildings, infrastructure, etc.),

    o **Human Capital** (i.e., human activities engaged in producing and disseminating knowledge),

    o **Intellectual Capital** (i.e., knowledge, mathematical formulas, patents, software, laws, etc.), and

    o **Financial Capital** (i.e., money, stocks, bonds, contracts, etc.).

- **Entrepreneurship**. Entrepreneurship is also a knowledge-based system of human activities, coordination, and analysis that enhance the realization of goods and services. Bringing a project to financial life could be considered analogous to organizing the confluence of the conditions for life.

For our purposes, it is meaningless to distinguish capital and entrepreneurship. Therefore, for convenience, we shall consider both factors to be capital.

7.1.1 Rates of Human Evolution and Capital Development

Environments vary and change in response to the laws of nature. Humans (as all organisms) evolve - not to generally improve - but to increase their probability of natural selection by conforming more closely to their environment. The rate of evolution is sporadic.

The creation of capital is motivated by moral propensities and realized as knowledge and its manifestations. Knowledge accretes from *discovery*, just as matter accretes from *gravity,* and money (that is lent) accretes from *interest*. They all change in proportion to the amount present. That is, they change exponentially.[143]

Whereas moral behavior is behavior that increases the probability of freedom, the judicious application of capital augments that probability.

The rate of capital development is usually much faster than the rate of evolution.

7.1.2 Capital is Uniquely Productive

Productivity is perhaps the most significant economic performance parameter. It is a measure of efficiency, and it is usually measured as the amount of production per worker (i.e., labor).[144] The nature of labor is fundamentally different from the nature of capital: For a specific task, the production due to a typical laborer is essentially *constant* over time. Obviously, it varies, somewhat, but it is essentially the same as it was thousands of years ago. Any permanent increase in productivity is necessarily caused by innovations (i.e., capital) that are available to labor. Most authors and economists do not distinguish labor and capital as precisely as we do. For example, Jerome Powell, Chairman of the Federal Reserve System commented that any increase in productivity should be matched by increased wages to labor! He seems to believe that labor generally increases productivity; it doesn't.

Our research shows a shocking result: For every one dollar paid to the capital-entrepreneur factor-pair for innovations that increased productivity, 122.1 dollars are paid to the other factor-pair, land-labor – even though they did not increase productivity! [145] [146]

The nature of the factor-pair, land-labor, is *linear*, and the nature of the factor-pair, capital-entrepreneurship, is *exponential*. Productivity is exponential.[147]

---

[143] The word exponential is currently used carelessly to describe a rapid or a large change. In this book, we use the word only as it is intended - to indicate an exponent in mathematics. For example, x is the exponent of a in the expression a^x. It is used when something increases or decreases in proportion to the amount present (i.e., a), such as a bank account that grows by drawing interest or a radioactive substance that decays.

[144] Productivity is one of the Federal Reserve System's three primary performance parameters: productivity, employment, and prices.

[145] *The Nature of Economics*, Martin J. Miles, Table 13.3.3-1

[146] The definition of productivity with respect to labor should be revised.

[147] If we compensated innovators, instead of labor for the amount gained by increased productivity, we would have to seriously restructure our economy.

Productivity is the ratio of the amount produced-to-the amount consumed in the process:

Productivity = (Amount Produced) / (Amount Consumed).[148]

Even though energy is continually supplied to the ecosystem by the Sun and thermal vents in the Earth, the ratio of the amounts produced and consumed over time are relatively constant. That is, productivity of the ecosystem is essentially 1. Capital allows productivity in our economy to be greater than 1. Knowledge, and one of its manifestations, productivity, is the reason humans live in a world that is so different from that of the remainder of the ecosystem. Note that Figure 7.3-1 is a graph of the per capita Worldwide Gross Domestic Product over the last 7,000 years. It increases exponentially.

Since knowledge is boundless, we can expect capital to augment both moral behavior and constrained freedom - at exponential rates.

7.2 Capital Augments Moral Behavior

The morality of capital can be measured by at least two related metrics: The increased population and the increased probability of natural selection. Figure 7.2-1 is a schematic diagram of the worldwide human population and the probability of human natural selection.

7.2.1 The Metric of Increased Population

Probably the most conclusive evidence of the morality of capital is the rapidly increasing human population. By our definition of morality, some types of capital must have been employed morally because capital is rapidly increasing the population. Figure 7.2-1 shows that 7,000 years ago, Earth had an estimated 5 million people and now it has an estimated 7.7 billion people. If, r, represents the average annual rate of increase of population over this period,

$$(1+r)^{7,000} = (7,700,000,000/5,000,000) = 1,540$$

$$(1+r) = 1,540^{(1/7,000)} = 1,540^{0.00014286} = 1.00105$$

$$(1+r) = 1.00105$$

$$r = 0.00105 = 0.105\%.$$

That is, over these 7,000 years, the average annual increase of population was 0.105%.

---

[148] The amount consumed is usually computed as the amount labor is paid. (See Table 13.3.3-2 in *The Nature of Economics*, Martin J. Miles.)

7.2.2 The Metric of Increased Probability of Natural Selection

To measure the morality of capital, we use a second type of evidence - the probability of *mortality* of human females prior to the end of their child-bearing years. This is the probability of natural *rejection*. Then we estimate the probability of natural selection as the complement of the probability of natural rejection:

Figure 7.2-1 diagram of the worldwide human population over the last 15 million years and the probability of natural selection over the last 15 million years

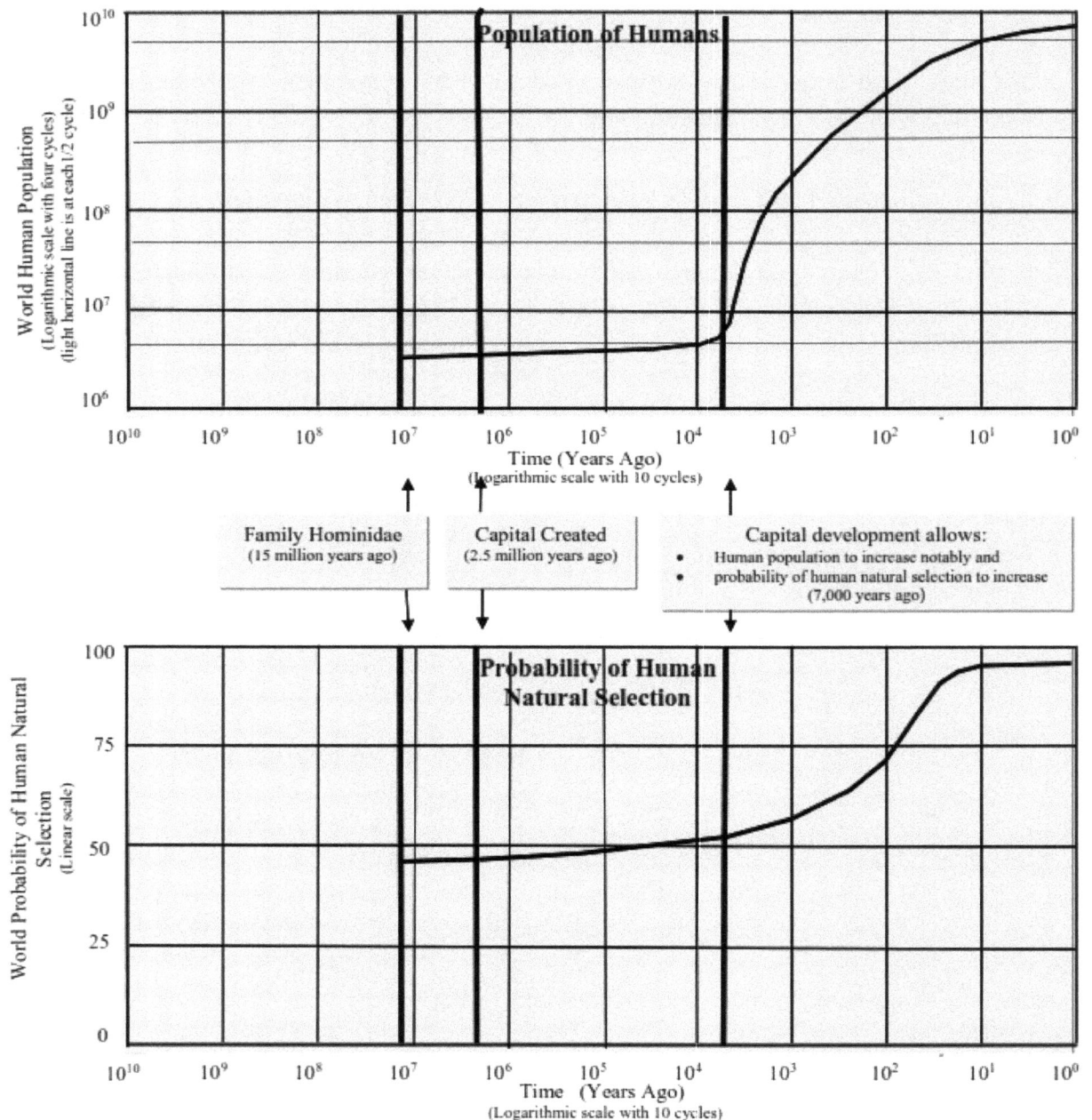

(Probability of Natural Selection) = 100% - (Probability of Natural Rejection).

We have estimated the probability of natural rejection from data obtained for the period from the beginning of family Hominidae (i.e., 15 million years ago) to the present.

Data for the probability of natural *rejection* come largely from three sources:

- **Earliest Part of this Period:** research of non-human primates who are still in the wild, [149]

- **Next Earliest Part of this Period:** research of current hunter-gather societies from various locations on Earth,[150] and

- **Latest Part of this Period:** research of modern data of mortality collected by governments. [151] [152]

Throughout most of this period of family Hominidae, the data are remarkably constant. The exception to this constancy is the effect of capital in the last 7,000 years ago when population began to increase and mortality rates began to decrease.

Figure 7.2-1 also depicts that the development of capital has decreased the *mortality* rate of young females, and, therefore, increased the probability of natural selection. Time is depicted by a logarithmic scale because it covers billions of years.[153]

---

[149]   The family Hominidae includes humans, chimpanzees, bonobos, gorillas, and orangutans. Some 14 million years ago humans split from orangutans; some 8 million years ago humans split from gorillas: and some 7 million years ago humans split from chimpanzees and bonobos.

[150] *Wealth Transmission and Inequality: Among Hunter-Gatherers*, Eric Aiden Smith, et al. Curr. Anthropol. 2010 February; 51(1): 19-34

[151] *Child and Infant Mortality*, Max Roser, Hannah Ritchie and Bernadeta Dadonaite, https://ourworldindata.org/child-mortality

[152] *Is Child Death the Crucible of Human Evolution?* Anthony A. Volk and Jeremy Atkinson https://www.researchgate.net/publication/256643424_Is_child_death_the_crucible_of_human_ evolution

[153] The nature of the probability of natural selection over time is similar to the Logistic function. However, keep in mind that our curve is drawn on a logarithmic scale, whereas the Logistic function is defined on a linear scale. A logistic function, f(x), is a common S-shaped curve (i.e., Sigmoid curve). That is,

$$f(x) = L / [1 + e^{-k(x - x_0)}]$$

where

x is the independent variable,

L= maximum value of the function,

At the beginning of humans, the probability of natural selection is estimated to have been approximately 45%. The increased probability of natural selection from capital in most Sub-Saharan African countries lags far behind the increase in other underdeveloped countries. Worldwide, the current probability of natural selection is approximately 95%, and in the USA it is approximately 99%. Our knowledge of pathogens is probably the most significant cause of this increase.

7.3 Capital Augments Constrained Freedom

As discussed in Section 6.2.3.C, moral behavior, freedom, and capital can all increase exponentially. Moreover, capital can enhance moral behavior and reduce the constraints on freedom.

The Moral Dilemma Space

As discussed throughout much of this book, the moral benefits from capital can be enormous. However, Chapter 8 discusses 13 types of situations that were novel during the last 7,000 years, but for which, our system of moral propensities has not yet evolved. (Many of these novel situations were made possible from our increased migrations.) The relatively slow rate of evolution allowed a 7,000-year lag in our moral propensity system. The delay is suspected of allowing as many as one billion deaths from conflicts with strangers.

Constrained Freedom

Fortunately, this lag in moral propensity is augmented by increased knowledge and freedom obtained from the migrations. That is, we can view the increased migrations and conflicts with strangers as a problem enhanced by capital, but we can also view the knowledge gained from migrating and interacting with strangers as a benefit by enhancing capital and freedom. (Freedom can be denied by death, by restraint from authorities, or by constraint from insufficient individual resources relative to individual desires.)

Productivity without capital is essentially unity. The introduction of capital has increased Worldwide Gross Domestic Product (GDP) from $130 per capita 7,000 years ago to $8,175 in 2,000, and $12,968 per capita in 2,010 AD - which, in the absence of restraint, increases individual freedom proportionately. Figure 7.3-1 depicts this dramatic increase in per capita GDP and several corresponding innovations. The dramatic increase really corresponds with the Industrial Revolution (1760-1840 AD) and the consequential reduction of slavery (1750-1950

---

k = logistic growth rate (i.e., steepness) of the function, and

x_0 = Sigmoid curves at the midpoint of the function.

https://en.wikipedia.org/wiki/Logistic_function

AD). It also notes that the increase in GDP/capita is a good estimate of the decrease in per capita constrained freedom

Figure 7.3-1 Productivity (Real-world GDP/capita) from 5,000 BC to 2,000 AD
(Horizontal scale is linear, and vertical scale is logarithmic.)
This figure is also a good estimate of Real-world GDP/capita freedom!

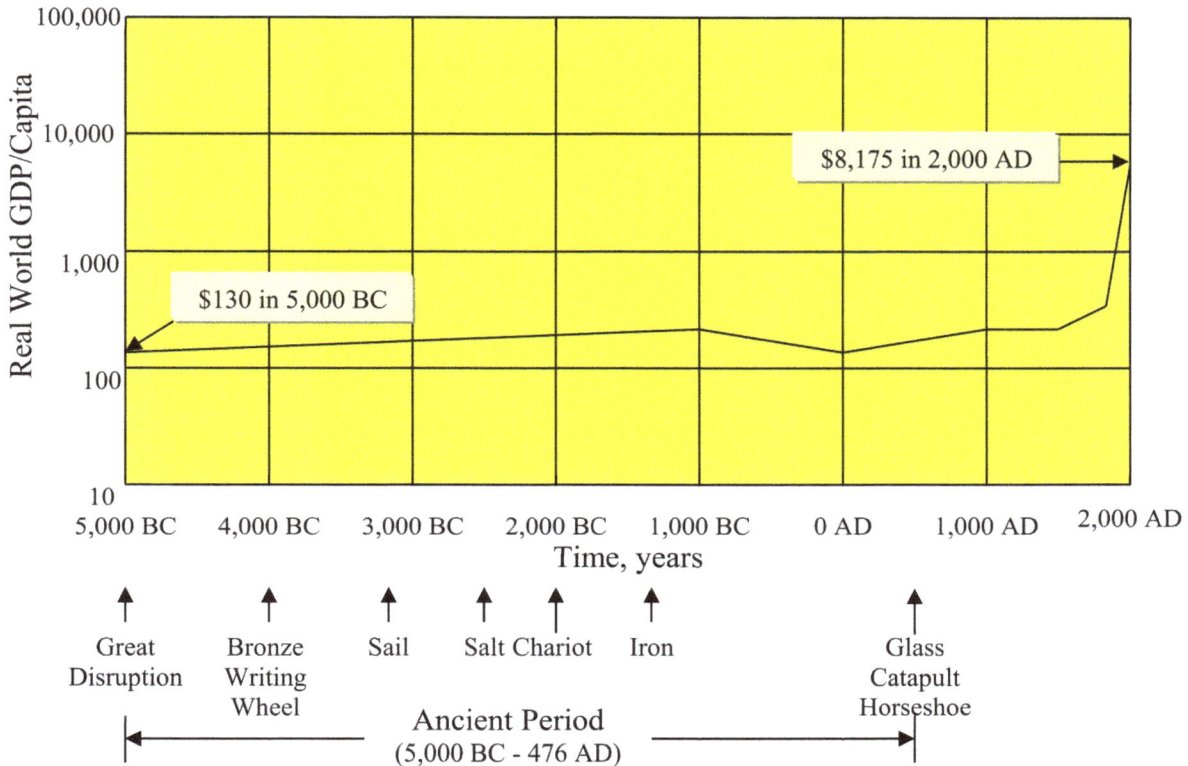

Figure 7.3-2 is Figure 4.4-1 except it also shows a graph of per capita Worldwide Gross Domestic Product over the last 7,000 years (expressed in International Dollars for the year 2000 AD).[154]

Figure 7.3-2 is a 3-dimensional schematic depiction of the Moral Propensity Space, the Moral Dilemma Space, and Worldwide GDP per capita over the last 7,000 years, expressed in International Dollars for 2000 AD. The productivity increases exponentially, and it can increase moral behavior and constrained freedom correspondingly.

---

[154] Data for this figure are obtained from Section 13.2.5-1 in The Nature of Economics by Martin J. Miles. Worldwide productivity is expressed in International Dollars for 2000 AD. The value in 2,010 AD was $12,968. The GDP for each of 11 years are: (5,000 BC, $130); (1,000 BC, $160); (1AD, $135); (1,000 AD, $165); (1,500 AD, $175); (1,800 AD, $250); (1,900 AD, $850); (1950 AD, $2,030); (1975 AD, $2,189); (2,000 AD, $8,175); and (2010 AD, $12,968).

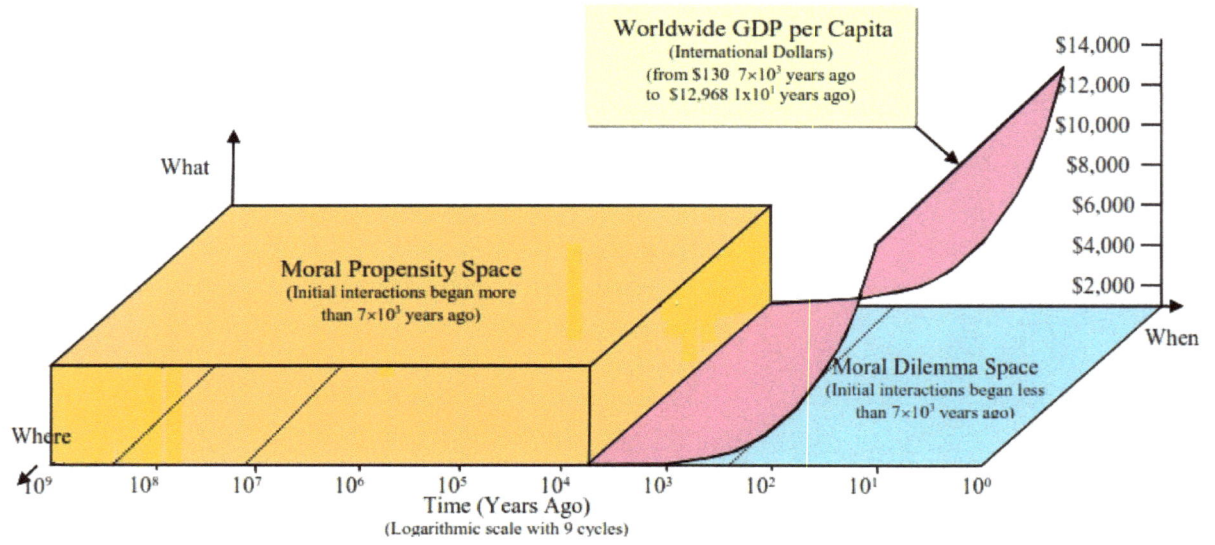

Worldwide GDP per Capita
(International Dollars)
(from $130 7×10^3 years ago
to $12,968 1×10^1 years ago)

What

Moral Propensity Space
(Initial interactions began more
than 7×10^3 years ago)

Where

Moral Dilemma Space
(Initial interactions began less
than 7×10^3 years ago)

When

$14,000
$12,000
$10,000
$8,000
$6,000
$4,000
$2,000

10^9 10^8 10^7 10^6 10^5 10^4 10^3 10^2 10^1 10^0

Time (Years Ago)
(Logarithmic scale with 9 cycles)

Chapter 8 Capital-Enabled Novel Types of Situations Pose Moral Dilemmas

The purpose of this chapter is to explore the dilemmas and adjustments caused by the rapid and exponential rate of capital development relative to the sporadic rates of evolution.

As discussed in the previous chapter, capital has increased the probability of worldwide human natural selection to a remarkable extent - from approximately 45% to greater than 95% Worldwide and 99% in the USA. Capital has been indescribably beneficial for humans.

Our system of moral propensities includes individual morality and group morality – but it seems not to include either species morality or ecosystem morality. Only recently have we been able to interact with strangers of our species, and to experience the damage we have caused to the ecosystem. For novel types of situations, we have no moral propensities – only moral dilemmas.

Capital develops so rapidly that human evolution (i.e., changing our genes) cannot occur quickly enough to conform to these novel situations. This is the practically unsolvable problem capital creates for us.

As we noted in Section 4.2, a system is a logical system if and only if its elements, such as moral propensities, are independent, consistent, and complete. Consequently, our innate moral system is now somewhat inconsistent for group morality. It is also incomplete for species morality and ecosystem morality - and it is rapidly becoming less complete as more novel types of situations occur.

By far, the most significant type of novel situation is our interaction with strangers. The problems with these interactions are exacerbated by the tens of thousands of years during which humans have evolved in countless diverse environments throughout the World – causing great differences with respect to race, gender, culture, morality, and abilities (i.e., identity).

Judging the Morality of Past Human Behavior

It seems that we can't resist judging past human behavior. Our judgment of the past probably depends upon our view of morality and whether the behavior was voluntary.

- **View of Morality.**
  - **Traditional View.** If you believe that morality is universal in time and space, you might consider the morality of the past behavior to be largely independent of the circumstances at that or any time.

- o **Innate View.** If you believe that morality is innate and you apply our definition of morality, the circumstances at that time necessarily affect the morality. Simply, did the behavior increase or decrease the probability of freedom – under the existing circumstances?
- **Freedom of Behavior.** If the behavior was involuntary, the moral judgment would apply only to the authority that caused the behavior to be involuntary.

Finally, if the behavior involves situations that are novel within the last 7,000 years, our moral propensities do not exist, and we are incapable of judging the morality of behavior accurately – regardless of our views or whether the act was voluntary: How can our judgment hit the bull's eye if the target has yet to evolve!

Timelines of the Two Rates: Human Morality and Capital Development

Figure 8-1 depicts significant evolutionary events and some significant developments of capital. The figure covers the period from the beginning of Earth to the present. The period is divided into 10 cycles of a logarithmic scale. Each cycle is a period between consecutive powers of 10 (i.e., from 1 to 10, from 10 to 100, from 100 to 1,000, etc.). The figure has three types of illustrations:

- **Two Eras of Capital Development and Periods of Four Levels of Morality.** Bar graphs indicate the periods covering two eras of capital development and four levels of moral behavior.
  - o **Two Capital Eras.**
    - **Primitive Capital Era (i.e., scraping flesh).** Tools (i.e., stones fashioned for scraping flesh and killing) were created 2.5 million years ago – hence, the Primitive Capital Era.
    - **Modern Capital Era (i.e., enhanced migration).** Tools were not sufficiently developed to enable groups to migrate and interact with strangers until about 7,000 years ago – hence, the Modern Capital Era.
  - o **Four Levels of Morality.** All levels of morality still exist, but their times of origin differ greatly.
    - **Individual Morality.** Life began 3.5-4.0 billion years ago, but complex organisms did not exist until 0.5-1.0 billion years ago. We assume that some individual morality existed in the period 0.5-1.0 billion years ago. (The earliest evidence of a brain structure dates to 0.526 billion years ago.)
    - **Group Morality.** Humans began 15 million years ago (i.e., the family Hominidae). We assume some group morality existed then.

- **Species Morality**. Since capital allowed groups to mingle with strangers 7,000 years ago, we assume this is the beginning of species morality – but it is still very immature.

- **Ecosystem Morality**. The Industrial Revolution began about 260 years ago. Since pollution began to increase greatly then, we assume this is the effective beginning of ecosystem morality.[155]

- **Human Population.** The estimated population of humans increased much more rapidly about 7,000 years ago.

- **Times of Significant Events.** The time of occurrence of 13 significant events are shown.

---

[155] It is true that primitive tools allowed humans to affect the ecosystem in many small ways (e.g., alter the food cycle (2.5 million years ago), domesticate animals (17,000 years ago), and domesticate agriculture (10,000 years ago)).

Figure 8-1 estimated periods and times of some significant events during the last 10 billion years

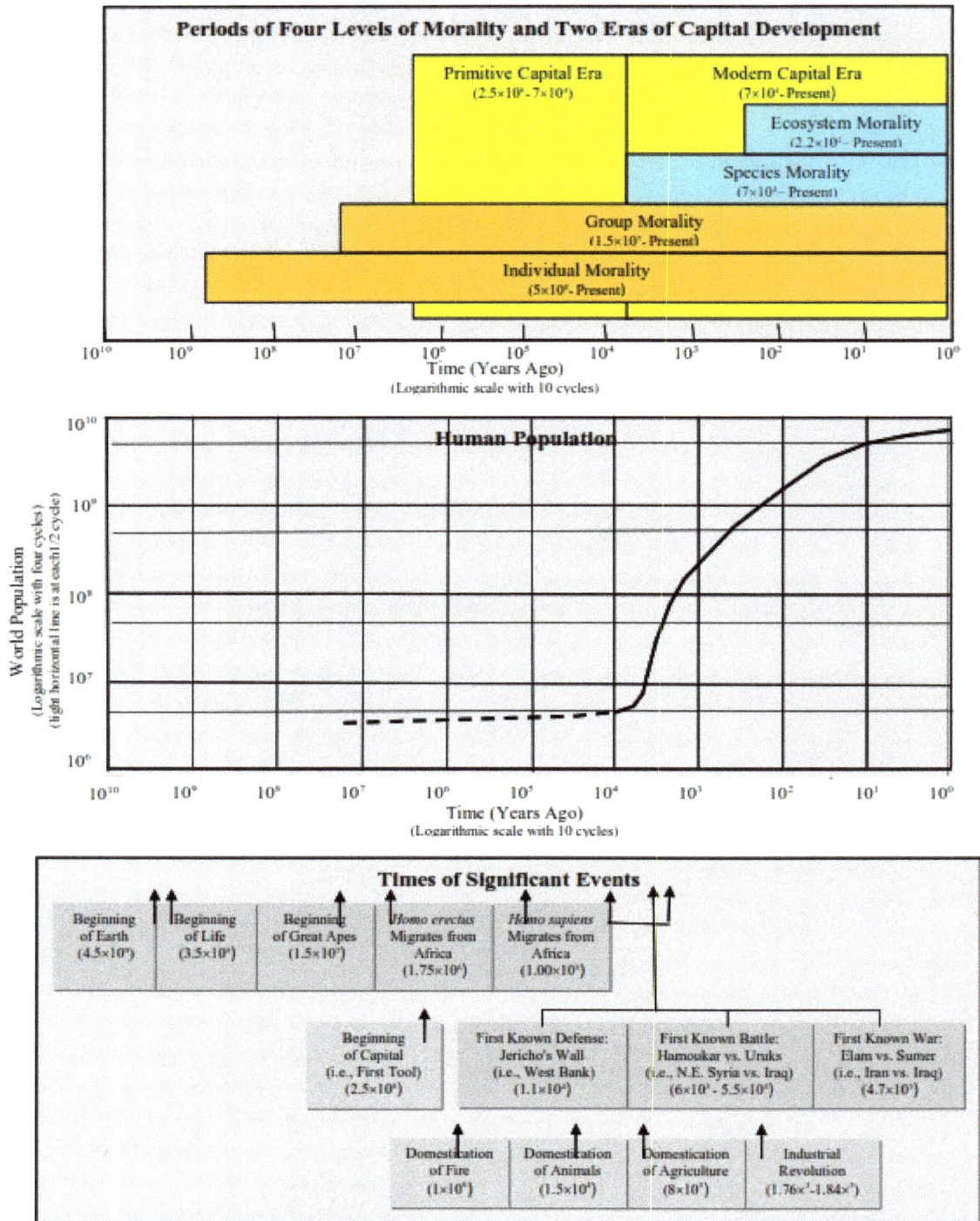

Table 8-1 lists some unnatural types of situations caused or cured by capital that would cause moral dilemmas. The table is organized according to the four levels of morality: individual morality, group morality, species morality, and ecosystem morality.

Of the 13 sections of this chapter, seven sections deal with species morality. It is convenient that all seven sections pertain to only two types of situations: Three situations occur because capital *brings us together*, and four situations occur because capital enables us to *separate* binary states that naturally occur together and provide balance.

Humans need help with these moral dilemmas – but none is readily available. None of us caused these dilemmas, and I think we should be patient with each other because we are all wallowing in dilemmas.

Table 8-1 capital-enabled novel types of situations (CENTS) pose moral dilemmas

			Caused by Capital	Cured by Capital	Solution
Capital-Enabled Novel Types of Situations (CENTS) Causes Moral Dilemmas	8.1 Individual Morality	8.1.1 Hubris	Unnatural success	-	Act intelligently
		8.1.2 Inactivity	Unnatural success	-	Act intelligently
	8.2 Group Morality	8.2.1 Abortion	-	More people are not needed. Baby is killed.	Be Responsible.
		8.2.2 Homosexuality	-	More people are not needed.	-
		8.2.3 Gender Roles Merge	Capital replaces some strenuous labor.	-	Be understanding.
	8.3 Species Morality — A. Novel Interactions Occur	8.3.1 Slave Labor	Capital enabled migration and mixing with strangers.	Capital is now more efficient than labor (i.e., Industrial Revolution).	-
		8.3.2 Conflicts and Conquests (Foreign)	Capital enables migration and mixing with strangers.	-	Be understanding.
		8.3.3 Moral Conflicts (Domestic)	Capital enables migration and mixing with strangers.	-	Be understanding.
	8.3 Species Morality — B. Natural Bonds are Separated	8.3.4 Consume-Produce are Separated	Capital replaces labor.	-	Be understanding.
		8.3.5 Rights-Responsibilities are Separated	Capital enables governments whose laws can be immoral.	-	Be responsible.
		8.3.6 Risk-Reward are Separated	Capital enables governments whose laws can be immoral.	-	Forbid separation.
		8.3.7 Supply-Demand are Separated	Capital enables separation.	-	Accommodate separation.
	8.4 Ecosystem Morality	8.4.1 Ecosystem Damage	Capital damages some life with chemicals and lost habitat.	Capital can increase capital's efficiency.	Act intelligently with empathy.

8.1 Individual Morality

Specifically, individual morality concerns the needs of existence - acquiring protection from the physical environment, acquiring protection from predators, and acquiring nutrition. Capital aids these needs for much of humanity – and, thereby, it greatly reduces the barriers to natural selection. Capital affects all levels of natural selection, but it affects individual selection most of all.

We divide the issues for individual morality into two types, mental (i.e., hubris) and physical (i.e., inactivity).

The sub sections of this sections are

> 8.1.1 Hubris

> 8.1.2 Inactivity

8.1.1 Hubris

Figure 2.3.4-1 is a diagram of decision-making in the ventromedial prefrontal cortex of the human brain. It decides between emotion and reason. Hubris is the "unreasonable" reliance upon emotion at the expense of logic - including the disregard of individual responsibility.

Truth

Probably the most important casualty of hubris is a type of irresponsibility - the disregard for truth – our fundamental moral compass!

Identity Selection

The practice of awarding benefits to individuals according to their identity rather than their merit is extremely reckless and immoral – if it endangers others.[156] With the possible exception of group selection, natural selection is *always* achieved by individual merit. This is important for our continued success. If an authority were (foolish enough) to choose winners or employees according to their identity, one couldn't trust the competence of such an individual or organization. People can be needlessly harmed or killed by such emotional and immoral behavior. Identity selection creates a biased market. Natural selection is a primary law of life. It is merit-based.[157]

---

[156] e.g., Affirmative Action is a prime example.

[157] Section 6.5.3 measures the morality of identity selection.

Less Need for Group Morality

To an increasing extent, capital augments individuals and enables us to live a "less than disciplined" life - which leaves us vulnerable to the biased judgments of hubris. [158]

As a means to achieve natural selection, group morality has evolved in humans for 15 million years. Since tools were realized 2.5 million years ago, humans have increasingly relied on capital to lower the barrier of natural selection. Correspondingly, group morality is increasingly less important to individual natural selection. A greater percent of humans survives, but their abilities are correspondingly less.

8.1.2 Inactivity

The more that capital increases the probability of natural selection, the less fit is the gene pool relative to natural selection, and the more dependent we become on capital. Not only are physically unfit individuals selected, but our subsequent life style allows us to become less fit from relative inactivity.

After some Negroids emigrated from Sub-Saharan Africa, those who left had human resources of almost the whole earth for themselves. Consequently, those who remained had much more human competition for resources than those who left. We discuss this in Section 8.3.3.

8.2 Group Morality

Table 2.2-1 lists the seven classifications of humans and their estimated dates of origin. The earliest classification of humans is family Hominidae. Its estimated date of origin is 15 million years ago. Since group morality undoubtedly existed 15 million years ago, and since capital is estimated to have begun 2.5 million years ago, we have approximately 12.5 million years (i.e., 15.0-2.5 = 12.5) of group morality propensities before capital could allow any novel types of situations to occur. Because of capital, we also have some group propensities that are no longer needed and which cause troublesome inconsistencies (e.g., dilemmas).

---

[158] Referring to hubris, the late great UCLA basketball coach, John Wooden, told his players: Talent is God-given; be humble. Fame is man-given; be grateful. Conceit is self-given, be careful.

The sub sections of this section are:

8.2.1 Abortion

8.2.2 Homosexuality

8.2.3 Gender Roles Merge

8.2.1 Abortion

Abortion is the deliberate termination of a human pregnancy. It causes one or two potential moral issues:

- denying the group another member, a fact that was very important to survival in the past, and

- killing a baby.

In the absence of resource shortages, a group probably preferred that pregnancy resulted in a healthy live birth; this additional member could have rendered the group more robust and more likely to survive. Innate group morality of abortion is determined by its effect on the survivability and freedom of the group, but today this depends largely on the effectiveness of applied capital rather than group size.

Conversely, in the presence of resource shortages, a group might prefer that a pregnancy be terminated by abortion.

Primitive Times

Pregnancy always creates a physically compromised situation for the mother and the baby, and, consequently, for the group. In primitive times, situations could occur in which a normal birth would decrease the group's expected probability of freedom (i.e., survival) – and an abortion would be moral. That is, abortion would be moral if continuing the pregnancy would substantially reduce the group's probability of survival (e.g., from exposure to climate, predation, conflicts, competition, starvation, etc.).[159]

Modern Times

On the other hand, capital has created a world in which most of humanity has advanced from a state of *need* to a state of *want*. In modern times, the killing of a baby by abortion is still practiced, but pregnancy almost never endangers the mother's or the group's survival. That is, in modern societies, the *need* for an abortion (i.e., to increase the probability of a mother's or group's survival) is so rare. Therefore, according to innate group morality, an abortion in modern times

---

[159] See Section 3.2 *Primitive Morality was Practical.*

would almost always be motivated simply by the mother's *want*, not *need*: It denies all freedom for the baby in order to maintain freedom for the mother.

Some Ancient History

The earliest induced abortions have been traced to China (2,700 BC) and Egypt (1,550 BC). The Greek Pythagoreans opposed all abortions because they believed the human soul entered the fetus at the time of conception, and they believed abortion was similar to homicide. On the other hand, the Romans were not opposed to abortion because they did not consider the fetus to be human.[160] The first known laws concerning abortion were documented in the Code of Hammurabi (1,772 BC).

Conclusion

Since humans existed for 12.5 million years before capital, we have inherited the moral propensities to kill the baby only to save the group. But in modern times, we almost never have the need to save the group. Consequently, when we kill the baby, it is almost always without necessity (but for convenience), and we undoubtedly have considerable guilt. This scenario seems immoral according to innate morality, and, if so, the feeling of guilt should be expected.

8.2.2 Homosexuality

Innate group morality probably had trouble with homosexual behavior because it did not increase the group's size and, consequently, it did not increase the probability of natural selection and freedom of its members. However, because of capital, we now have so many people, and the size of the group is irrelevant to its probability of natural selection or freedom.

Now, moral propensities that disapprove of homosexuality are needless and unfortunate. These moral propensities cannot soon be replaced.

8.2.3 Gender Roles Merge

Since the beginning of humanity there have been two genders that have many complementary functions. They are appropriate and effective. In the absence of capital, the genders and their roles seem to be well-designed. The efficiency of capital is gradually allowing it to complement and replace many activities of labor. First, it replaced heavy and unpleasant labor. Then, it

---

[160] Science has not settled on a definition of life, but when it does, it will almost certainly include at least one of the following properties: metabolism, irritability, reproduction, adaptability, growth, and organization – all of which are potentially possessed by the human fetus. Alternatively, life could be identified by its use of energy.

replaced much of the lighter labor - blurring some functions of the genders. (For obvious reasons, the opposite type of replacement is rare.)

Capital has allowed many females to join males in the workforce. Figure 8.2.3-1 depicts this trend.[161]

Figure 8.2.3-1 graph of male worker participation, all worker participation, and female worker participation over 62 recent years in the U.S.

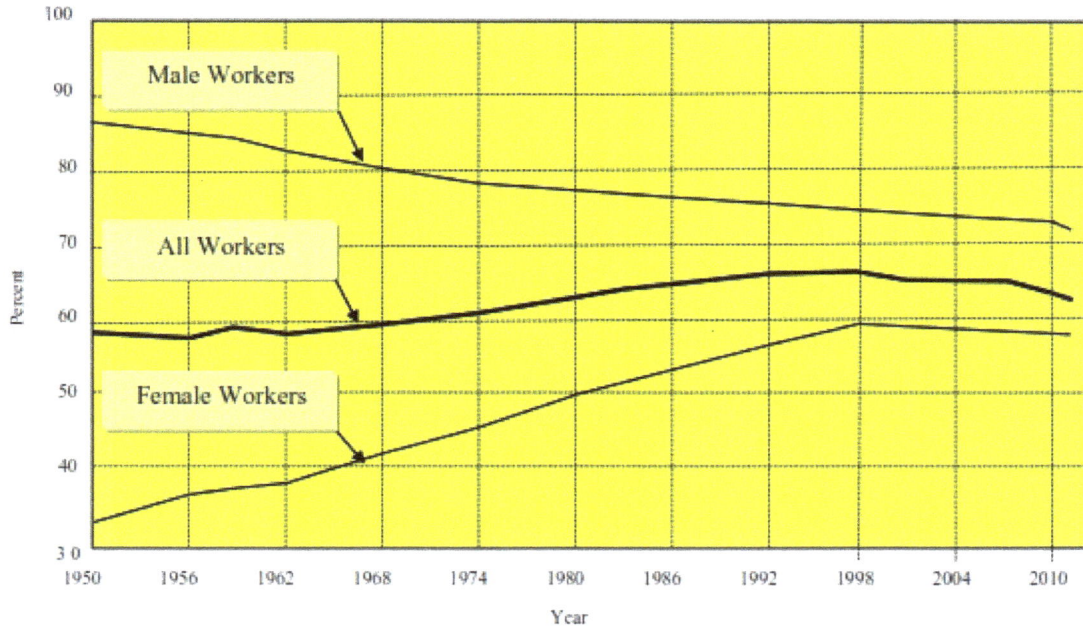

Since all individuals are necessarily territorial and some males are also chauvinistic, merging can cause gender conflicts. We can't expect our amygdala to remain idle during threats of the loss of a job, income, or identity.

The purpose of this section is not to judge the merging of gender roles but to note that we have no moral propensities to guide us through this novel type of situation.

8.3 Species Morality

Capital allowed human groups to migrate more easily approximately 7,000 years ago. Capital-enabled novel types of situations (CENTS) for species morality are divided into two types of

---

[161]The labor force participation rate is the ratio of (national labor force)-to-(national population) that is within the same age range. Some disincentives to work are food stamps, social security disability, Pell grants, and unemployment benefits.

situations (i.e., some bring us *unnaturally* together and others separate our relationships *unnaturally*):

    A. Unnatural Interactions Occur

        8.3.1 Slave Labor

        8.3.2 Conflicts and Conquests (Foreign)

        8.3.3 Moral Conflicts (Domestic)

    B. Natural Bonds are Separated

        8.3.4 Consume-Produce are Separated

        8.3.5 Rights-Responsibilities are Separated

        8.3.6 Risk-Reward are Separated

        8.3.7 Supply-Demand are Separated

A. Unnatural Interactions Occur

Because evolution has formed our group moral propensities for at least 15 million years (i.e., family Hominidae), our system of moral propensities has evolved as a logical system. But, since the application of capital beginning 2.5 million years ago, our relationships with our environments have changed. Capital has allowed humans to migrate and interact more easily, creating unnatural types of situations for which we have no moral propensities. We must develop species morality, but this can require many millennia.

Primary Migrations[162]

Homo erectus migrated throughout Africa 1.75 million years ago but it is now extinct. However, the primary (i.e., first) migration of *Homo sapiens* out of Sub-Saharan Africa is thought to begin 100,000 years ago and continued across the Bering Straits until it finally spread to South America approximately 11,000 years ago. Humans evolved to be compatible with their adopted environments. But because the migration was primary, it did not encounter other humans (i.e., strangers). Therefore, species morality didn't effectively begin during primary migrations.

Secondary Migrations

Approximately 7,000 years ago secondary migrations throughout the World did encounter strangers, and some war-like encounters began to modify human evolution with respect to

---

[162] https://en.wikipedia.org/wiki/History_of_human_migration

strangers. This was essentially the beginning of the development of species morality. Secondary migration is labeled the Great Moral Disruption in Figure 8.3.2-1.

Human Evolution is being Modified by Secondary Migrations that Encountered Strangers[163]

An allele is one of two or more alternative forms of a gene that arise by mutation (and occupy the same location on a chromosome). Modifying a human allele (i.e., a result of evolution) requires, at least, many generations and possibly thousands of years, depending upon the advantage of selection of the allele.

From these conditions (i.e., the time since encountering secondary migrations and the time to evolve from those encounters), we have probably modified genetically very little. A recent scientific paper shows that our genes differ by only 7% from those of humans that populated the Middle-East 40,000-50,000 years ago. At this time, the function of these new genes is not known.[164]

Probably the most significant novel type of situation caused by capital is the increased ability of groups of humans to migrate and interact. This ability accelerated 7,000 years ago.

Consider two measures of our period with strangers:

- **Hominidae.** If we assume that group morality has existed for 15 million years (i.e., family Hominidae), and species morality began 7,000 years ago, we have spent only 0.0047% of our time with strangers.

- *Homo sapiens sapiens.* Alternately, if we assume that group morality has existed for only 0.2 million years (i.e., *Homo sapiens sapiens*), and species morality began 7,000 years ago, we have spent only 3.5% of our time with strangers.

In either case, 7,000 years is not much time to evolve propensities for species morality. See the amygdala in Section 2.3.2 and Figure 2.3.4-1.

8.3.1 Slave Labor

There have been multiple motives to enslave humans. Labor is the most common, but indebtedness, amusement, prisoners of war, and sex are others.

---

[163] https://en.wikipedia.org/wiki/Recent_human_evolution

[164] *An ancestral recombination graph of human, Neanderthal, and Denisovan genomes*, Nathan Schaefer, Beth Shapiro, Richard E. Green

The Beginning

In a primitive form, slavery began when members of one group were captured by another group. Otherwise, it is difficult to know when slave labor began and to what degree it involved neighboring groups or true strangers. Even though we believe that interactions with strangers accelerated about 7,000 years ago, it could have started earlier.

Slave labor could have begun with the domestication of animals (15,000 BC), but some believe it was practiced in earnest with the domestication of agriculture (8,000 BC) – due to the increased need for labor after the domestication of agriculture.

Profitability

Slave labor was clearly a successful business model that was practiced worldwide for 10,000-17,000 years, during which time it also provided necessary protection and nourishment for the slaves.

Morality

The reference to slavery in the code of Hammurabi demands death for anyone who helps a slave escape. In Ancient times, slavery was considered moral by many scholars, religious leaders, and philosophers - including Aristotle.

Life, the basic freedom, is more important than ancillary freedoms. When we contemplate the morality of slavery, we should contemplate it under what we believe were the prevailing conditions – if that is possible:

- **Quantity of Life.** Did enslavement increase or decrease the individual's/group's probability of freedom (i.e., remaining lifespan)?

- **Quality of Life.** Enslavement caused individuals/groups to lose some freedoms, but they undoubtedly received protection and nourishment.

The Ending

Slavery began to lose favor worldwide *immediately* following the Industrial Revolution (1760-1840 AD). Eight significant industrial innovations that occurred during that period are:

- **Canal Engineering.** James Brindley was a civil engineer who created canals.

- **Ceramics.** Josiah Wedgwood pioneered the industrial production of ceramics.

- **Machine Making.** Henry Maudslay recognized that metal was needed for machine precision. He designed machines for lathes, drills, planes, machines, etc. These machines, in turn, made many machines.

- **Manufacturing.** Matthew Boulton was a factory owner and engineer who facilitated the manufacture of James Watt's steam engines.

- **Railways.** George Stephenson developed several aspects of rail transport, including flanged wheels and the standard gauge.

- **Road Building.** John McAdam created methods of building roads that could be used in most weather conditions.

- **Steam Engineering.** James Watt could be considered the father of the steam age.

- **Textiles.** Richard Arkwright invented the 'water frame' for spinning cotton. He could be considered the father of the industrial revolution.

Figure 8.3.1-1 depicts three significant periods for slavery whose times we should correlate:

- **A Histogram of the Periods of the Abolishment of Slavery by Countries.** A histogram depicts the frequencies (e.g., a probability density function) of the dates of legal abolition of slavery in 102 countries. The frequencies are shown as bar graphs. The table in the upper left of the figure shows how the frequency of each period is determined. Except for the first short and wide bar on the left, each bar represents a 50-year period.

- **The Period of the Industrial Revolution.** The black bar graph depicts the 80-year period of the Industrial Revolution.

- **The Period of the U.S. Civil War.** The narrow black bar (or line) graph depicts the four year period of the U.S. Civil War, which resulted in the freeing of the slaves in the U.S.

Figure 8.3.1-1 conjures a few observations and questions:

- Slavery, for the purpose of labor, undoubtedly ended because capital became more efficient than labor. The Industrial Revolution dramatically increased productivity relative to human labor – which, like the food cycle, is essentially always near 1. (See Section 7.1.2.) If slavery for labor ended because of the conscience of humanity, it would have coincided with the end of slavery for other purposes (i.e., indebtedness, amusement, war, sex, etc.)

- Slavery was essentially a worldwide practice for perhaps 10,000-17,000 years, and all ethnic groups were enslaved at various times. The United States abolished slavery essentially at the median of the dates on which the 102 countries abolished slavery.

- If slave labor was no longer efficient, perhaps, the U.S. civil war was unnecessary; it started approximately 40 years after the end of the Industrial Revolution. Generally, entrepreneurs who would hold slaves beyond the time that it was no longer efficient would fail economically.

- Abolishing slave labor because of innovation is an older version of job loss from innovation. (See Section 8.3.4.)

- Like all practices of the past, slave labor should be judged *only* in its context (e.g., its economic environment), and, perhaps, not even then if we also believe that humans do not yet possess species morality!

Figure 8.3.1-1 The blue bars depict a histogram of the dates of legal abolition of slavery in 102 countries. The wide black bar depicts the period of the Industrial Revolution, a period that allowed the efficiency of machines to often exceed the efficiency of slavery. The narrow black bar depicts the period of the U.S. Civil War.

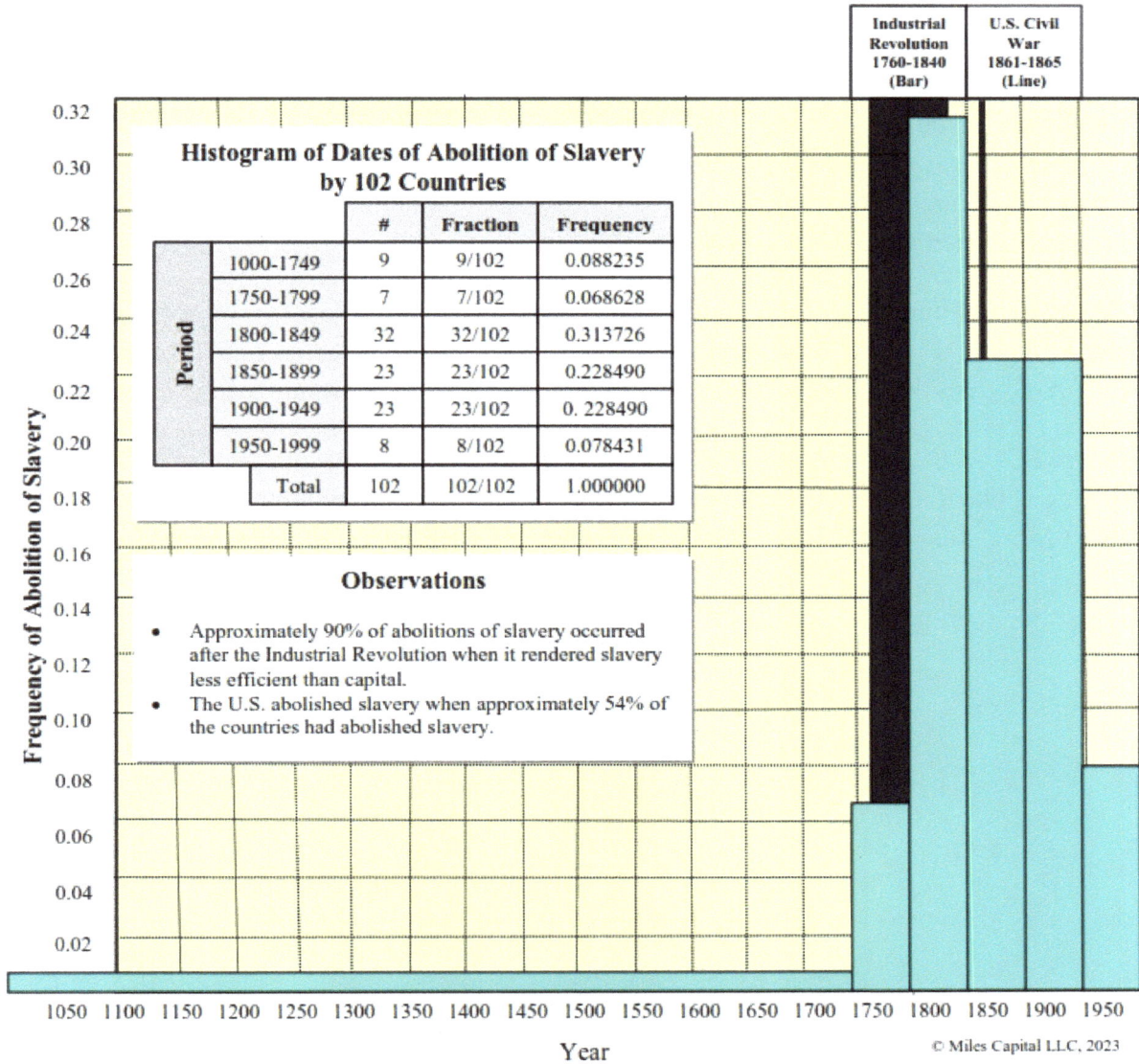

Histogram of Dates of Abolition of Slavery by 102 Countries

Period	#	Fraction	Frequency
1000-1749	9	9/102	0.088235
1750-1799	7	7/102	0.068628
1800-1849	32	32/102	0.313726
1850-1899	23	23/102	0.228490
1900-1949	23	23/102	0.228490
1950-1999	8	8/102	0.078431
Total	102	102/102	1.000000

Observations

- Approximately 90% of abolitions of slavery occurred after the Industrial Revolution when it rendered slavery less efficient than capital.
- The U.S. abolished slavery when approximately 54% of the countries had abolished slavery.

© Miles Capital LLC, 2023

Source of data: https://en.wikipedia.org/wiki/Timeline_of_abolition_of_slavery_and_serfdom

The practice of slavery throughout known history clearly reveals that group morality is magnanimous and species morality is mundane!

Since slave labor essentially no longer exists, it is not a moral situation that needs new propensities.

175

8.3.2 Conflicts and Conquests (Foreign)

There have been many motivations for migrations, but most migrations that followed the domestication of animals (15,000 BC) and the domestication of agriculture (8,000 BC) were motivated by droughts, conflicts, or conquest.

Since 5,000 BC, there are estimates of 1.25 billion humans either dead by war or dead by disease from war. Capital (i.e., technology) enabled conflicts to be more violent after states were formed. Probably states were formed for protection. Even today, all governments consider protection of citizens to be their primary responsibility. This section is relatively brief only because so much has already been written about conflicts and conquests.

The history of humans is loaded with tragic examples of our problems with territory, resources, and strangers. Figure 8.3.2-1 depicts evidence of the first five types of conflicts with strangers (i.e., A-E) , and the estimated dates of conflicts are indicated by small "explosions."

Figure 8.3.2-1 estimated sizes of human societies from groups to empires (The horizontal scale of time is linear, and the vertical scale of size of societies is logarithmic with five cycles.) "The Great Moral Disruption" refers to the initial merging of groups.

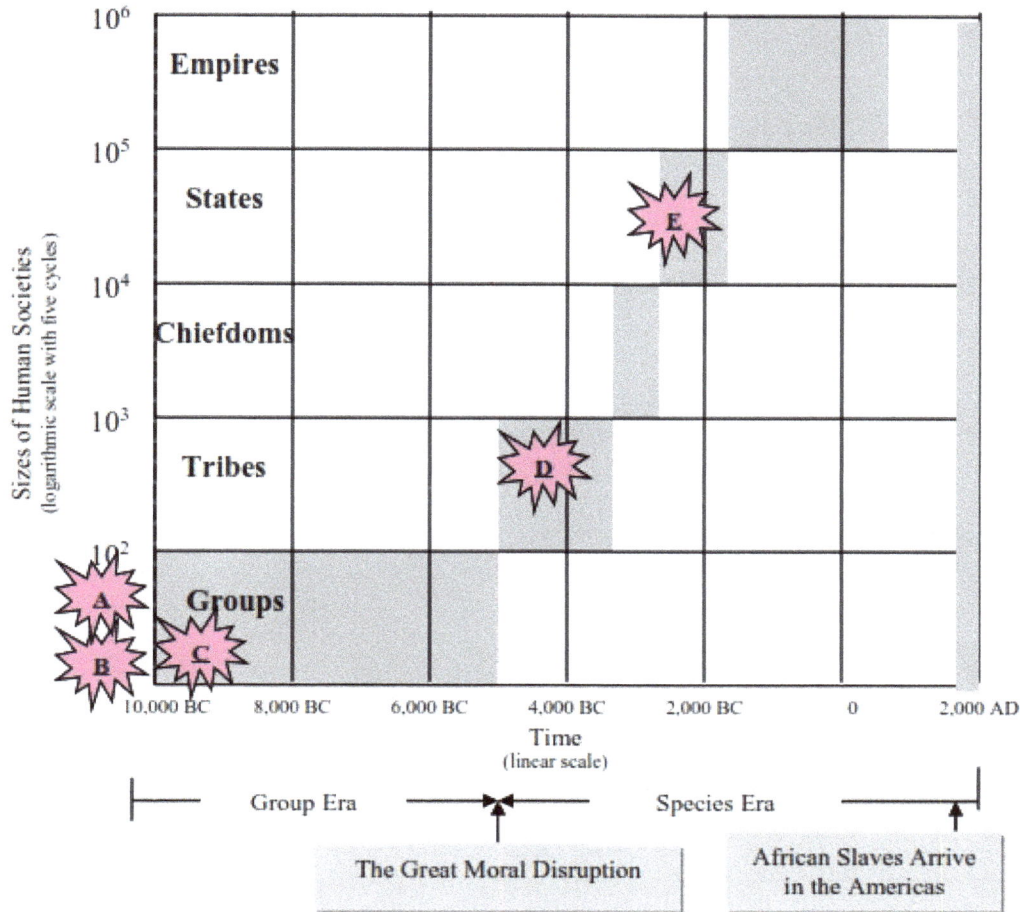

The chart shows "Sizes of Human Societies (logarithmic scale with five cycles)" on the vertical axis (10^6 Empires, 10^5 States, 10^4 Chiefdoms, 10^3 Tribes, 10^2 Groups) versus "Time (linear scale)" on the horizontal axis (10,000 BC, 8,000 BC, 6,000 BC, 4,000 BC, 2,000 BC, 0, 2,000 AD). Stars labeled A, B, C, D, and E are plotted. Below: "Group Era" and "Species Era" with "The Great Moral Disruption" and "African Slaves Arrive in the Americas."

Following are five types of evidence from early human conflicts:

A. Inter-Group Conflict. There is almost no evidence (i.e., damage to skeletons, artifacts, or cave paintings) of inter-group conflicts until perhaps 10,000-11,000 BC. The first evidence, near the present-day border of Egypt and Sudan, is many skulls of both males and females with arrowheads embedded in them.

B. **Observation Tower.** The first (mass) warning is apparently an observation tower that was constructed between 11,000 BC and 9,650 BC near Aleppo (in present-day Syria).

C. Wall. The first defense was apparently a 15-foot wall that is four feet thick. It was constructed in 9,000 BC in the West Bank city of Jericho.

D. Battle. The first battle apparently occurred between 4,000 BC and 3,500 BC in the city of Hamoukar in the north eastern portion of present-day Syria when it was invaded by the Uruks from Mesopotamia in present-day Iraq.

E. War. The first war occurred in 2,700 BC. It was in Basra in present-day Iraq between Sumer and Elam (in present-day Iran).

177

Battles and wars could not exist until societies became large and innovations permitted advanced weapons.

Merged groups have increased in size with time. The capabilities (for conquest, enslavement, and persecution of selected groups) of these large organizations also increased with time.

Even though the first known inter-group conflict, an observation tower, and a wall were known to exist earlier than 5,000 BC, we believe that inter-group conflicts were so rare that they had a minor role in evolving our moral propensities for strangers.

As conflicts and wars have increased in frequency, so also have the efforts of humans to reduce or mitigate them: The League of Nations was created after WWI (1920). It failed to prevent WWII, and it ceased to exist when the United Nations was formed in 1946.

These efforts are well-intentioned, but the immaturity of species morality, natural mistrust, inequalities, racism, and discrimination are present in almost all interactions of strangers. This can't be helped – and neither can the presence of competing interests that usually exceed common interests.

8.3.3 Moral Conflicts (Domestic)

Because moralities vary among environments, immigration tends to increase domestic moral conflicts. As a reminder of this type of situation, we repeat Figure 2.2.4-1 which depicts primary migrations to most environments inhabited by *Homo sapiens* from 100,000 years ago to 7,000 years ago. Table 2.1-1 lists the origin of many significant events during this period.

History of Human Migrations

Humans evolved in Africa 15 million years ago. Approximately 100,000 years ago some modern humans (i.e., *Homo sapiens*) migrated from Sub-Saharan Africa to the Middle-East.[165] The varied environments inhabited by migrations caused *Homo sapiens* to differentiate and evolve into three races. According to forensic archaeologists, *Homo sapiens* that evolved in Sub-Saharan Africa are now called Negroids. Those Negroids that left Sub-Saharan Africa migrated and evolved in the Middle-East until approximately 70,000 years ago when some migrated farther east to evolve in Asia as Mongoloids (and some of those migrated even farther and crossed the Bering Straits and to the Americas to evolve as American Indians). Similarly, approximately 40,000 years ago some migrated west from the Middle-East to evolve in Europe as Caucasoids.

Before about 12,000 years ago, the Americas were populated by Mongoloids which led European adventurers to believe that they had landed in the "Indies" of Asia. The New World (i.e., the

---

[165] https://www.worldhistory.org/image/6605/map-of-homo-sapiens-migration/

Americas) was apparently "discovered" by Christopher Columbus in 1492 AD and soon became populated by Europeans. At that time, we had no propensities for the morality of inhabiting occupied (but relatively undeveloped) land.[166] Then, approximately 200-400 years ago, slave traders forced some Negroids to be brought from Sub-Saharan Africa to the Americas as slaves for the European inhabitants.

Figure 2.2.4-1 where and when *Homo sapiens* migrated during the last 100,000 years

- Most *Homo sapiens* remained in Africa and continued to evolve as Negroids during this 100,000 period.
- In this primary migration, *Homo sapiens* migrated from Sub-Saharan Africa approximately 100,000 years ago to the Middle-East. Approximately 70,000 years ago some moved east to Asia and evolved as Mongoloids, and approximately 40,000 years ago, some of those migrants moved west to Europe and evolved as Caucasoids. Some Middle-Eastern people remained.
- In many secondary migrations, approximately 7,000 years ago, groups dispersed and caused many strangers to interact – causing human conflicts to begin evolving propensities for species morality.
- From 200-400 years ago, the slave trade brought some Sub-Saharan Africans to the Americas. (This forced migration is depicted by the very, very short line segment, resembling a dot, on the right side.)

Legend

Era of Evolution due to Physical Environments (i.e., Group Era) (100,000-7,000 years ago)

Era of Evolution due to Physical Environments & Conflicts with Strangers (i.e., Species Era) (7,000-0 years ago) (See Section 8.3.2.)

Environments in which *Homo sapiens* have evolved over the Last 100,000 Years

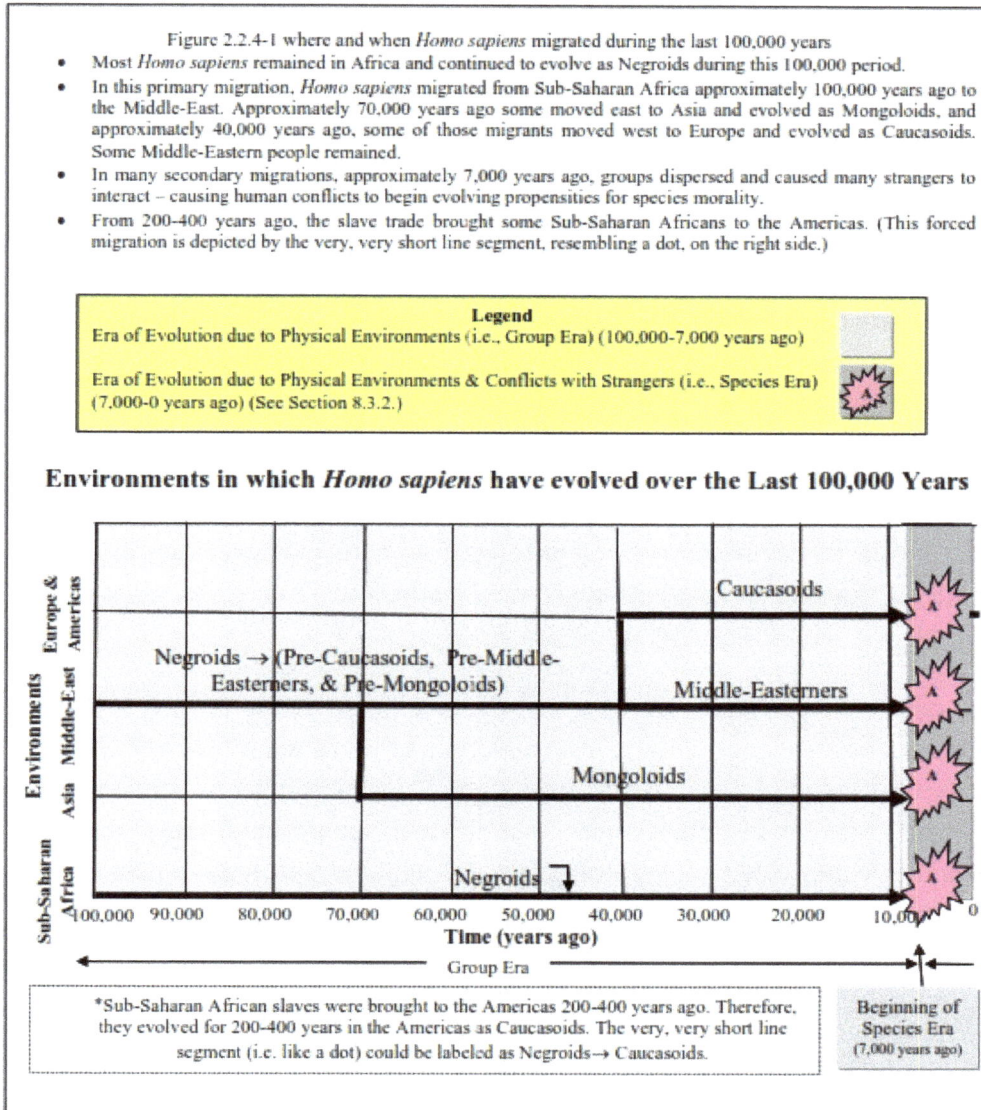

*Sub-Saharan African slaves were brought to the Americas 200-400 years ago. Therefore, they evolved for 200-400 years in the Americas as Caucasoids. The very, very short line segment (i.e. like a dot) could be labeled as Negroids→ Caucasoids.

Beginning of Species Era (7,000 years ago)

---

[166] Perhaps the best indication that we have essentially no propensities for species morality is this: Group morality very clearly exists. The relationships of individuals within groups are universally magnanimous. Conversely, species morality, the relationship between individuals from different groups is almost always wary, sometimes hostile, and has been responsible for more than one billion deaths worldwide from conflicts and wars. A level of morality with a scenario such as this could never be called mature or complete.

Morality Varies among Environments

Since morality is innate, different human environments create different levels of moralities:

- There is a version of human morality for every human environment. This also means that a universal morality does not exist.

- Immigrants bring their morality with them. Morality usually requires millennia to evolve. That is, if a human allele is very advantageous to human survival, it could become widespread in a population after a few centuries, but if a human allele is less advantageous to survival, it could require millennia to become widespread in a population.[167]

- The optimum environment for an individual is the environment that designed it.

Capital Development Enables More Frequent Immigrations

Capital enables novel types of situations, and since capital develops at an exponential rate, novel types of situations occur with a corresponding frequency. Also, because these situations are novel, moral propensities have not yet evolved to guide us – leaving dilemmas. Many of these novel types of situations enable humans to migrate and merge with domestic societies. These migrations began to occur more frequently approximately 7,000 years ago as what we call secondary migrations and the beginning of the Species Era.

Probably most migrations have been considered acceptable to societies because their differences were assumed to be cultural (i.e., transitory) rather than genetic (i.e., essentially permanent). Genetic differences will endure for at least hundreds of years and often for millennia. This means that differences that might have been considered acceptable because they were assumed to be transitory will exist far into the future. Conflicts will endure, and there will be pressures for societies and governments to skew laws from the relatively normative behavior of natives and toward the migrants' foreign behavior.

An Example of Cultural Conflicts

The most appropriate example of domestic cultural conflicts seems to be the Black and White homicide rates in the USA because these data are most significant, available, and reliable.[168] That is, homicide is not a matter of degree or a matter of opinion (i.e., as are some other crimes).

---

[167] An allele is an alternative form of a gene that arises by mutation. *"How We Are Evolving"*. *Scientific American. November 1, 2012. Retrieved May 27, 2020.*

[168] Over the past 100,000 years, Negroids and Caucasoids evolved almost exclusively in different environments.

Consequently, we don't need to be concerned with third-party biases and judgments that could taint the data.

Obviously, the levels of morality vary among human environments, but the magnitude of some differences, such as these homicide rates, really should be explained. According to published data from the U.S. Justice Department, the homicide rates of Blacks and Whites in 2018 in the USA are very different:

- **Between Races.** Blacks killed Whites at a rate that was 12.57 times the rate that Whites killed Blacks.

- **Within Races.** Blacks killed other Blacks at a rate that was 5.56 times the rate that Whites killed other Whites.

These two rates are derived in the following table, Table 8.3.3-1, which has three subtables (i.e., a, b, and c). The above homicide rates are derived in subtable (c) after the ratio in each cell in subtable (a) is multiplied by the population in the corresponding row in suitable (b).

Table 8.3.3-1(a) Homicides/100,000 Population			Table 8.3.3-1(b) Population	
	Victim			**U.S. Population**
	White	**Black**	**Race**	
Offender — White	2,677/100,000	234/100,000	White	250,446,755
Offender — Black	514/100,000	2,600/100,000	Black	43,784,096

Table 8.3.3-1(c) Homicide Rates: Each cell of subtable (c) is the product obtained by multiplying the expression in each cell in each row of subtable (a) by the number in each cell in each row of subtable (b).

		Victim	
		White	**Black**
Offender	**White**	$(2,677/100,000) \times 250,446,755 = 1.069$	$(234/100,000) \times 250,446,755 = 0.0934$
Offender	**Black**	$(514/100,000) \times 43,784,096 = 1.174$	$(2,600/100,000 \times 43,784,096 = 5.938$

Table 8.3.3-1 (continued)

Lastly, data from subtable (c) show:

- Blacks were 12.57 times more likely to kill Whites than Whites were likely to kill Blacks. That is, 1.174 / 0.0934 = 12.57
- Blacks were 5.555 times more likely to kill other Blacks than Whites were likely to kill other Whites. That is, 5.938 / 1.069 = 5.555.

These results are depicted in Figure 8.3.3-1.

https://ucr.fbi.gov/crime-in-the-u.s/2018/crime-in-the-u.s.-2018/tables/expanded-homicide-data-table-3.xls
https://ucr.fbi.gov/crime-in-the-u.s/2016/crime-in-the-u.s.-2016/tables/expanded-homicide-data-table-3.xls

Figure 8.3.3-1 This figure depicts the large difference in homicide rates between the races as computed in Table 8.3.3-1.

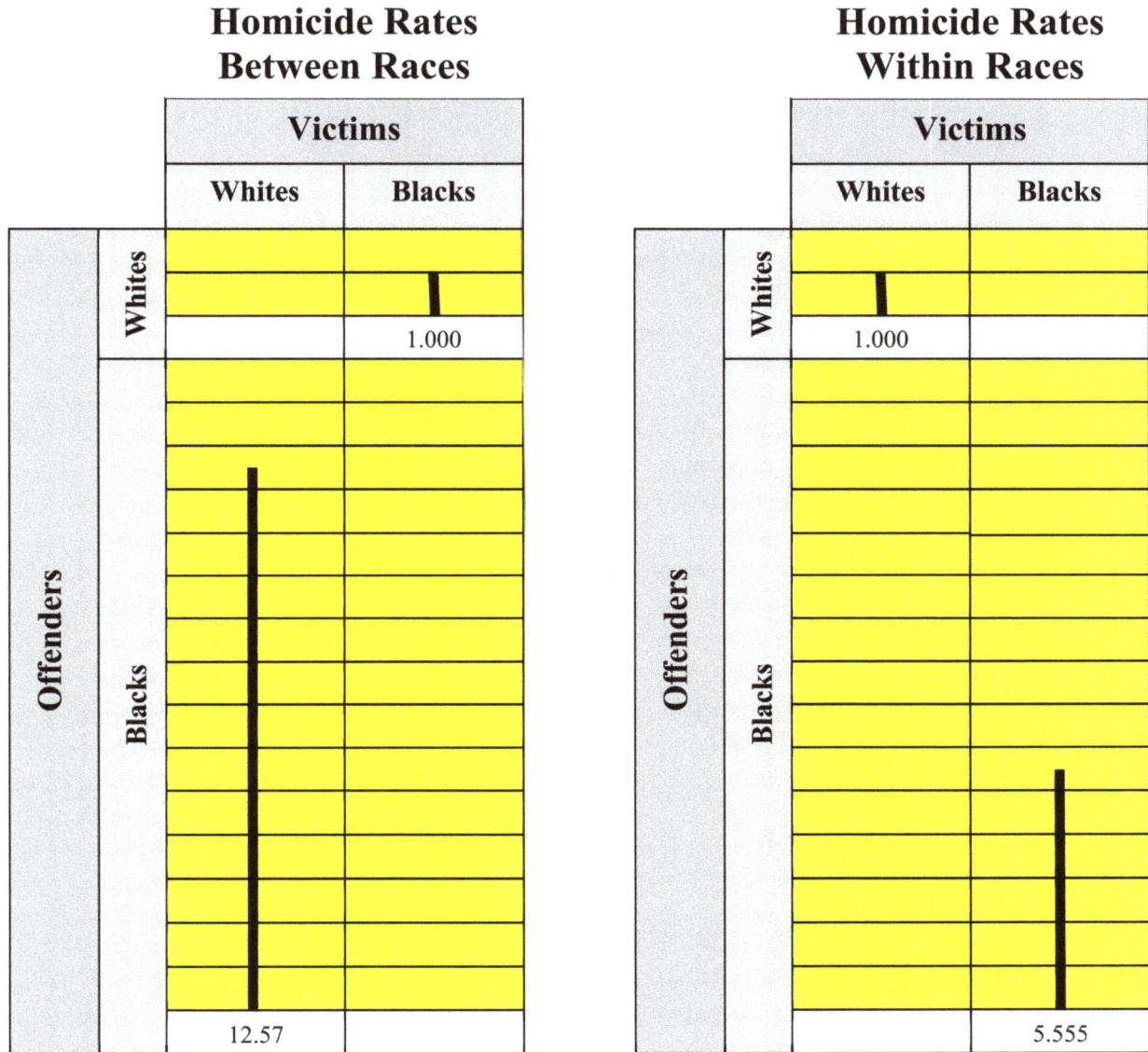

Homicide Rates Between Races

		Victims	
		Whites	**Blacks**
Offenders	**Whites**		1.000
	Blacks	12.57	

Homicide Rates Within Races

		Victims	
		Whites	**Blacks**
Offenders	**Whites**	1.000	
	Blacks		5.555

Figure 5.2.2-1 depicts worldwide homicide rates for 18 regions. Blacks in Sub-Saharan Africa killed other Blacks at a rate that was 38% higher than the 5.555 rate in the USA. (The homicide rate of Blacks in the USA might have exceeded the homicide rate of Negroids in Sub-Saharan Africa if the incarceration rate of Blacks in the USA were not 29.69 times that of the incarceration rate of Negroids in the Sub-Saharan African countries!)

183

In Figure 5.2.2-1, the region labeled "Americas" includes the Caribbean, Central America, North America, and South America. It should be noted that, except for North America, the Americas have homicide rates approximately the same as Sub-Saharan Africa. Specifically, the Caribbean region, which is 65% Black, has the highest homicide rate in the world at 26.12 per 100,000 persons. Note that the ancestors of essentially all Blacks in the Americas left Sub-Saharan Africa only 200-400 years ago.

Possible Reason for this Large Difference in Homicide Rates

The difference between the homicide rates of Whites and Blacks in the USA is so large that one feels compelled to explain it. Even though the purpose of this section is to discuss problems between different moralities within the same society, this section also contains the data needed to examine the reason for the large discrepancy. I pose this possible explanation: Consider the evolution of the following two populations over the last 100,000 years:

- **Negroids Who Remained.** Negroids who remained in Sub-Saharan Africa continued to have *human competition* for resources for the last 100,000 years. Perhaps they "solved" their competition problem by killing each other. Those are the Negroids that were brought to the Americas 200-400 years ago. [169]

  They also developed relatively little capital to relieve resource shortages. For example, it is noted in Section 7.2.2 that the current rate of natural selection in Sub-Saharan Africa is still very small.

- **Negroids Who Emigrated.** Conversely, Negroids who emigrated from Sub-Saharan Africa to the Middle-East and, subsequently, to either Europe (as Caucasoids) or Asia (as Mongoloids) had *no human competition* for resources for much of the next 100,000 years (because there were no other humans outside of Sub-Saharan Africa)! This fact seems most significant.

  Almost all societies farther from the Equator developed considerably more capital than those in Sub-Saharan Africa. Capital alone can cause productivity; productivity can greatly increase the production of natural resources – and this decreases resource shortages.

In summary, the difference in human competition for resources could have caused two very different levels of competitiveness that is manifested by two very different rates of homicide.

---

[169] The Negroids who were brought to the Americas 200-400 years ago descended from those Negroid populations who continued to evolve with *human competition* in Sub-Saharan Africa. The land mass of Sub-Saharan Africa is 9.4 million square miles – only 4.8% of the 196.9 million square miles of the land mass of Earth!

Whites and Blacks were designed by their respective environments. Individuals from neither race should be blamed nor credited for their evolutionary *moral propensities*, but a society must hold them responsible for *behavior* that is not normative in that society.

Observations

- **Observation #1.** The human amygdala warns us to be wary of strangers and strange things. We should be patient with those who behave accordingly. They are not to be blamed for being wary. Graphs of political freedom (Figure 5.2.3-1) show how societies in different regions of the world feel about strangers and security.

- **Observation #2.** Because environments design morality, individuals are not responsible for their *moral propensities*. I believe that knowing this fact could mitigate some ill feelings.

- **Observation #3.** Sub-Saharan African environments designed the morality of their inhabitants. Environments design levels of characteristics – not characteristics. Since evolution is efficient it is rare that individuals inherit extraneous characteristics.

- **Observation #4.** An individual and its moral propensities are inseparable (i.e., its phenotype and its genotype are inseparable). Knowing this is important because we can rationally dislike an individual's moral *behavior* without blaming the individual for its inherited moral *propensities*.

- **Observation #5.** An individual's genes usually require many millennia to change.

- **Observation #6.** Sub-Saharan Africans were sold by their fellow Sub-Saharan Africans and brought to the USA 200-400 years ago from Africa against their will. (Who is more morally responsible, the seller or the buyer?)

- **Observation #7.** The optimum environment for an individual is the environment that designed it.

B. Natural Bonds are Separated

Capital affects all four levels of morality, but, as it develops, it affects them in significantly different ways. Some types of situations involve what is known as naturally opposing binary states, but capital enables the opposing states to separate – causing moral issues. Examples of naturally opposing states are on-off, up-down, inside-outside, true-false, and, most significantly, "for every action there is an equal and opposite reaction."[170] To be considered natural, each of

---

[170] Newton's Third Law of Motion

the two unary states must apply to the same entity or situation. We shall consider four such opposing states: consume-produce, rights-responsibilities, risk-reward, and supply-demand.[171]

8.3.4 Consume-Produce Are Separated

Capital is so effective and so alien to nature that it enables the fundamental opposing binary states, consume-produce, to be separated.

The Food Cycle Consists of Naturally Opposing States: Consume-Produce

Life began about 3.5 billion years ago, and complex organisms evolved about 0.5-1.0 billion years ago. The manner in which organisms obtain nutrition is probably their most fundamental characteristic. Autotrophs (i.e., "self-nourishers") are producing organisms (i.e., plants, algae, and some types of bacteria) that produce their nutrients from the sun, thermal vents in the oceans, and minerals in the soil. Heterotrophs (i.e., "nourished from others") are consuming-producing organisms (i.e., animals, fungi, and archaea) that produce themselves by consuming producers or other consumers (i.e., herbivores, carnivores, and decomposers). Decomposers are consuming organisms (i.e., bacteria and fungi) that consume all deceased organisms and reduce them to minerals. Within the biological system, the following organisms define the food cycle:

- **Producers:** The first type of organism in the food cycle is a producer (i.e., autotrophs).

- **Consumer-Producers:** The next type of organism in the food cycle is at least one consumer-producer (i.e., heterotrophs).

- **Consumers:** The final type of organism in the food cycle is a consumer (i.e., decomposers).

Figure 8.3.4-1 depicts the food cycle.

Figure 8.3.4-1 the food cycle within the physical system and the biological system.

---

[171] In modern societies, rights are often divided into natural rights and legal rights. This chapter concerns legal rights because laws and behavior often don't link responsibilities and rights. Legal rights and their associated responsibilities must reside naturally in the same entity. (It is unthinkable that an entity would have either a natural or a legal right to unearned benefits that others must provide.) Charity definitely has a place but "required charity" does not.

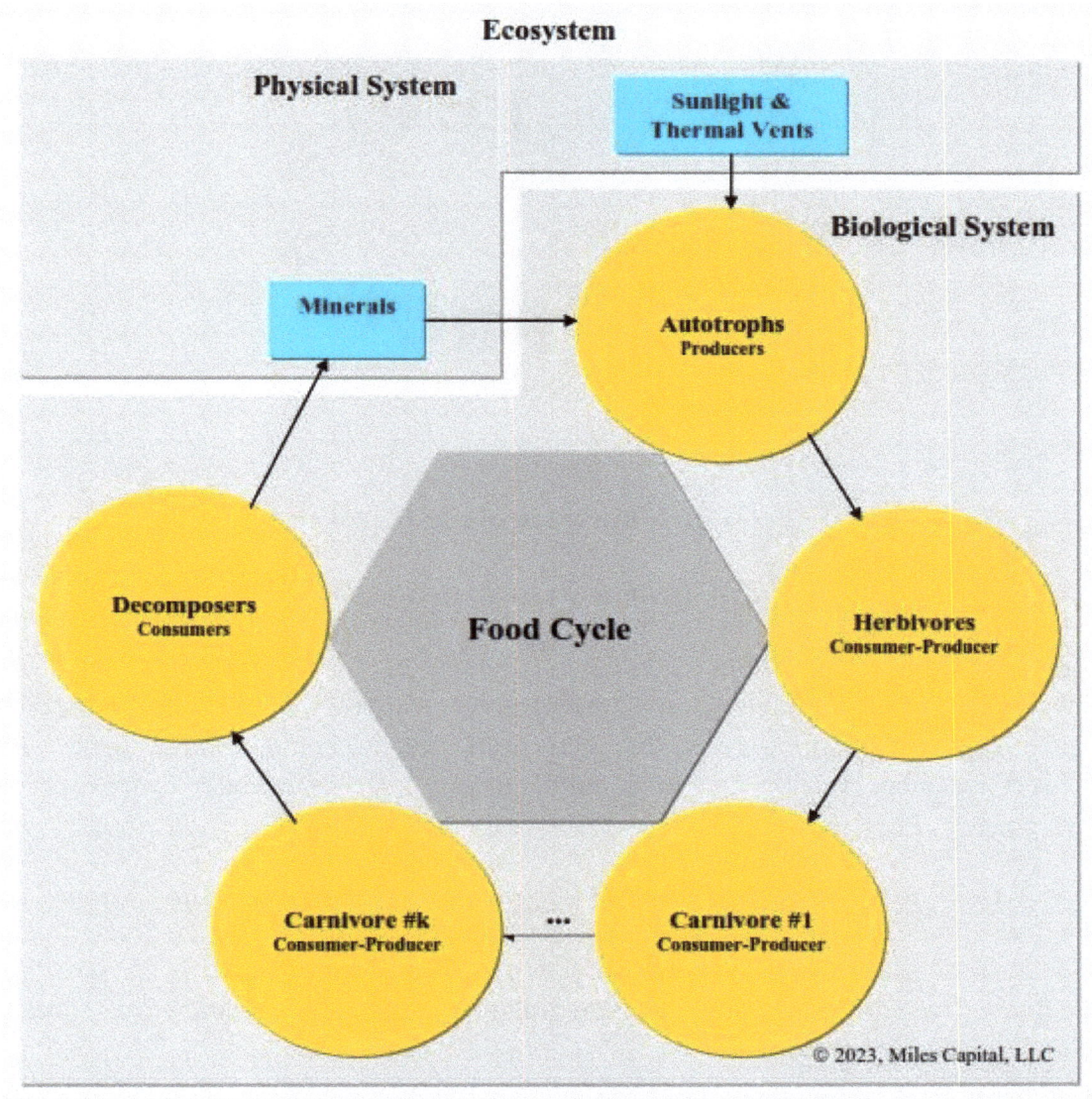

The consumer-producer behavior of heterotrophs is an example of naturally opposing binary states. We can depict naturally opposing binary states by forming a two-sided band from a strip of paper whose ends are united. Then, we can write PRODUCE on one side and CONSUME on the other side. Such a band is depicted in Figure 8.3.4-2.

Figure 8.3.4-2 a two-sided band depicts the naturally opposing binary states, produce-consume

The Effectiveness of Capital

Capital increases Productivity

Capital, one of the four factors of production, was created 2.5 million years ago. Initially it allowed humans to more easily kill potential predators and prey – behavior that allowed humans to move higher in the food cycle. For many years, capital complemented labor, but it now competes with labor. Section 7.1.2 describes the unique power of capital to increase productivity above unity.

Capital is Separating Naturally Opposing Binary States in the Economy

Capital is becoming so efficient that it is replacing many activities formerly performed by labor (i.e., the food cycle or human labor). It is separating the naturally opposing binary states because capital produces, but it essentially doesn't consume. The participation rate for employment has been declining for some years. See Figure 8.2.3-1. Even though some jobs are being created by capital, it is likely that many more jobs will be lost to capital. The economic and moral dilemma is that capital needn't be paid much for production, and the displaced labor cannot afford to consume what has been produced. As noted in Section 7.1.2, labor is already being subsidized hugely by the innovations of others.

We can depict a broken state by forming a band from a strip of paper whose ends are united - but only after we have twisted the strip by 180° (i.e., a half turn). The twisted band, called a Möbius band, has only one side - which serves as a metaphor for a single state.[172] Figure 8.3.4-

---

[172] When innovations replace a human production activity, we can say (as a metaphor) that a möbot has been created.

3 depicts a Möbius band for the single state, produce. Of course, a similar band can also be created for the single state, consume.

Figure 8.3.4-3 A one-sided band (i.e., a Möbius band) depicts the unary state, PRODUCE, from the separated binary states. A similar one-sided band exists for CONSUME.

Examples of Five Performance Parameters for Three Principal Parties when the Fraction of Job Loss Varies from 0 to 1

When human activities or jobs are lost, economic and moral dilemmas are created. We have developed a mathematical model to measure the economic results of job loss for three principal parties and their five performance parameters for the U.S. economy:

- **Labor:** The performance parameter for labor is *wages*;

- **Entrepreneur:** The two performance parameters for the entrepreneur are *profit* and the *rate of return*; and

- **Economy:** The two performance parameters for the economy are *production* and *productivity*.

Figure 8.3.4-4 depicts how the model is constructed when

- the fraction, x, of job loss varies between 0 and 1;

- four relative incomes to the factors of production (i.e., R, W, I, and P) are specified; and

- four scenario assumptions (i.e., σ, α, β, and τ) are specified.[173]

---

[173] Page 324, *The Nature of Economics*, Martin J. Miles

Figure 8.3.4-5 depicts the resulting graphs of each of the five performance parameters as the fraction, x, of job loss varies from 0 to 1, and the values are as stated above.[174]

How would a society function when consume-produce are separated? There would be psychological and economic adjustments, and individuals would no longer have to function as they are designed. Fortunately, the separation will occur gradually.

---

[174] Page 326, *The Nature of Economics*, Martin J. Miles

Figure 8.3.4-4 Scenarios for the U.S. Economy

Relative Incomes to Factors of Production

Factor		Relative Income
Factor	Land	R = 3
	Labor	W = 66.7
	Capital	I = 5.3
	Entrepreneurship	P = 25
	C = R+W+I = 75	GDP = 100

Scenario Assumptions

Condition			Assumption
Condition	Subsidy for Job Loss	Sigma	$\sigma=0.1$
	Fraction of Consumption: (Domestic)/(Total)	Alpha	$\alpha=0.90$
	Profit Advantage from Foreign Consumption	Beta	$\beta=1.2$
	Tariff	Tau	$\tau=0.10$

Schematic Diagram of Factors of Production with Scenario Assumptions

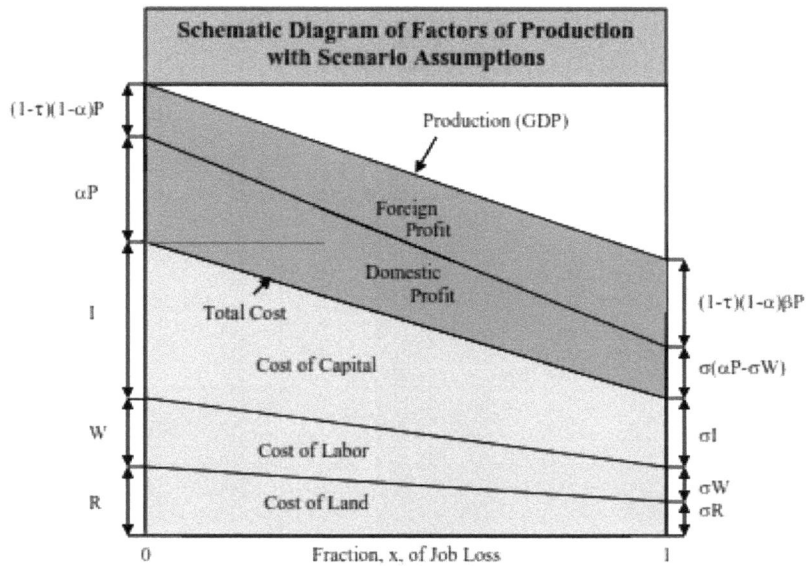

Equations of Performance Parameters from Job Loss

Party			
Party	Employees	Wages	$V = W[(\sigma-1)x+1]$.
	Entrepreneurs	Profit	$Q=\{[(1-\tau)(1-\alpha)\beta P+\sigma(\alpha P-\sigma W)]-P[(1-\tau)(1-\alpha)+\alpha]\}x+P[(1-\tau)(1-\alpha)+\alpha]$. In this scenario, $\alpha=0.90$ and $\tau=0.10$. Therefore, $Q_0=\{[2.25\beta +\sigma(22.5-\sigma66.7)]-24.75\}x+24.75$.
		Rate of Return	$T=Q/\{C[(\sigma-1)x+1]\}$.
	Economy	Production	$GDP=Q+C[(\sigma-1)x+1]$.
		Productivity	$D=GDP/\{W[(\sigma-1)x+1]\}= \{Q+C[(\sigma-1)x+1]\}/\{W[(\sigma-1)x+1]\}$.

191

Figure 8.3.4-5 Scenarios for the U.S. Economy

Values of Performance Parameters
(The fraction of job loss, x, varies from 0 to 1.)

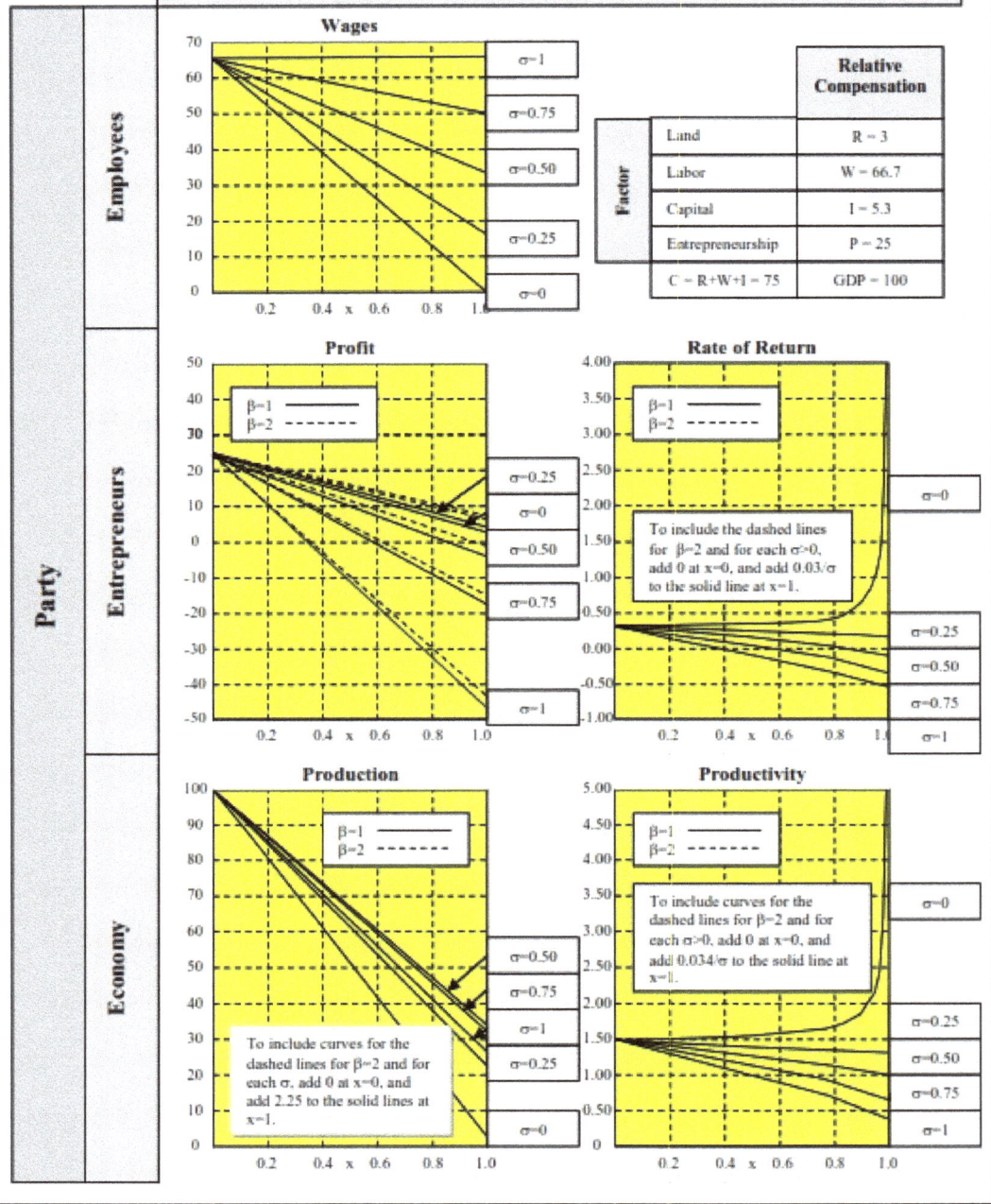

Party

Employees

Wages

σ=1
σ=0.75
σ=0.50
σ=0.25
σ=0

Factor		Relative Compensation
Land	R = 3	
Labor	W = 66.7	
Capital	I = 5.3	
Entrepreneurship	P = 25	
C = R+W+I = 75	GDP = 100	

Entrepreneurs

Profit

β=1 ———
β=2 - - - -

σ=0.25
σ=0
σ=0.50
σ=0.75
σ=1

Rate of Return

β=1 ———
β=2 - - - -

To include the dashed lines for β=2 and for each σ>0, add 0 at x=0, and add 0.03/σ to the solid line at x=1.

σ=0
σ=0.25
σ=0.50
σ=0.75
σ=1

Economy

Production

β=1 ———
β=2 - - - -

To include curves for the dashed lines for β=2 and for each σ, add 0 at x=0, and add 2.25 to the solid lines at x=1.

σ=0.50
σ=0.75
σ=1
σ=0.25
σ=0

Productivity

β=1 ———
β=2 - - - -

To include curves for the dashed lines for β=2 and for each σ>0, add 0 at x=0, and add 0.034/σ to the solid line at x=1.

σ=0
σ=0.25
σ=0.50
σ=0.75
σ=1

8.3.5 Rights-Responsibilities are Separated[175]

Rights and responsibilities are naturally opposing binary states. Capital enables situations to occur in which the two states can be easily separated (e.g., by governments). That is, organizations, such as governments, provide an alternative for individual responsibility. Separating rights-responsibilities occurred so recently (i.e., well within 7,000 years) that there are no suitable moral propensities to guide us.

Rights and Responsibilities are Subsets of Freedom and Moral Behavior[176]

Rights are specific freedoms, and responsibilities are specific moral behaviors. That is, rights and responsibilities are subsets of freedom and moral behavior, respectively. They are naturally opposing states. Not only can freedom and moral behavior be logically united (i.e., Figure 6.2.2-2), but they are naturally united! We have shown that freedom can be a function of moral behavior, and moral behavior can be a function of freedom (i.e., Figure 6.2.2-2 and Figure 6.2.3-1).

Natural Rights

Some philosophers believe there are natural rights (i.e., rights such as life, liberty, the pursuit of happiness, speech, association, etc.). They believe we "deserve" these rights because we are human. Natural rights cannot include material value (that would be provided by others).

We believe that natural rights are implied in individual and group morality (i.e., among members of the group), but, due to our immature species morality, we should have no expectation that strangers will respect those rights.

Legal Rights

On the other hand, there are legal rights (i.e., rights that governments believe are created by certain conditions). Legal rights can include material value.

Socialism

We are responsible for ourselves. Could it be that the magnanimous morality that we feel from group morality, causes us to assume that strangers will feel group morality for us? They won't.

---

[175] Some of this discussion is taken from a comprehensive 37-page chapter in *The Nature of Economics* written by this author. It discusses redistributions to individuals and organizations.

[176] The slogan, *peace through strength*, is similar to *freedom through moral behavior*. It was first described by the Roman Emperor Hadrian in the second century and by President Ronald Reagan in the 1980s.

How did it happen that we could believe that strangers are responsible for us? This is quite unnatural. If we allow strangers to assume responsibility for us, they can (and do) take our rights.[177] (Thus maintaining the balance of the naturally opposing binary states.) Does this mean that losing our rights is inevitable in a socialist government? History shows that it is. Since species morality does not yet exist, our "rights" are not respected outside of our group (e.g., by others or governments). Freedom can be lost unless we behave responsibly. Socialism is a decidedly unnatural system. It is similar to government-sponsored slavery because it often begins voluntary and invariably becomes involuntary.

Figure 8.3.5-1 is a version of Figure 6.2.2-2. It depicts rights as a function of responsibility. The two block arrows at the bottom indicate that decreased responsibility leads to serfdom as predicted by the famous Austrian economist. Frederich A. Hayek, and increased responsibility leads to increased freedom.

---

[177] Socialist governments attack the family structure; that is, they attack their competition, - group morality.

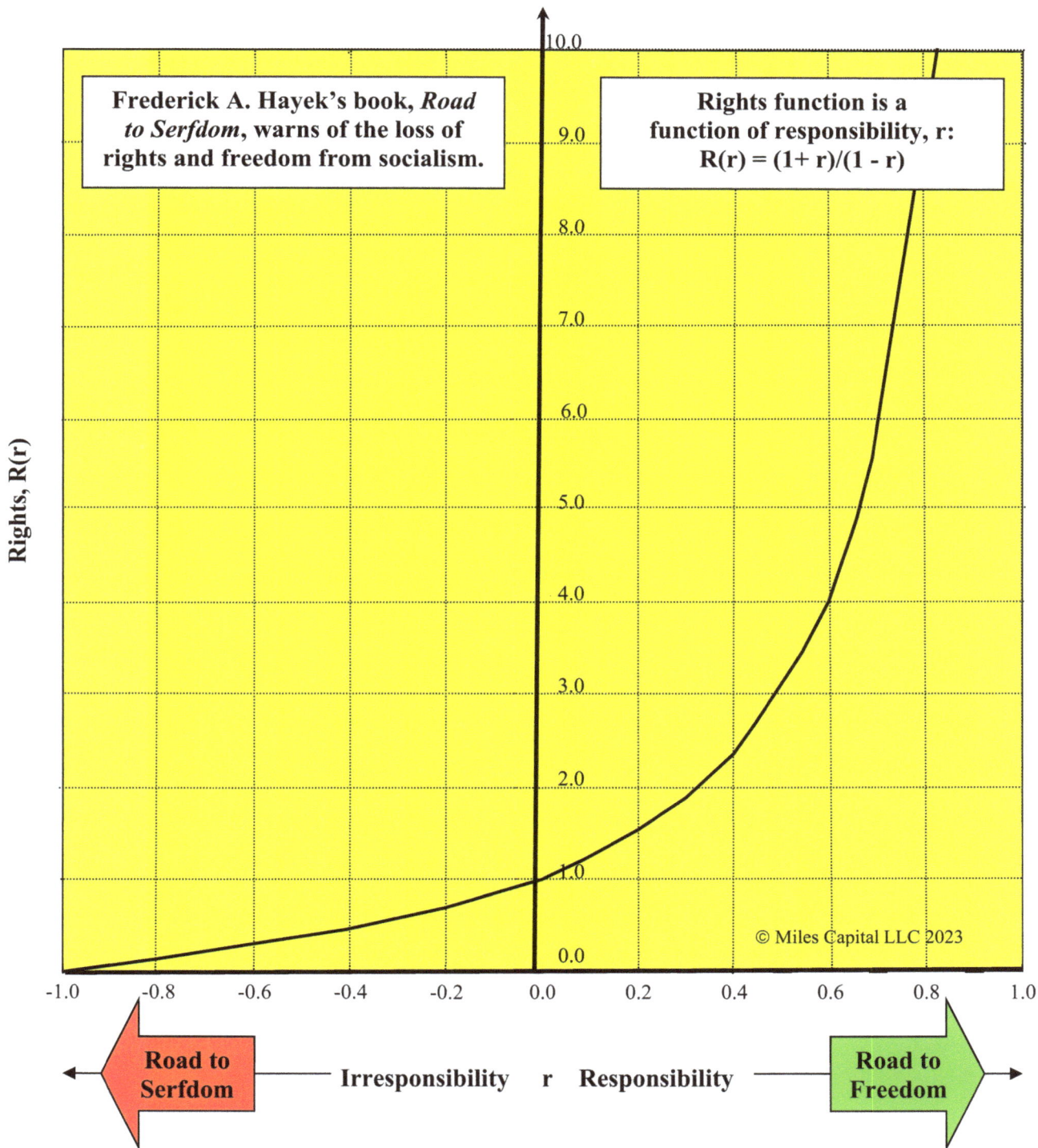

Figure 8.3.5-1 The Rights function, R(r), is a function of responsibility, r. It is defined over the interval -1≤ r < 1.

Frederick A. Hayek's book, *Road to Serfdom*, warns of the loss of rights and freedom from socialism.

Rights function is a function of responsibility, r:
$$R(r) = (1+ r)/(1 - r)$$

© Miles Capital LLC 2023

Rights, R(r)

Road to Serfdom

Irresponsibility   r   Responsibility

Road to Freedom

Table 8.3.5-1 lists the "opposing levels" of three characteristics of two natural societies and two unnatural societies. The natural societies are based on freedom: They are the ecosystem and capitalism. The unnatural societies are based on equality: They are slavery and socialism.

Table 8.3.5-1 characteristics of four societies whose purposes are either freedom or equality

Type of Society			Characteristics		
			Purpose	**Dependent Behavior**	**Entity Selection**
Natural		**Ecosystem**	Freedom	Competition	Merit Selection**
		Capitalism			
Unnatural		**Slavery**	Equality*	Cooperation & Force	Identity Selection
		Socialism			

* Because genetic variation is natural, equality is unnatural.
** Natural selection is merit selection.

Section 1.3.4 discusses genetic variation in living entities. Even though variation is purposeful and natural, socialists refuse to recognize this in their quest to make everybody equal. Economist and presidential advisor, Art Laffer states: "When we take from those who have more, they produce less. When we give it to those who produce less, they produce less (i.e., reduced incentive). We could redistribute to zero, just trying to make everybody equal."

Moral Problems

Governments can and do decide that certain individuals have a legal right to the wealth of others. These legal rights have enormous moral implications. This is possible in a democracy; if voters believe they will benefit from financial redistributions from others, they will be inclined to vote for them.

Due to capital, populations and governments continue to grow. Sometimes governments, such as the U.S. government, provide unearned benefits to selected citizens. As listed in Table 8.3.5-

2, they receive these benefits in the form of Affirmative Action, home mortgage interest deductions, public education, public health care, subsidies, and welfare.

It is universally agreed that the first, and perhaps, only, responsibility of government is to protect its citizens from external threats. However, many other government provisions are questionable. If unearned benefits are provided, it is less objectionable if they are provided voluntarily as charity by individuals – rather than from wealth confiscated from taxpayers.

Voluntary contributions are especially important in a country like the United States, because it is not a true nation (i.e., a nation is a country whose citizens are native, have common descent, history, culture, and language).[178]

Economic Problems from Unearned Benefits

Granting unearned benefits can cause three types of economic problems:

- biased values of resources,

- inappropriate responsibility, and

- unfair practices.

Biased Values of Resources

Friedrich Hayek's observation concerning the importance of knowing value demonstrates a reason that command economies (e.g., socialist, communist, fascist, state capitalistic, and other dictatorial economies) are unsuccessful: Because production and consumption are commanded by a central authority rather than demanded by consumers, the artificially increased demand from unearned benefits causes values to be unknown. Therefore, economic resources can't be accurately allocated.[179] The inaccurate allocation of resources causes poor decisions to be compounded throughout the economy (i.e., accuracy = (bias)^2 + (precision)^2). See Section 6.5.2.

Inappropriate Responsibility

---

[178] This section exists because some countries, like the U.S., do not have a homogeneous population. The propensities of group morality are inconsistent with involuntary sharing in countries of strangers. If it were not paradoxical, we would say that involuntarily taking resources from taxpayers to provide unearned benefits for selected citizens (i.e., strangers) is immoral behavior because we have little or no species morality.

[179] The preferred definition of accuracy consists of two independent parameters, bias and precision. Since bias is one of two parameters of accuracy, it is a significantly immoral result of redistributions.

Inappropriate responsibility can occur as *misplaced* responsibility and/or as *reduced* responsibility (e.g., causing inappropriate diligence and care).

- **Misplaced Responsibility.** Misplaced responsibility exists when one party makes a decision, but another party is responsible for losses that might result from that decision. Misplaced responsibility is often a moral hazard. [180] Perhaps a moral hazard is actually immoral only if the premiums are insufficient to compensate for the misplaced responsibility.

- **Reduced Responsibility.** Reduced responsibility results from either a flawed contract or flawed legislation. Generally, unearned benefits received by an individual encourage his/her behavior to be less than satisfactory. Even though the common plea, "Please, don't feed the animals," might seem offensive when applied to humans, the reduced responsibility caused by unearned benefits applies to all species.

Inappropriate responsibility causes immoral behavior from a variety of irresponsible behaviors (e.g., error, diminished effort, carelessness, inadequate care, hubris, etc.) and possible subsequent loss.

Unfair Practices

Unfair practices, as considered here, are unfair governmental practices. Using tax receipts to provide unearned benefits to others is, itself, an unfair practice, but levying taxes at unequal rates (e.g., graduated income tax rates) to provide unearned benefits to others compounds the unfairness.

Both types of unfair practices (i.e., giving unearned benefits by taking earned benefits and also taxing at a greater rate) are forms of discrimination.

Of all entities that should never discriminate among individuals, it is government. Yet, it is replete with discriminatory practices. And, ironically, it is government that takes action against individuals who discriminate.

Table 8.3.5-2 lists the above three types of immoral economic behavior caused by several types of unearned benefits.

---

[180] The term moral hazard was introduced by the insurance industry: Individuals who become insured tend to take less care of the insured property than otherwise - because the insurer, rather than the insured, is now responsible for the loss.

Table 8.3.5-2 types of immoral economic behavior caused by several types of unearned benefits given to certain citizens

		Types of Immoral Economic Behavior		
		Biased Value	Inappropriate Responsibility	Unfair Practices
Types of Unearned Benefits	Affirmative Action	√	√	√
	Home Mortgage Interest Deduction	√	-	√
	Public Education	√	√	-
	Public Health Care	√	√	-
	Subsidies	√	√	√
	Welfare	√	√	√

8.3.6 Risk-Reward are Separated

Risk and reward are naturally opposing binary states. Capital enables situations to occur in which the states can be separated. Nature did not anticipate this, so there are no suitable moral propensities to protect us.

A rational individual assumes a risk only if the reward is expected to exceed the risk. That is,

(Expected Value of Reward) > [(Value of Asset at Risk) x (Probability of Loss)].

Now, if one party assumes the risk, another party may be entitled to the reward. This is another example of misplaced responsibility as defined in Section 8.3.5.

Governments and some branches of the financial industry transfer the responsibility of risk from investors to others (e.g., to taxpayers, creditors, or other investors).

Due to laws, reward is the surviving unary state from the risk-reward state. Laws provide unfair protection for investors when they misplace their responsibility for risk to others.

Table 8.3.6-1 lists and analyzes the following misplaced responsibilities:

- **Bank Bailout.** Taxpayers are not legally responsible for bank bailouts, but they are financially responsible for bank bailouts. They are financially responsible because politicians fear a depression might occur if they do not bail-out the bank. According to the *World Bank*, there have been nearly 100 banking crises in the last 20 years. All were "resolved" by taxpayer and creditor bailout. Governments and, ultimately taxpayers, have covered the direct costs of bank bailouts. The *World Bank* estimates that in the year 2000, governments in 40 countries spent an average of 12.8% of their national GDPs to bail out their banks!

- **Bankruptcy.** The legal ability of individuals and businesses to declare bankruptcy creates a moral hazard - but some consider the legal ability a benefit of entrepreneurship (by reducing the high risk of an entrepreneur) - but bankruptcy, correspondingly, increases the risk for creditors.

- **FDIC Insured Bank Deposits.** The Federal Deposit Insurance Corporation (FDIC) is a federal government corporation that insures each depositor's accounts in each member bank for a maximum of $250,000 for each ownership category. Because the government insures the deposits, the bank can engage in riskier behavior (i.e., riskier loans and/or a larger amount of loans relative to the size of deposits) than if the bank insured the deposits.

- **Government Redistribution**. Modern governments redistribute taxed income or wealth to other citizens or organizations as politicians choose. The probability that this act causes loss to the taxpayer is virtually 100%.

- **Insurance.** In the 17th century, the moral hazard concept was realized to be inherent to the insurance industry. The term describes misplaced responsibility for risk (rather than immoral behavior). By virtue of the insurance contract, the insured reduces his/her risk. Hence, the insured becomes less responsible - and the risk for the insurer increases. Of course, the premiums can be increased to cover the hazard.

- **Rating Agencies or Schools.** Organizations that issue bonds *hire an agency to rate (or grade) the quality (or safety) of those bonds*. This poses a clear conflict of interest for the rating agency - which can benefit by over-rating the bonds. Similarly, schools are hired by students or their families to teach and grade the student. Unreasonably high grades (sometimes identified as "grade creep") are evidence of the propensity to provide high grades to the "customer."

- **Securitized Mortgages.** Before the worldwide financial crisis that began August 9 2007, originators of risky (i.e., sub-prime) loans sold them without having to bear any risk for their performance (i.e., making required payments). If the originators had been vested in their performance, they undoubtedly would have been more careful about the quality of the borrowers and, hence, of the loans. (Private Label securitization passes responsibility to investors, but Agent securitization does not.)

Table 8.3.6-1 types of misplaced responsibility and conditions that cause the responsible party to lose

Type of Misplaced Responsibility		Conditions		
		Deciding Party (Benefiting Party)	**Responsible Party** (Losing Party)	**How Deciding Party Might Cause Loss**
	Bank Bailout	Owner	Taxpayers / Creditors	Riskier Investments
	Bankruptcy	Owner	Creditors	Riskier Investments
	FDIC Insured Bank Deposits	Bank / Depositors	Taxpayers / Creditors	Riskier Investments
	Government Redistribution	Politicians	Taxpayers	Taxpayers' Income Taken
	Insurance	Insured	Insurer	Contract to Insure Encourages Careless Behavior
	Rating Agencies / Schools	Rating Agency / School	Purchaser of Bond / Employer of Student	Sells to Unqualified Borrowers / Certify Unqualified Graduates
	Securitized Mortgages[*]	Originator / Seller	Investor	Originator Sells to Unqualified Borrowers

[*] Private Label securitization passes responsibility to investors, but Agent securitization does not.

8.3.7 Supply - Demand are Separated

Supply and demand is a quintessential example of naturally opposing binary states. It is also at the heart of a free market. Supply and demand can be separated by manipulation. A market is a moral market if and only if it is a free market (that estimates the true value of a resource). If either supply or demand is manipulated, the value is not true. The free market is discussed in Section 6.5.3 with the derivation of the Market Freedom function. The value of the Market Freedom function measures the morality of the market – the accuracy of supply and demand.

The value of the Market Freedom function is

$$T(a) = (1-a)/(1+a)$$

where $a = \beta^2 + \sigma^2$ is the Accuracy function. In Section 6.5.3 we assume that some prices have been manipulated and some prices are true. That is, we do not attribute the price to either supply or demand - we treat the two opposing binary states as a unit.

8.4 Ecosystem Morality

If the ecosystem is not selected, we are not selected.

Now, that we realize the adverse consequences for the ecosystem from some of our innovations (i.e., capital), we should seriously assess what we are doing. Until recently, it seemed unthinkable that we should not develop a "good" idea. However, some innovations can create unintended consequences for us and the ecosystem.

Adverse consequences of capital for the ecosystem bring us directly to the concept of ecosystem morality. Ecosystem morality is cooperation between humans (who develop capital) and individuals of other species to increase the probability of freedom for the ecosystem

It is necessary and achievable to respect all life. We needn't favor other species, but we should respect them. And certainly, we should protect ourselves from them. (Nobody told them that we moved higher in the food cycle, but are still below the decomposers.)

The human species is one of possibly 10 million species in the ecosystem. It seems that relatively few humans have *yet* developed an appreciation of and respect for the ecosystem. Many humans seem to believe that other species are either a nuisance or exist only for the benefit of humans.[181] [182] Thus far, the human species resembles a very bad neighbor to almost all other species.

8.4.1 Ecosystem Damage

Some types of damage from capital are obvious and others, such as climate change, are less obvious. Currently, the solutions for ecosystem damage usually involve reducing or eliminating some uses of capital. This leaves many workers, companies, and nations economically more vulnerable – and less willing to cooperate. A solution requires people to understand that they will be less successful if they do not cooperate. A company or country cannot decide to move forward unless their competitors cooperate. Beginning 2.5 million years ago, the effects of the

---

[181] Disregard for other species (i.e., speciesism) could result from the belief that God granted a license to humans to treat nonhuman life merely as a means to human ends. Such an attribute is expressed in this statement from Genesis (the first book of the Hebrew Bible and the Christian Old Testament): God gave humans *"dominion over the fish of the sea, and over the fowl of the air, and over the cattle, and over all the Earth, and over every creeping thing that creepeth upon the Earth."*

[182] In Greek mythology, Icarus is the son of the master craftsman, Daedalus. Icarus and his father attempt to escape from the island of Crete by means of wings that his father constructed from feathers and wax. Icarus' father warns him first of *complacency* and then of *hubris*, asking that he fly neither too low nor too high, because the sea's dampness would clog his wings or the sun's heat would melt them. Icarus ignored instructions not to fly too close to the sun, and the melting wax caused him to fall into the sea where he drowned.

first capital were noticed rather quickly in the food cycle because these tools were used to defend humans from predators (members of the food cycle) and to kill prey (members of the food cycle). The food cycle is depicted in Figure 8.3.4-1.[183] Now it seems that our concerns for the ecosystem began with pollution from the Industrial Revolution (1760-1840). Since this is relatively recent, it should not be surprising that we lack sufficient moral propensities to care for the ecosystem as we should.

Table 8.4.1-1 lists four types of effects on the ecosystem from capital for several ecosystems.[184]

Table 8.4.1-1 effects of capital on the ecosystem (except for increasing the human population while essentially solving human natural selection)

		Type of Ecosystem Effects			
		A. Decreased Resources	B. Increased Resources	C. Modified Resources	D. Contaminated Resources
Affected Resources	Forests	√	-	-	-
	Habitats	√	-	-	-
	Minerals	√	-	-	-
	Species	√	√	√	-
	Soil	√	-	-	√
	Atmosphere	-	-	√	√
	Nutrient Resources	-	-	√	√
	Water	-	-	-	√

---

[183] Life begins and ends with sunlight and minerals in the physical system. In the biological system, autotrophs are plants; herbivores are plant eaters; and carnivores are meat eaters (and the figure allows for between one or more carnivores). Decomposers are bacteria and fungi that convert dead biological material into minerals for new autotrophs.

[184] Worldwide Earth Day (April 22) is a manifestation of ecosystem morality.

Part IV
Summary and Conclusions

Chapter 9 Summary

The sections of this chapter are

9.1 Part I Entropy and Evolution

The Earth's physical and biological systems design the evolution of life and morality.

9.1.1 The Physical System

The Big Bang occurred 13.8 billion years ago.

Entropy (i.e., the Second Law of Thermodynamics) states that energy continually flows to regions of lesser energy.

The Earth was formed about 4.5 billion years ago.

9.1.2 The Biological System

Freedom (i.e., life) appeared approximately 1 billion years after the Earth was formed. Life occurred because some maverick molecules were able to divert energy (from energy that would have flowed directly to regions of lesser energy). It, then, flowed for the purposes of creating and maintaining life!

All life must constantly replace its energy that has flowed from them. The primary purpose of moral behavior is to counter entropy by enabling the constant acquisition of necessary resources. Life must be continually protected and maintained because it cannot be restarted.

9.1.3 Evolution of Humans

Evolution is a combination of one-to-four processes that tend to design individuals to be increasingly compatible with their native environment – but nothing more. Natural selection is by far the most important process of evolution. One of the three components of natural selection is genetic variation. It assures job security for socialists who strive to make everybody equal.

The first brain-like structure appeared about 500 million years ago.

Humans evolved in present-day Ethiopia about 15 million years ago (i.e., family Hominidae).

The minimum goal of all living individuals is selection by natural selection (i.e., living long enough to pass their genes to the next generation – as passing a baton to the next teammate in a relay race).

There are three (constant) criteria for the natural selection of an individual:

- **Criteria #1.** Constant protection from the physical environment;
- **Criteria #2.** Constant protection from predators – including microscopic predators that we call pathogens; and
- **Criteria #3.** Constant acquisition of necessary resources (e.g., prey).

The last two criteria are caused by entropy – the force that also designs the food cycle.

9.2 Part II Morality and Freedom

Because life cannot be restarted, the criteria for freedom require that necessary natural resources are continually available. It is difficult to overstate the importance of the *continual* availability of necessary natural resources. Because of this, the autocorrelation of lag 1 is the obvious model for moral behavior.

9.2.1 Morality is Innate

Even though it is logical that morality would evolve just as all other parts of the human body evolve, this book provides evidence that morality is inherited and evolves for us to fit our environment.

The brain evolves with propensities for moral behavior. Obviously, the first moral propensities inherited by the individual are individual moral propensities. However, there is strong evidence that we have inherited group morality as well as individual morality. That is, cooperation among group members tends to increase the group's probability of natural selection. (Members within a group usually compete only for mates.)

The purpose of morality is to increase the probability of freedom. Behavior is moral behavior if and only if it increases the probability of freedom.

We define four nested genetic levels of morality:

- Individual,
- Group,
- Species, and
- Ecosystem.

Our empathy toward other individuals naturally decreases with increasing genetic distance between us. We assume that individual morality (0.5 billion years ago) and group morality (15 million years ago) both exist, but we are very far from having evolved species morality (7,000 years ago) and ecosystem morality (260 years ago). Whereas group morality helped some individuals be selected there is no meaningful evidence that species morality helps groups be selected.

In reference to the moral propensity space, the interrogative, *what*, is the system of moral propensities, and the interrogative, *how*, is the cooperation of individual and group morality – including the behavior that is documented in natural law and moral codes - such as religious commandments, precepts, yamas, and niyamas.

Because evolution designs individuals to be compatible with their environment, there are countless versions of moral propensities.

9.2.2 Measuring Moral Behavior

Organizations, such as religions, appeared about 10,000 years ago and governments appeared about 4,000 years ago.

Moral propensities are implicit, but organizations are practical. That is, they need the propensities to be explicit so they can guide and control their members.

At the least, documentation is a textual description, and at the most, it is a mathematical model that can measure moral behavior - the manifestation of our moral propensities.

We use a mathematical model to take the documentation of the moral propensities all the way to measurement. Specifically, we define moral behavior as accurately as is possible relative to a situation. For example, the autocorrelation function can measure the constancy of a sequence of individual activities: The function is positive when the sequence of activities is relatively constant, and it is negative otherwise. Behavior can be moral when the autocorrelation is positive (i.e., between 0 and 1) and immoral when the autocorrelation is negative (i.e., between -1 and 0).

A few types of dependent behavior can affect moral behavior:

- **Individual Behavior.** (i.e., when a sequence of activities is performed dependently over time by the same individual)

- **Competition and Cooperation.** (i.e., when sequences of activities are performed dependently by two individuals or two parties).

The Moral Behavior function is the autocorrelation of lag 1:

$$m = [\Sigma(x_i - t_x) \cdot (x_{i+1} - t_x)] / [\Sigma(x_i - t_x)^2],$$

where

m = moral behavior,

$i = 1, \dots, k,$

x_i, x_{i+1} = consecutive observations, and

t_x = mean of observations.

9.2.3 Measuring Freedom

Freedom can apply to many types of situations, but they all imply the ability to behave morally. The Freedom function expresses the long-sought relationship of freedom with moral behavior. Section 6.2.3 shows that, not only are they linked, but freedom is a function of moral behavior, and moral behavior is a function of freedom.

Freedom is measured by the individual's ability to behave morally:[185]

- Moral behavior requires constancy of acquiring necessary resources.

- Constancy of these acquisitions is inversely proportional to the variance of these acquisitions:

    o When acquisition is uniform (i.e., constant), the variance of the acquisitions is near zero and morality is near 1.

    o When acquisition is erratic (i.e., inconstant), the variance of the acquisitions is large and morality is near -1.

The Freedom function is

$$F(m) = (1+m)/(1-m)$$

where $-1 \leq m < 1$ is the interval of moral behavior.

9.2.4 Measuring the Morality of a Market

The Accuracy function is defined in Section 6.5.2 and in Table 9.2.4-1. We also derived the Market Freedom function that is a function of accuracy. It can measure markets of goods and services (e.g., manipulation) and markets of entity selection (e.g., selecting on the basis of identity rather than selecting on the basis of merit). The Market Freedom function is

$$T(a) = (1 - a)/(1 + a),$$

where $0 \leq a < \infty$.

Whereas Figure 6.2.2-2 depicts the Freedom function as a function of moral behavior, Figure 6.5.3-1 depicts the Market Freedom function as a function of accuracy.

---

[185] The function also increases the accuracy of the confidence limits of the covariance of observations.

The Market Freedom function increases as the accuracy becomes small (i.e., the bias is small and the variance is also small). A market is a free market if and only if a = 0.

Table 9.2.4-1 lists the formulas for four important functions - moral behavior, freedom, accuracy, and market freedom.

Table 9.2.4-1 functions of important parameters

<table>
<tr><td rowspan="5">Parameter</td><td></td><td>Functions</td></tr>
<tr><td>Moral Behavior function</td><td>m = autocorrelation of lag 1
$= [\Sigma(x_i - t_x) \cdot (x_{i+1} - t_x)] / [\Sigma(x_i - t_x)^2]$,
where $i = 1, \dots , k$; x_i, x_{i+1} = observations, and t_x = mean.</td></tr>
<tr><td>Freedom function</td><td>$F(m) = (1 + m) / (1 - m)$, where m = moral behavior</td></tr>
<tr><td>Accuracy function</td><td>$a = \beta^2 + \sigma^2$, where β = bias & σ = precision</td></tr>
<tr><td>Market Freedom function</td><td>$T(a) = (1 - a) / (1 + a)$, where a = accuracy</td></tr>
</table>

9.3 Part III Capital

9.3.1 Morality and Capital

Some 2.5 million years ago, some humans demonstrated unusual motivation and intelligence that caused the invention of the first tool - the beginning of an incredible system that we now call capital.

9.3.2 Capital Can Augment Moral Behavior

The Benefits of Capital

Capital is unique to humans, and it is usually designed by humans to increase their probability of freedom.

Capital accretes from *knowledge* just as matter accretes from *gravity,* and money (that is lent) accretes from *interest*. They all increase in proportion to the amount present. That is, they increase exponentially.[186] The quantity and quality of knowledge are unlimited.

---

[186] The word, exponential, is currently used inappropriately to describe rapid or large change. In this book, we use the word as it is intended - to indicate an exponent in mathematics. For example, x is the exponent of a in the expression a^x. It should be used only when something

Increased Population

Just as capital is unique to humans, productivity greater than unity is unique to capital: Only capital can increase productivity. Capital allowed us to move up in the food cycle, and it allows populations to increase – which is evidence of its moral applications to humans.

Productivity is the reason populations have increased so much (i.e., from five million 7,000 years ago to nearly eight billion currently).

Increased Probability of Natural Selection

Throughout most of the period of the family Hominidae, the data concerning natural selection are remarkably constant. The exception to this constancy is caused by capital approximately 7,000 years ago when the population began to increase and mortality rates began to decrease.

Near the beginning of humans, the probability of natural selection is estimated to be approximately 45%. Capital has allowed humans to increase their probability of natural selection by more than 220% over the last 7,000 years. It also increases our life span and our freedom from constraints! Now, the worldwide probability of natural selection is approximately 95%, and, in the USA, it is approximately 99%. The increased probability of natural selection from capital in most Sub-Saharan African countries still lags far behind the increase in other under developed countries.

Measuring the Probability of Natural Selection

The probability of natural selection can also be measured by the probabilities of rejection from the three criteria of natural selection (i.e., R_1, R_2, and R_3). That is, the probability of rejection is R, and the probability of selection is S, where

$$S = 1 - R = 1 - \{(R_1 + R_2 + R_3) - [(R_1 \cdot R_2) + (R_1 \cdot R_3) + (R_2 \cdot R_3)] + (R_1 \cdot R_2 \cdot R_3)\}.$$

Capital has greatly increased the constancy of the acquisition of necessary resources and the probability of natural selection. Even though capital can be misused, it is easy to find applications of capital that are exceedingly moral!

9.3.3 Capital Can Augment Freedom

During the morality lag (in the last 7,000 years ago), we have been greatly handicapped. However, during this time, capital has allowed per capita Worldwide GDP to increase, from

---

increases or decreases in proportion to the amount present (i.e., *a*), such as a bank account that grows from drawing interest or a radioactive substance that decays.

$130 7,000 years ago to $12,968 International Dollars in 2010 AD. In the absence of restraint, capital has provided so many assets that allow individual freedom to increase greatly. Figure 7.3-2 depicts this phenomenon.

Figure 7.3-2 a 3-dimensional schematic depiction of the Moral Propensity Space, the Moral Dilemma Space, and Worldwide GDP per capita over the last 7,000 years, expressed in International Dollars for 2000 AD

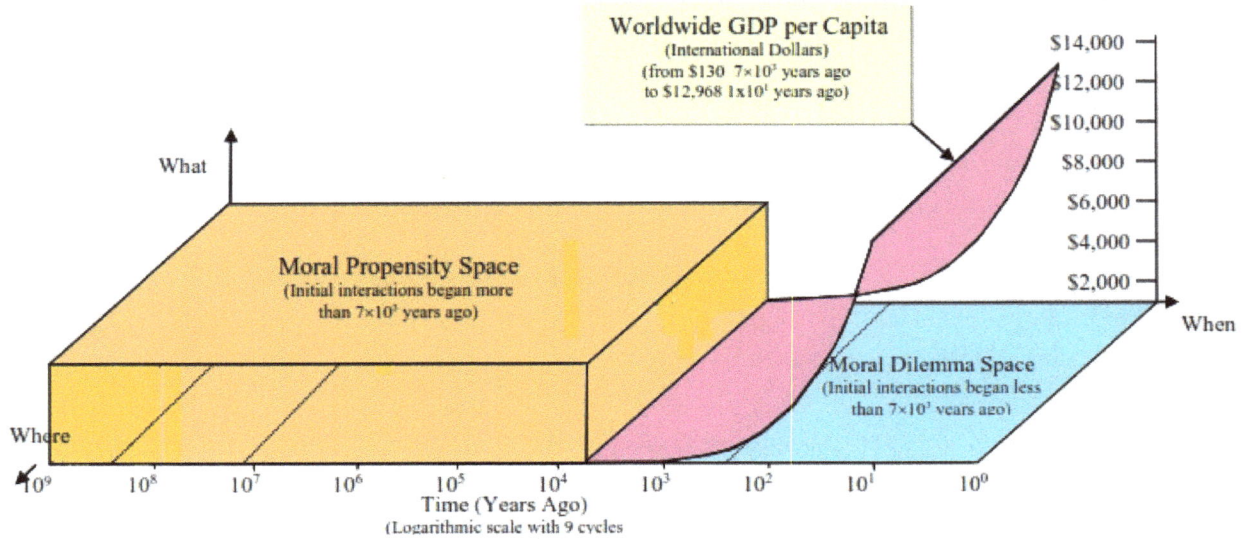

9.3.4 Capital Can Create Moral Dilemmas

Logical Systems

For the first 12.5 million years of human existence (i.e., until capital was created), morality was a logical system that evolves in our brain and whose properties require that its moral propensities are

- independent,

- consistent, and

- complete.

As capital develops, it alters human relationships and environments - and *confuses our moral propensities*. In a logical system, capital might not affect the logical properties of independence and consistency, but it definitely affects the logical property of completeness. Consequently,

- some needed propensities do not exist,

- some existing propensities need to be modified, and

- some existing propensities are no longer needed.

The Moral Propensities Space

Table 4.4-1 is a list of the moral propensities as defined by interrogatives (e.g., dimensions). The interrogative, when, terminated 7,000 years ago – leaving us with countless serious dilemmas.

Table 4.4-1 six dimensions of the moral propensity space as defined by interrogatives

		Dimensions of the Moral Propensity Space	
Interrogatives	Why	The purpose of moral propensities is to increase the probability of freedom for the individual.	
	How	An individual's moral propensities may be manifested and augmented by multi-level moral behavior.	
	What	Moral propensities are manifested by the constancy of acquiring necessary resources for the individual. (See Section 5.3.3.or Section 6.1.2)	3-dimensions of Figure 4.4-1
	When	Moral propensities are available for all types of situations that have existed for at least 7,000 years.	
	Where	Moral propensities are available for all types of situations that have existed for at least 7,000 years in the environment that designed the individual.	
	Who	Moral propensities are available to all individuals for all types of situations that have existed for at least 7,000 years in the environment that designed the individual.	

Multi-Level Morality

Groups were limited in their migrations until about 7,000 years ago when capital reached a level that allowed them to migrate more easily. It allowed groups to interact with strangers – causing a need for species morality!

As depicted in Figure 7.3-2, we have no moral propensities – only moral dilemmas – for types of situations that were novel after 7,000! (Our genes are 99% the same as they were 7,000 years ago.)

This book discusses approximately 13 serious situations enabled by capital which confuse our moral propensities. See Table 8-1. Three of those situations result from human interactions with strangers and four of those situations enable naturally opposing binary states to be separated. A most serious example is the separation of rights and responsibilities that has a seemingly necessary consequence of the loss of rights (i.e., freedom) when responsibilities (i.e., moral behavior) are surrendered to strangers (e.g., socialism). Life and freedom must coexist, but both can be lost without responsible (i.e., moral) behavior.

*****

Since 7,000 BC we have very few of the necessary propensities for species morality and ecosystem morality – and we do not know it!

Families (e.g., groups) generally get along well; however, we are swamped with crimes, conflicts, and wars. Perhaps this is the best evidence that our species morality is woefully immature! When we are judging interactions with strangers, how can we hit the bull's eye while the target is still evolving?

Chapter 10 Conclusions

The sections of this chapter are

(Please excuse the repetition of some discussions, but the Summary and Conclusions are not, at all, mutually exclusive.)

Three types of processes dominate the subjects of this book: entropy, evolution, and capital development.

10.1 Innate Morality

Because morality is innate, it varies with environments – so there is no universal morality. Also, because of capital, we have only limited species morality and almost no ecosystem morality.

10.1.1 Morality and the Brain

Figure 2.3.4-1 is a structured diagram that depicts the parts of the human brain involved in decision-making. In fact, those parts are often considered the location of morality. The figure is repeated here because it is relevant to many topics of this book.

Why do intelligent people often make poor decisions? As shown in Figure 2.3.4-1, the dorsolateral prefrontal cortex provides logic, and the amygdala provides emotion. Then, the ventromedial prefrontal cortex weighs logic and emotion to make the decision. That is, different regions of the prefrontal cortex provide logic (i.e., the dorsolateral PFC) and decisions (i.e., the ventromedial PFC).

Figure 2.3.4-1 structured diagram of the human brain's decision process between a logical and an emotional response to a sensory stimulus

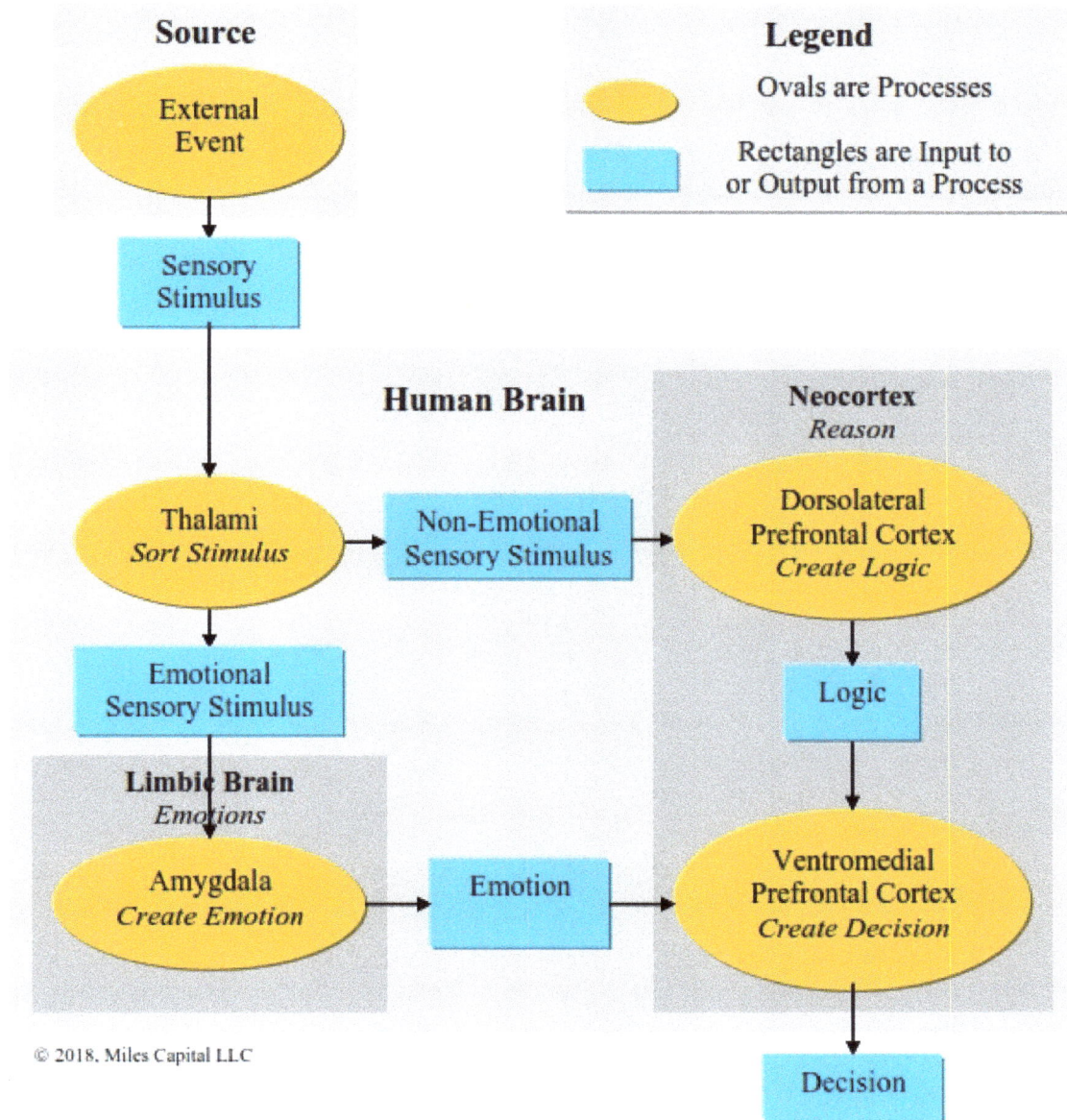

Table 5.3.1-1 lists the precepts of the five largest religions. The three Abrahamic religions, Judaism, Christianity, and Islam, advocate both faith and morals. The other two, Buddhism and Hinduism, simply advocate morals.[187] There is an interesting relationship between the two

---

[187] Some scholars wonder if the reason the god proffered by the Abrahamic religions is described as so awesome (e.g., all-knowing, all-seeing, all-powerful, etc.) is to intimidate strangers (who are worrisome to our amygdale) and "encourage them to behave."

concepts, "faith" and "morals," of Table 5.3.1-1 and the two concepts, "emotion" and "logic," of Figure 2.3.4-1: That is,

Faith is emotional, and morals are logical.

10.1.2 Natural Selection is Merit Selection

The genotype (i.e., the set of genes) of an organism is manifested as its phenotype (i.e., the organism). Natural selection occurs when an organism has passed its genes to a descendant. That is, natural selection allows both the phenotype and its genotype to continue individual freedom. Natural selection is by far the most significant of the four types of evolution.

To be selected by natural selection, the following three criteria must be met *continually* until an individual procreates:

- **Criterion #1.** Environmental Protection

- **Criterion #2.** Predator-Pathogen Protection

- **Criterion #3.** Prey Acquisition

If an individual is selected, the individual's genes are considered sufficiently compatible with its native environment (i.e., to continue living).

Laws of gravity and thermodynamics are physical laws. Natural selection is the law of the evolution of life; it is merit selection: Moral behavior increases the probability of freedom.

Before capital, humans had a natural place in the food cycle: We could defend ourselves from some large predators and some familiar pathogens, and we could obtain some prey. As capital develops, we can defend ourselves from additional predators and pathogens and obtain additional prey.[188] Our research shows that when capital was still primitive, fewer than 45% of humans were selected by natural selection. Due to developing capital, that percentage is now about 95% worldwide and 99% in the USA.

10.1.3 Moral Behavior

We discuss six types of evidence that morality is innate. For example, experiments with infants and young children show that they are born with preferences for situations similar to their natural situations: They prefer people who belong to their race, eat the same food, speak the same

---

[188] In the 1850s Louis Pasteur discovered that microorganisms caused food spoilage and Joseph Lister discovered that sterilization could kill bacteria. However, even though we did not realize it, our *innate* immune system was killing many pathogens, and our *acquired* immune system would work with vaccines to also increase our probability of natural selection.

language, and wear the same clothes. (Some believe that morality is not innate - but why would all human characteristics be inherited except the essential characteristic, moral behavior?)

Levels of Morality

The empathy between an individual and an individual of a different level of morality decreases as the genetic distance between them increases. An individual's empathy with an individual of these four levels could be described by the following moralities:

- Individual morality is *self-interest morality.*

- Group morality is *magnanimous morality.*

- Species morality is *mundane morality.*

- Ecosystem morality is *necessary morality.*

We have an innate duty to be responsible for ourselves and a necessary responsibility to respect our ecosystem. This is the only ecosystem we have.

Logic of an Innate Moral Propensity System

Moral propensities constitute a system that has evolved as a logical system in humans for 15 million years. That is, its propensities should constitute a logical system. As such, the propensities should be

- independent,

- consistent, and

- complete.

The moral propensity system does not evolve unless external forces are introduced. Capital was introduced about 2.5 million years ago, and it has increasingly done wonderful things for humanity. However, it also has introduced novel situations that occurred so recently that moral propensities have not yet evolved. Now, we have no moral propensities for these novel situations – and evolution requires millennia to develop them (i.e., external forces).[189] (A very beneficial allele could become widespread in a population after a few centuries whereas an allele that is less beneficial might require millennia to become widespread.)

---

[189] *"How We are Evolving" Scientific American. November 1, 2012. Retrieved May 27,2020.*

The Moral Propensity Space

Figure 10.1.3-1 is a depiction of our moral propensity space (that has probably not increased since 7,000 years ago) and the assumed concept of universal morality (a concept that we reject because moralities are designed by environments).

The figure also includes the dates of two significant interactions of strangers. If you believe in innate morality and the lag in evolution, you can believe, for example, that neither Christopher Columbus nor the Indians possessed moral propensities for their interactions as strangers.

Figure 10.1.3-1 a 3-dimensional schematic depiction of (1) the four levels of morality, (2) the innate moral propensity space for initial occurrences of novel situations that began more than 7,000 years ago, moral dilemmas for initial occurrences of novel types of situations that occurred less than 7,000 years ago, and two types of species interactions, and (3) the universal moral space *assumed* to exist by some philosophers and religions who do not believe in innate morality.

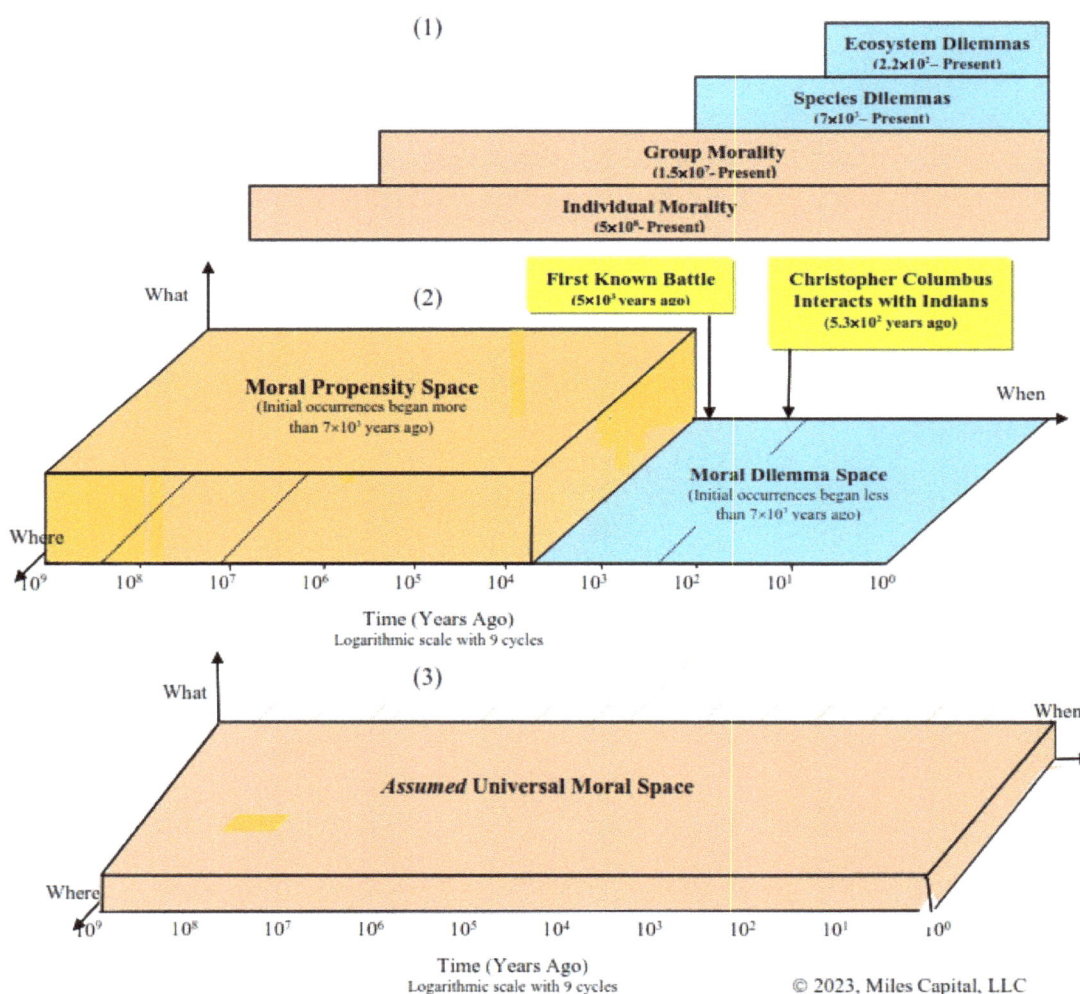

10.1.4 Measuring Moral Behavior

When life is lost it is lost forever. Consequently, the necessary quality of moral behavior is the constancy of acquiring necessary resources. If constancy is not achieved, no other behavior matters. Since morality is innate, it is implicit. To express it, we must document it. This book documents moral behavior as precisely as possible in the following three steps:

- **Define Moral Behavior:** Behavior is a sequence of activities. Moral behavior is a sequence of activities that is expected to increase the probability of freedom.

- **Model Moral Behavior:** A model of moral behavior is a function of a sequence of activities that is isomorphic to moral behavior. The autocorrelation function is the function that is isomorphic to moral behavior because it models individual constancy.

- **Measure Moral Behavior:** The value of the autocorrelation function measures moral behavior. The value is defined in the interval $[-1, 1] \equiv$ [total immorality, total morality].

10.1.5 Dependent Behavior

Because constancy is so important to life, dependency is also important. There are essentially four types of dependent behavior:

- Individual

- Cooperation

- Competition

- Force

Individual

Individual behavior is serially dependent within the individual. That is, it occurs in the individual as a sequence in time (rather than between two sequences from two individuals). Constancy is usually measured by the autocorrelation function of lag 1.

Cooperation (It helps us get *along*.)

Cooperation is similar to group morality:

- It allows less freedom of behavior than competition.

- It is more passive and more risk-avoidant than competition.

- It is often responsible for the same inaccurate markets that result from monopolies and unions.

Competition (It helps us get *ahead*.)

Choosing between competition and cooperation often involves decisions as described in Figure 2.3.4-1: weighing logic and emotion.

Because the participants in each type of dependent behavior (i.e., cooperation/competition) have the same goal, their activities tend to be correlated. However, the reward from competition is usually greater than that from cooperation.

Competition is more similar to individual morality, species morality, and capitalism than is cooperation:

- It is freedom of behavior.

- It is active and risk-acceptant.

- It provides motivation for innovation (i.e., "necessity is the mother of invention"), causing productivity to accelerate.

- It causes prices to be lower.

- It encourages accurate market values.

Force

Force occurs when an authority (e.g., government) compels an individual to behave in a certain way without his/her implied or explicit consent. The individual loses freedom (i.e., the ability to behave morally): The individual must behave as compelled rather than as desired. Force is behavior of the enforcer to the extent discussed in Section 5.4.4.

10.1.6 Moral Behavior Applied to the Criteria of Natural Selection

Table 5.5-1 is a two-dimensional matrix that matches the three criteria of natural selection to the four types of dependent moral behavior that may achieve it.

10.2 Freedom

Freedom exists if and only if Moral Behavior can exist.

Ideally, freedom is the ability to behave morally. When our freedom is limited, our ability to behave morally is limited. Constancy requires dependent behavior. (Dependent behavior occurs frequently, but, for convenience, analysts usually treat behavior as independent behavior.)[190]

10.2.1 Measuring Freedom

When behavior is a sequence of activities from an individual, dependence of the activities can be measured by the autocorrelation function. (The autocorrelation function is an example of an isomorphic model of individual moral behavior.)

- **Define Freedom.** Freedom is the ability to act or behave. Ideally, freedom is the ability to behave morally.

- **Model Freedom.** The Freedom function must be isomorphic to the value of freedom.

- **Measure Freedom.** The Freedom function is measurable by moral behavior.

10.2.2 Criteria of the Freedom Function

A function that models freedom must satisfy the following criteria:

- It must be continuous.

- It must be non-negative.

- It must change monotonically with moral behavior.

- When the Freedom function equals 0, moral behavior must equal -1 (i.e., totally immoral behavior).

- As the Freedom function approaches infinity, moral behavior must approach 1 (i.e., totally moral behavior).

- The values of the Freedom function must be isomorphic to the values of freedom.

We derived the Freedom function in Appendix A. As far as we know, it is the only function that models freedom and models it as a function of moral behavior. We believe the best model of freedom is what we call the Freedom function:

---

[190] A probability distribution has two independent parameters, the mean and the variance. Dependence does not alter the mean, but it alters the variance – and, hence, it alters the confidence limits of the mean.

$$F(m) = (1+ m)/(1- m)$$

where m is moral behavior, and $-1 \leq m < 1$.

10.2.3 Freedom and Moral Behavior are Naturally Opposing Binary States

For thousands of years, philosophers have been intrigued by the concept of duality in nature. In the East, duality is called Yin-yang, and in the West, it is often called naturally opposing binary states.[191] Generally, duality maintains balance between two opposing (and, sometimes, *complementary*) states. Sometimes one state is active, and the other state is passive. The concept of duality is important to moral behavior and freedom. We consider the following four types of naturally opposing binary states:

- Consume and Produce

- Rights and Responsibilities (which are subsets of Freedom and Moral Behavior, respectively)[192]

- Risk and Reward

- Demand and Supply

To maintain balance, the states must remain as a pair. For example, we can't consume unless we produce; if we are not responsible, we will lose our rights; we shouldn't risk unless success is expected to provide an acceptable reward; and the supply of a good or service should equal the demand; etc.

Each state can be considered to be a function of the other. That is, each state can be the independent variable, while the other state would be the dependent variable. The validity of this dual role (i.e., switching of freedom and moral behavior from either independent variable or dependent variable) is possible because of the monotonic criterion stated in Section 10.2.2.

The type of duality that is of special interest in this book is rights and responsibilities: A right is a specific freedom, and a responsibility is a specific moral behavior. That is, freedom and moral

---

[191] Projective (i.e., non-Euclidian) geometry has no parallel lines or planes. Since lines and planes intersect, it also has a system of duality:
- In two dimensions, two points define a line, and two lines define a point.
- In three dimensions, two lines define a plane, and two planes define a line; three points define a plane, and three planes define a point.

[192] We consider that the holder of a right is responsible for himself / herself. But some others assume this responsibility lies with the state!

behavior are also naturally opposing binary states. Table 6.2.3-1 is two tables that show that each state can be either an independent variable or a dependent variable.

For convenience, we repeat Figure 6.2.2-2 which depicts freedom as a function of moral behavior and Figure 6.2.3-1 which depicts moral behavior as a function of freedom.

Figure 6.2.2-2 The Freedom function, F(m), is a function of moral behavior, m.
It is defined over the interval -1≤ m < 1.

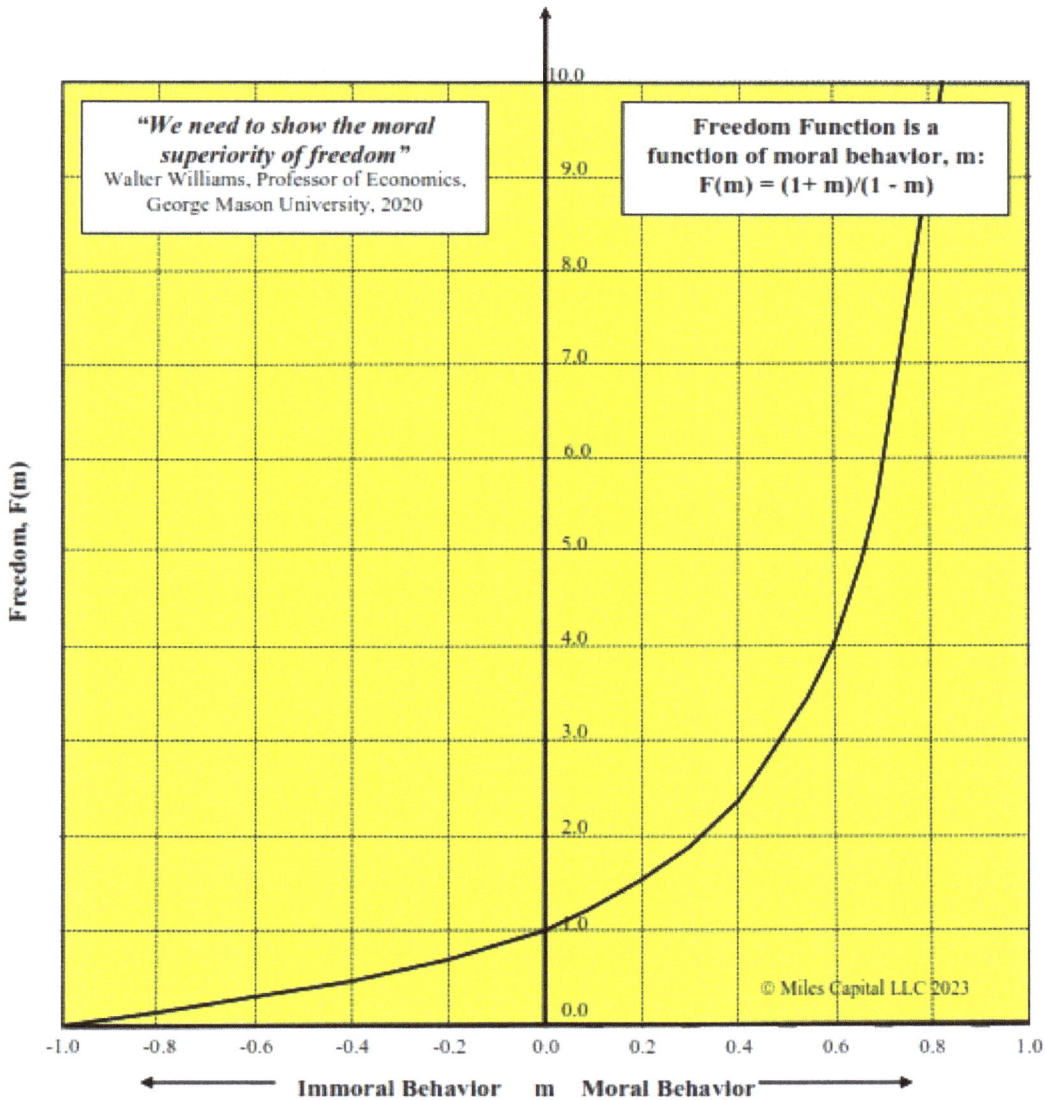

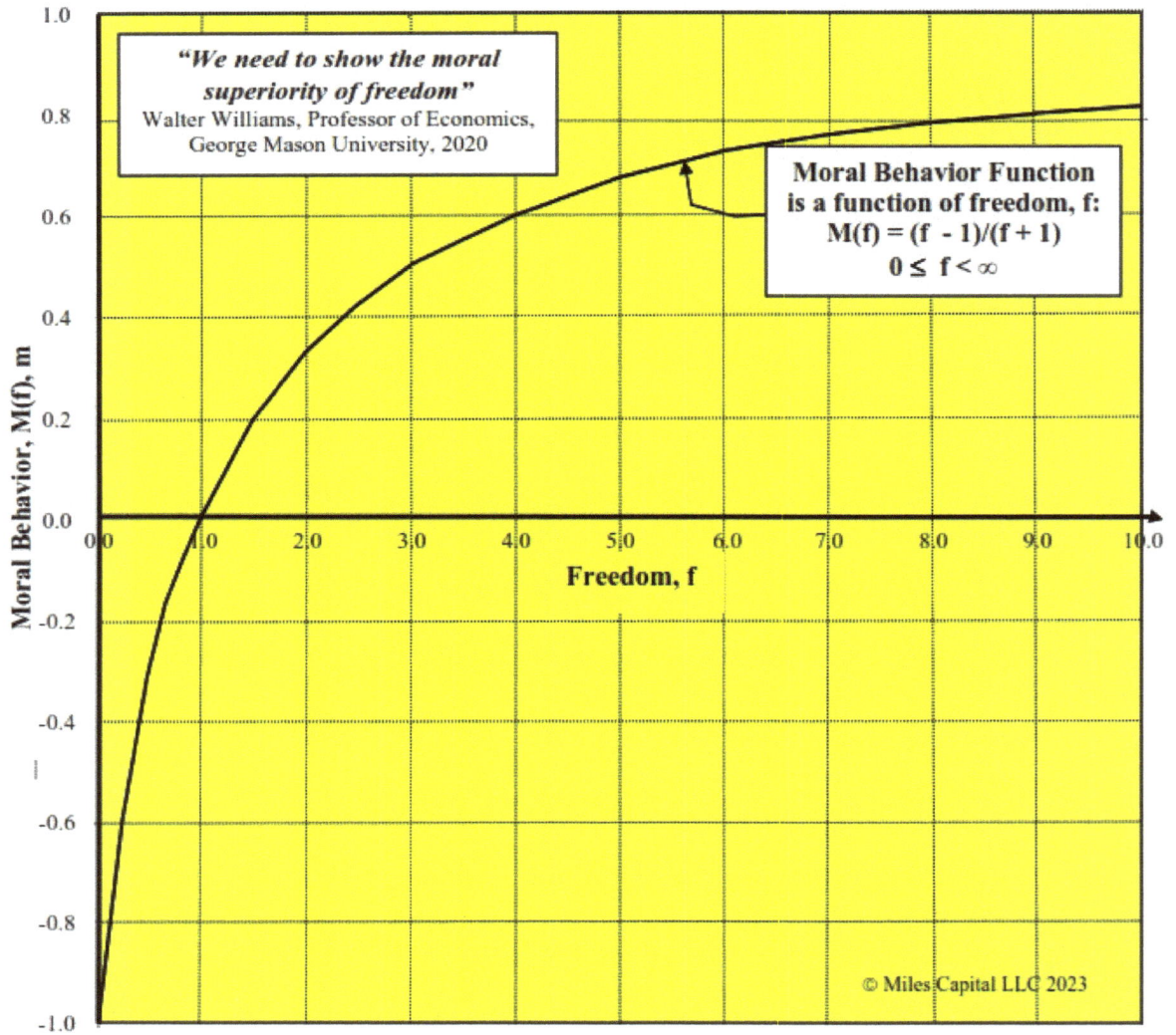

Figure 6.2.3-1 Moral Behavior Function, M(f), is a function of freedom, f. It is defined over the interval $0 \leq f < \infty$.

"We need to show the moral superiority of freedom"
Walter Williams, Professor of Economics, George Mason University, 2020

Moral Behavior Function is a function of freedom, f:
$$M(f) = (f - 1)/(f + 1)$$
$$0 \leq f < \infty$$

© Miles Capital LLC 2023

10.2.4 Measuring the Morality of a Market

A Market is a Moral Market if and only if it is a Free Market.

A decision is a "good" decision if and only if it allows moral behavior. Knowledge is an important ingredient of morality. However, critical knowledge is not always available when markets are controlled and manipulated – truth is also a victim.

We discuss two types of markets (i.e., trading goods and services and selecting entities). In Section 6.3 we discussed how accuracy can estimate the degree to which a market is free. We have been careful to define accuracy as the expected value of the random squared error - a function of the bias and the precision (i.e., variance).[193] Consequently, we distinguish true values of market resources from manipulated values. It is also serendipitous that accuracy and moral behavior both seek the truth, and both are achieved by constancy (i.e., precision). Therefore, we are able to measure these four important parameters:

- moral behavior,

- freedom,

- accuracy, and

- market freedom.

The Market Freedom function is

$$T(a) = (1-a)/(1+a)$$

where a = accuracy = $(bias)^2 + (precision)^2$.

A free market exists if and only if a = 0, in which case, T(0) = 1 (i.e., 100% morality).

Figure 6.5.3-1, the Market Freedom function, is depicted on the following page.

---

[193] The variance is small when constancy is large.

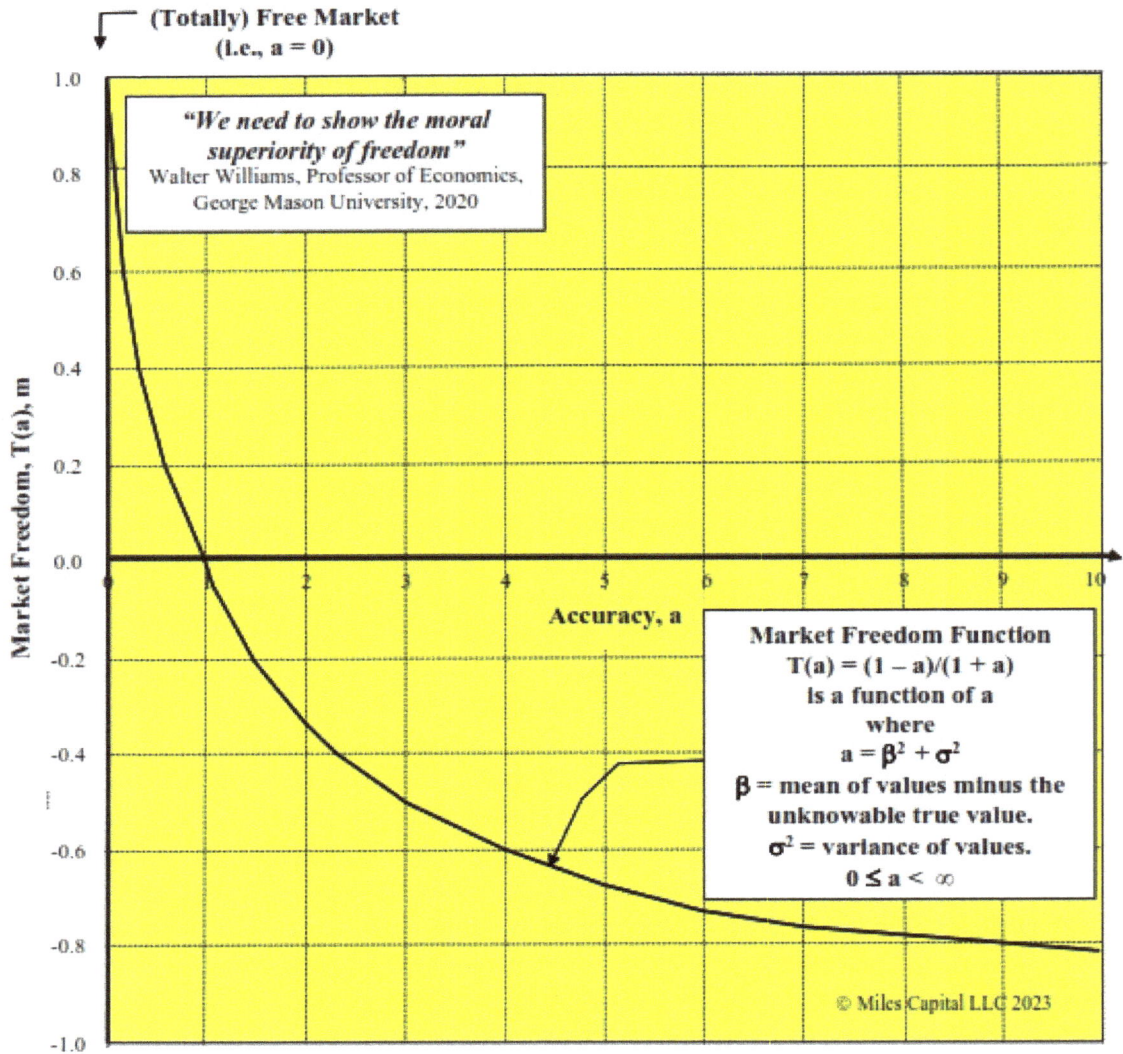

Figure 6.5.3-1
The Market Freedom Function, T(a), is a function of accuracy, a.
It is defined over the interval $0 \le a < \infty$

(Totally) Free Market
(i.e., a = 0)

"We need to show the moral superiority of freedom"
Walter Williams, Professor of Economics,
George Mason University, 2020

Market Freedom Function
$T(a) = (1 - a)/(1 + a)$
is a function of a
where
$a = \beta^2 + \sigma^2$
β = mean of values minus the
unknowable true value.
σ^2 = variance of values.
$0 \le a < \infty$

© Miles Capital LLC 2023

Market Freedom, T(a), m

Accuracy, a

10.3 The Enormous Implications of Innate Morality

The implications of innate morality have been largely unknown, and they are enormous: They challenge the following important beliefs and relationships, including the universality of morality: It varies with environments, and it does not always exist!

10.3.1 Environments Design Morality

Due to natural selection, morality varies among human environments. An individual's morality is designed by its environment. Therefore, a universal morality does not exist. Just as there are countless environments, there are countless versions of morality.

This book shows that humans from different environments behave very differently with respect to, at least, the following important moral metrics:

- rates of homicide, [194]

- rates of incarceration,

- degrees of political freedom, and

- degrees of economic freedom.

If we believe that morality is universal, we judge individual behavior accordingly, but if we believe morality is innate, we should judge individual behavior according to the environment that designed the individual - but that doesn't mean we should accept that behavior in another environment.

Figure 2.2.4-1, a depiction of the environments in which *Homo sapiens* have evolved over the last 100,000 years, is repeated on the following page.

---

[194] When European colonists in Africa couldn't convince the natives to abide by European laws, they reluctantly allowed the natives to revert to their traditional ways as long as those ways did not conflict with European laws.

Figure 2.2.4-1 where and when *Homo sapiens* migrated during the last 100,000 years

- Most *Homo sapiens* remained in Africa and continued to evolve as Negroids during this 100,000 period.
- In this primary migration, *Homo sapiens* migrated from Sub-Saharan Africa approximately 100,000 years ago to the Middle-East. Approximately 70,000 years ago some moved east to Asia and evolved as Mongoloids, and approximately 40,000 years ago, some of those migrants moved west to Europe and evolved as Caucasoids. Some Middle-Eastern people remained.
- In many secondary migrations, approximately 7,000 years ago, groups dispersed and caused many strangers to interact – causing human conflicts to begin evolving propensities for species morality.
- From 200-400 years ago, the slave trade brought some Sub-Saharan Africans to the Americas. (This forced migration is depicted by the very, very short line segment, resembling a dot, on the right side.)

Legend

Era of Evolution due to Physical Environments (i.e., Group Era) (100,000-7,000 years ago)

Era of Evolution due to Physical Environments & Conflicts with Strangers (i.e., Species Era) (7,000-0 years ago) (See Section 8.3.2.)

Environments in which *Homo sapiens* have evolved over the Last 100,000 Years

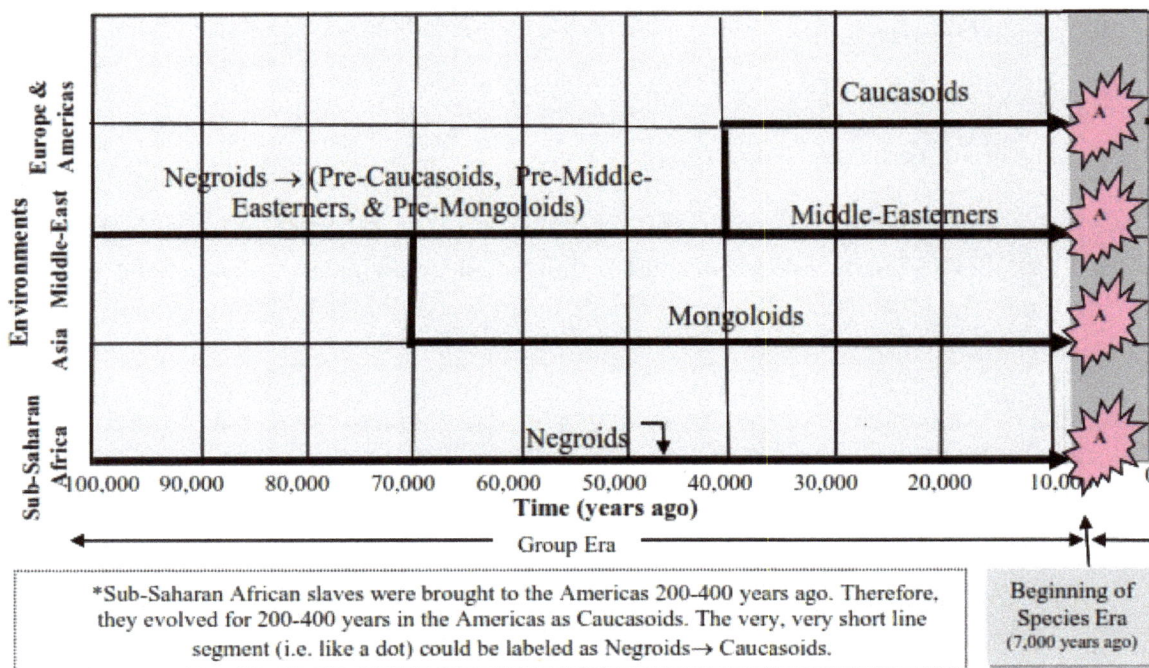

*Sub-Saharan African slaves were brought to the Americas 200-400 years ago. Therefore, they evolved for 200-400 years in the Americas as Caucasoids. The very, very short line segment (i.e. like a dot) could be labeled as Negroids→ Caucasoids.

Beginning of Species Era (7,000 years ago)

230

10.3.2 Capital Enables Novel Types of Situations - for which We Have Only Moral Dilemmas

Largely because of capital, our moral propensity system is not complete, and some moral propensities are now inconsistent! This means that, for some types of situations, we have been faced with moral dilemmas for approximately 7,000 years.

We consider four levels of morality. We have evolved as humans for 15 million years. When capital was introduced 2.5 million years ago, we had evolved individual morality and group morality to a fine degree. However, we have not yet evolved species morality and ecosystem morality. Until 7,000 years ago, there was little need for species morality and even less need for ecosystem morality.

Humans have not had sufficient time to evolve moral propensities to successfully navigate capital-enabled novel types of situations (CENTS) (e.g., situations that would require species morality and ecosystem morality to be judged or decided without moral propensities):

- **Species Morality.** Species morality has been needed since approximately 7,000 years ago when secondary migrations of *Homo sapiens* began. Today's humans have approximately 99% of the same genes as humans had 7,000 years ago. Perhaps the best evidence that we have immature species morality is that it is estimated that more than one billion strangers have killed and been killed in conflicts and wars. If this morality is mature, why has it not been effective. Of course, these deaths contribute to evolution, specifically, species morality. When undefended or indefensible lands are available, how should we behave toward its inhabitants and vice versa?

- **Ecosystem Morality.** Ecosystem morality has been needed for over 260 years (i.e., since 1760 AD) when the Industrial Revolution began.

Table 8-1 lists many novel situations that are enabled by capital and have caused moral dilemmas. These types of situations that pose dilemmas are summarized in the following pages.

Table 8-1 capital-enabled novel types of situations CENTS pose moral dilemmas

			Caused by Capital	Cured by Capital	Solution
Capital-Enabled Novel Types of Situations (CENTS) Causes Moral Dilemmas	**8.1 Individual Morality**	8.1.1 Hubris	Unnatural success	-	Act intelligently
		8.1.2 Inactivity	Unnatural success	-	Act intelligently
	8.2 Group Morality	8.2.1 Abortion	-	More people are not needed. Baby is killed.	Be responsible.
		8.2.2 Homosexuality	-	More people are not needed.	-
		8.2.3 Gender Roles Merge	Capital replaces some strenuous labor.	-	Be understanding.
	8.3 Species Morality — A. Novel Interactions Occur	8.3.1 Slave Labor	Capital enabled migration and mixing with strangers.	Capital is now more efficient than labor (i.e., Industrial Revolution).	-
		8.3.2 Conflicts and Conquests (Foreign)	Capital enables migration and mixing with strangers.	-	Be understanding.
		8.3.3 Moral Conflicts (Domestic)	Capital enables migration and mixing with strangers.	-	Be understanding.
	8.3 Species Morality — B. Natural Bonds are Separated	8.3.4 Consume-Produce are Separated	Capital replaces labor.	-	Be understanding.
		8.3.5 Rights-Responsibilities are Separated	Capital enables governments whose laws can be immoral.	-	Be responsible.
		8.3.6 Risk-Reward are Separated	Capital enables governments whose laws can be immoral.	-	Forbid separation.
		8.3.7 Supply-Demand are Separated	Capital enables separation.	-	Accommodate separation.
	8.4 Ecosystem Morality	8.4.1 Ecosystem Damage	Capital damages some life with chemicals and lost habitat.	Capital can increase capital's efficiency.	Act intelligently with empathy.

Individual Morality

Hubris. Capital enables a degree of leisure for which humans were not designed and for which many humans are not emotionally and intellectually prepared to accept. A dangerous level of hubris currently permeates advanced societies.

Inactivity. The relative ease of modern life allows many health issues to occur.

Group Morality

Abortion. Pregnancy creates a compromised condition for mother and child. In primitive societies group safety was a moral concern. Babies could cause societies to be vulnerable to external threats and inadequate resources, but grown children were probably an asset. Capital has eliminated the primitive concerns for group safety, which might have been considered justifications for abortion. Some mothers are now having their babies killed - apparently because the babies would temporarily diminish their freedom. Of course, the babies lose all of their freedom.

Homosexuality. Capital has eliminated the reason people believed homosexual behavior was immoral. That is, homosexual behavior does not produce offspring, which otherwise could have increased group size and safety – but we no longer need to increase group size.

Gender Roles Merge. Capital has eliminated most jobs that require strength, and it has provided a variety of machines to replace routine household activities. The merging gender roles are emotionally and financially difficult for some men, women, and children.

Species Morality

There are, at least, two types of capital-enabled situations for species morality – those that allow novel interactions to occur (with strangers) and those that separate naturally opposing binary states.

A. Novel Interactions Occur

Slave Labor. Slave labor is believed to have been practiced worldwide for 10,000-17,000 years. Since the Industrial Revolution (1,760-1,840 AD), developing capital has caused slave labor to become relatively inefficient. (Efficiency is important for living entities to remain competitive.) Apparently, inefficiency has caused slave labor to be abolished in at least 102 countries during the period 1,750-2,000 AD. The U.S. abolished slavery in 1864, which was about the median year in which the other 101 nations abolished it. Maybe the U.S. Civil War was unnecessary. (It seems that most Americans believe only Americans practiced slavery.)

Conflicts and Conquests (Foreign). Capital allows strangers to migrate and interact. Humans have not had sufficient time to develop species morality. Our amygdala keeps us alive by causing us to be wary of strangers and strange situations. Worldwide, the loss of human life from conflicts has been estimated at over one billion – results that, hopefully, have correspondingly accelerated the evolution of species morality.

Within the last 7,000 years, various groups have taken or occupied land that was occupied by others. (For example, European immigrants now occupy land in the Americas that Indians (i.e., Mongoloids) had occupied for 11,000-12,000 years.) We still have moral dilemmas about interacting with strangers and occupying land.

Moral Conflicts (Domestic). Approximately 200-400 years ago, the slave trade brought Sub-Saharan Africans (i.e., Negroids) to the Americas. The Americas have been recently populated by Europeans – who evolved for the last 100,000 years in environments different from those of the enslaved Negroids (i.e., different from Sub-Saharan Africans). Currently, the Black homicide rates in the USA are many times the White homicide rates – as much as 12.57 times higher. Undoubtedly, for these 100,000 years, Blacks evolved in a much more competitive and physical environment than Whites,

The homicide rate difference could have occurred because Negroids that migrated to the Middle-East 100,000 years ago had no competition from other humans for resources throughout the entire Earth - except for Sub-Saharan Africa. The land area of Sub-Saharan Africa is only 4% of the land area of the Earth. Moreover, inland waterways in these lands facilitated communication among humans, and the colder climates outside of Tropical regions probably motivated those humans to be more innovative than those who remained in Sub-Saharan Africa.[195] Capital allows productivity that exceeds unity: Productivity greatly increases the production of resources, and more resources reduce the need for competition. Of course, the Negroids who were brought to the Americas from Sub-Saharan Africa a few hundred years ago had evolved with great competition for nearly the same duration as those who had *not* migrated 100,000 years ago.

To summarize these observations, Blacks that came to America as slaves 200-400 years ago had competition for the last 100,000 years, whereas, Whites who inhabited the Americas, had far less competition in unoccupied lands during the same 100,000 years.

Because morality is innate, we should probably characterize the high homicide rate of the Blacks who were brought to the USA as misplaced behavior rather than misbehavior.

---

[195] The Tropics is a region within 22.5° on both sides of the Equator.

B. Naturally Opposing Binary States are Separated

The term, naturally opposing binary states, refers to two states that naturally provide balance for each other in nature. Examples of these states are up-down, in-out, on-off, "for every action there is an opposite and equal reaction," etc.[196] Each pair of naturally opposing states is intended to maintain a balanced and sustainable situation. (Unlike activities employing capital, nature tends to be balanced, and, therefore, sustainable.) We consider the following naturally opposing binary states:

- Consume-Produce

- Rights-Responsibilities (or, equivalently, Freedom-Moral Behavior)

- Risk-Reward

- Supply-Demand

Capital enables the situations that separate naturally opposing binary states. With the possible exception of consume-produce, this ability usually has an immoral result.

Consume-Produce are Separated. The efficiency of capital is supplementing and replacing human labor, thereby separating the naturally opposing states, consume-produce. How will replaced humans feel without meaningful work? How will humans afford to consume if they do not produce? Increased efficiency is moral, but how do we adjust to the lost work and income?

For any fraction of job loss (i.e., between 0.0 and 1.0) in the U.S. economy, Section 8.3.4 shows how to compute five basic economic parameters (i.e., wages for employees; profit and rate of return for entrepreneurs; and production and productivity for the economy). The formulas in Figure 8.3.4 allow the reader to adjust the relative contributions of the four factors of production (i.e., land, labor, capital, and entrepreneurship) and four other scenario assumptions (i.e., a subsidy, the fraction of domestic consumption, the profit advantage from foreign consumption, and tariffs).[197]

Rights-Responsibilities are Separated. Capital (specifically when employed by governments) enables the naturally opposing binary states, rights-responsibilities, to be separated. (Section 10.2.3 shows that the states, rights and responsibilities, are equivalent to the states, freedom and moral behavior.) Entropy imposes continual pressure on individuals to acquire necessary resources. By definition, weaker individuals are more likely to surrender their individual responsibilities to others or to the state. This is not so serious within groups, but it is very serious among strangers. Probably, most significantly, socialist governments redistribute individual responsibilities of their citizens and effectively enslave them by subsequently denying them their

---

[196] Newton's law of universal gravitation

[197] *The Nature of Economics*, Martin J, Miles, Chapter 16

natural rights. Life and freedom must coexist. Both can be lost without responsible (i.e., moral) behavior.

Over time, virtually all socialist governments have shown that separating rights and responsibilities causes the loss of individual rights (i.e., freedom): It seems inevitable. Are rights more likely to be lost if they have *not* been earned, and, consequently, are not cherished? Additionally, socialism is similar to the moral hazard that is inherent in the insurance industry. They both accommodate relaxed responsibility,

Figure 8.3.5-1 depicts rights and responsibilities and compares them to Hayek's "Road to Serfdom" when individual responsibilities diminish.

Risk-Reward are Separated. Governments have created laws that separate the naturally opposing binary states, risk and reward. For example, banks can reap rewards from profitable investments (using depositor's money), and, to avoid failing, banks can legally pass the responsibility for their bad investments (i.e., risk) to taxpayers. This is known as a bank bailout.

Supply-Demand are Separated. Capital provides the opportunity to more easily manipulate free markets. Manipulating markets is immoral because it biases prices. Biased prices propagate throughout the economy, causing subsequent transactions to present unexpected risk. Because the manipulated markets are inaccurate (i.e., biased prices are posing as legitimate values), they can increase individual losses. Section 6.5.2 discusses the interesting concept of accuracy and its role in measuring the morality of a manipulated market. This is the Market Freedom function, $T(a) = (1-a)/(1+a)$, where a is accuracy. Entity selection is another type of market that can be abused by favoring an entity's identity over an entity's merit. Where would we be if natural selection was abused as merit selection is abused? Life requires meritable competition!

Ecosystem Morality

Ecosystem Damage. During the Industrial Revolution some Europeans experienced environmental problems such as air pollution, but the world did not notice, until the 20th century, the variety and extent of ecosystem damage that has been occurring. This is all so recent that probably very little ecosystem morality has evolved in our human genome.

10.4 A Few Additional Observations

10.4.1 Relationship between Innate Morality and Documented Traditional Morality

Morality has been documented since the Ur-Nammu law code (2,100-2,500 BC), the Code of Hammurabi 1760 BC, the Ten Commandments (1,300-1,600 BC), the Golden Rule, Natural Law, etc. These documentations are all consistent with individual and group morality, but they do not include species or ecosystem morality. That is, we believe they are all examples of individual and group morality.

10.4.2 Manipulated Markets

Accuracy is the sum of the square of the bias and the square of precision. Accuracy helps to measure the moral behavior of the following two types of markets.

Markets of Goods and Services

Our definition of morality implies that manipulations of a market don't just cause inefficiencies, ineffectiveness, and inaccuracies - manipulations are also immoral because they *propagate more bias and less precision (i.e., more variation),* which reduce the probability of success (i.e., freedom).

Markets of Selection

Similarly, in the selection markets, our definition of moral behavior implies that the practice of placing an individual in a position because of the individual's identity (rather than the individual's merit) undoubtedly *reduces the effectiveness* of the position and reduces the probability of freedom for all affected – including the individual selected for the position.[198] Failing to fill a position on the basis of merit is immoral because it undoubtedly reduces the probability of freedom for all affected individuals. (Natural selection is merit-based, and as stated earlier, what would life be like if we ignored ability, intelligence, effort, efficiency, accuracy, truth, competition, etc.?)

Manipulated or abused markets are not free markets; they are immoral markets.

---

[198] Affirmative Action is a long-standing example of the increasing abuse of identity selection.

10.4.3 Natives and Strangers

When strangers inhabit a foreign society, the variance of moral behaviors in the society also increases. This can be morally concerning to natives and can decrease the stability of the society.[199]

Native Concern for Security

Members of all societies are naturally wary of strangers and strange situations. Our amygdala causes us to be wary of unusual situations. Natives of some societies are decidedly more wary than others. National security and political freedom are often considered to be conflicting goals. That is, governments that highly value security are more reluctant to allow political freedom. Figure 5.2.3-1 depicts political freedom for most regions of the world. I think we should realize that wariness of strangers is natural. It is an inherent, universal, and necessary fear. Consequently, reasonable wariness is moral rather than immoral.

Strangers' Behavior

If we believe that morality is learned rather than innate, we might blame strangers for their exotic or offensive behavior (believing that "they should act better"). On the other hand, if we believe that morality is innate, we might believe that strangers' behavior is moral in their environment but not necessarily in another environment - and it would be fair to dislike the behavior rather than to dislike the person. It is fair to understand the reason for the behavior, but that doesn't mean the behavior should be tolerated.

When humans merge, the variance of moral behavior in the larger group usually increases, and a larger variance tends to cause more conflicts. If conflicts increase in a society, there might be pressure on the domestic population to change its laws to accommodate the migrant's behavior.[200] This happens.

10.4.4 Capital and Moral Dilemmas

Even though our newly needed propensities will not be available for millennia, it should help enormously just to realize that the propensities are missing, and they are missing because of the relatively recent consequences of our creative human mind - which has also given us so many wonderful abilities.

---

[199] There can also be advantages to diversity. It can produce a more robust society.

[200] Changing laws occurred in the U.S. in 2021 when some governments released countless alleged law breakers rather than trying them. Subsequently, crime rates increased dramatically.

Our increased human life spans prove that capital can provide more beneficial solutions than it provides damaging problems.

Realizing that we are missing critical moral propensities, will not provide the propensities, but it will encourage us to be more careful and understanding. Hopefully, it will improve our relationships with each other.

Increasing our moral propensity space will require hundreds or thousands of generations. What will our moral propensities for strangers and the ecosystem be? It is eerie to realize that for certain situations, our moral judgment is immature and, perhaps, worthless.

10.4.5 A Mosaic of Observations

Perhaps some of the most important conclusions in this book are among the following:

- **Dependent Moral Behavior and Constancy**. Freedom requires dependent moral behavior, at least because life requires constancy of acquiring necessary resources.

- **Exponential Concepts.** Because capital is knowledge and its manifestations, capital increases exponentially. Behavior is moral behavior if and only if it increases the probability of freedom, and freedom is the ability to behave morally. Therefore, moral behavior begets moral behavior and freedom begets freedom: Moral behavior and freedom can change roughly in proportion to the amount present (i.e., exponentially). This provides a tremendous additional incentive to develop capital, behave morally, and obtain freedom!

- **Faith and Morals.**
    - Morality is consistent with logic, and faith is consistent with emotion.
    - Moral behavior increases the probability of natural selection, and some believe that faith increases the probability of supernatural selection.

- **Freedom.** Freedom exists if and only if moral behavior can exist. Freedom and moral behavior are augmented by capital.

- **Human Rights.** Human rights are concepts that are innate and implicit in individual and group morality. Human rights require freedom to exist and moral behavior to provide the responsible behavior.

- **Income Inequality.** Income inequality is a pejorative for the variance of incomes. For all common probability distributions, *the mean is independent of the variance*. That is, the mean income can increase or decrease, regardless of whether the variance of incomes increases or decreases. This is a mathematical fact. In any case, why should incomes for different types of labor, environments, and times be equal? Incomes should respond to supply and demand.

- **Labor and the Food Cycle.** The food cycle in the ecosystem is equivalent to labor in an economy. Both types of activities, the food cycle and labor, consume and produce, and neither can increase and sustain productivity beyond unity – without capital.

- **Life and Freedom.** Approximately 3.5-4.0 billion years ago, some molecules were able to divert some energy for their purposes. This was the beginning of life. Living entities still need to use energy for their purposes, and energy still flows to regions of lesser energy. We moved from the physical system, where the freedom of a rock is zero and to the biological system, where the freedom of a human life is essentially infinite. Life (i.e., the basic freedom) and freedom must coexist, and both require moral behavior.

- **Mathematical Models of our Four Important Parameters.**
  - **Moral Behavior.** We selected the appropriate function to model and measure moral behavior in terms of constancy. It is modeled and measured by the autocorrelation function of lag 1.

  - **Freedom of an Individual.** We derived the Freedom function to model and measure freedom as a function of moral behavior.

  - **Accuracy.** We selected the appropriate formula to model and measure accuracy (i.e., the expected value of the random squared error). It is also the formula selected by the International Standards Organization (ISO).

  - **Freedom of a Market.** We derived the Market Freedom function to model and measure the morality of a market as a function of accuracy. It measures markets of goods and services and markets of selection – such as the reduced morality resulting from selecting on the basis of identity rather than on the basis of merit as nature does.

Functions of the four Important Parameters

		Functions
Parameter	**Moral Behavior function**	m = autocorrelation of lag 1 $= [\Sigma(x_i - t_x)\cdot(x_{i+1} - t_x)] / [\Sigma(x_i - t_x)^2]$, where $i = 1, \ldots, k$; x_i, x_{i+1} = observations; and t_x = mean.
	Freedom function	$F(m) = (1 + m) / (1 - m)$, where m = moral behavior
	Accuracy function	$a = \beta^2 + \sigma^2$, where β = bias & σ = precision
	Market Freedom function	$T(a) = (1 - a) / (1 + a)$, where a = accuracy

- **Moral Propensities.** Humans have few moral propensities for any type of situation that began approximately within the past 7,000 years – and we haven't realized it. But, really, would these current behaviors exist if we possessed the moral propensities?

- **Moralities Vary.** Because morality is innate and natural selection exists, morality is designed by environments. We discuss a few examples of various moralities (i.e., homicides, political freedom, and economic freedom). We should realize that moralities from other environments are as valid in their environments as our morality is in our environment. It seems we could appreciate each other much more if we realize why our moralities differ. The optimum environment for an individual is the environment that designed it.

- **Rates of Capital Development and Evolution.** The rate of capital development is exponential because it increases in proportion to the amount of existing capital. On the other hand, the rate of evolution depends upon the rate of environmental change, and this is episodic - not exponential. The differences in results from the two rates will continue to increase.

- **Socialism.** Table 8.3.5-1 lists the three characteristics of two natural societies and two unnatural societies: The natural societies are based on freedom. They are the ecosystem and capitalism. The unnatural societies are based on equality. They are slavery and socialism. Even though nature provides a variety of human genomes, these societies discard the morality of merit selection to provide equal outcomes!

Table 8.3.5-1 characteristics of four societies whose purposes are either freedom or equality

Type of Society			Characteristics		
			Purpose	**Dependent Behavior**	**Entity Selection**
Natural		Ecosystem	Freedom	Competition	Merit Selection
		Capitalism			
Unnatural		Slavery	Equality*	Cooperation & Force	Identity Selection
		Socialism			

* Because genetic variation is natural, equality is unnatural.

241

10.4.6 It is Impossible to Accurately Judge the Morality of Past Interactions between Strangers

We believe that we have evolved essentially without species morality because conflicts with strangers (i.e., individuals from other groups) were rare until about 7,000 years ago. If we don't have propensities for species morality, we cannot accurately judge the morality of interactions between strangers that were novel within the last 7,000 years.

We may have an urge to judge the morality of some of these interactions (e.g., Christopher Columbus and the American Indians), but we can't. It is not merely difficult for us - it is impossible! How can our judgment hit the bull's-eye when the target has not yet evolved?

If you think this inability doesn't apply to you, you will proceed to judge these situations based on your *group* morality, rather than based on *species* morality – which you don't yet have.

Probably the best evidence that we do not possess species morality is that members of a group usually interact quite civilly with each other, whereas members of our species clearly do not.

We are so late to realize that we cannot accurately judge these past situations with strangers. Think of all of the humans killed, all of the accusations, all of the statues that have been destroyed, all of the monuments and buildings that have been renamed, all of the demands for reparation, etc.

This book explains why we believe that morality is innate. If morality is innate, there is no universal morality - either over space or time. Countless environments design our moralities to increase our probability of freedom in the environment in which we evolved.

Knowing that our moralities are necessarily varied and that we do not possess species morality should encourage us to judge each other with more understanding. I really hope it will.

Appendix A Derivation of the Freedom Function

Estimation

We can draw random samples from a population and then use these samples to estimate parameters of the population. A sample statistic is a function of values from a sample - that does not include parameters from the population to be estimated. The probability distribution of a sample statistic is often called the sampling distribution of the sample statistic.

Generally, Greek letters represent values of population parameters, and Roman letters represent values of the sample statistics that estimate the population parameters. We use θ to represent an arbitrary population parameter. Suppose $\theta^\wedge$ is an estimator of the parameter, θ.

If a statistic is designed to estimate a parameter, it is called a point estimator. The value of an estimator is called the estimate. An estimator can have several desirable properties, some may be practical and some must be mathematical. Practical properties would include the ease of calculation. Mathematical properties would include, at least, that the estimate is in the possible range of values of the parameter, and the maximum property would be that the estimate always equals the parameter - but that would violate the condition that the statistic must not include the parameter.

The Expected Value of the Random Squared Error is

the Mean Squared Error

Suppose $\theta^\wedge$ is an estimator of the parameter, θ. Then consider, $(\theta^\wedge\text{-}\theta)^2$, the random squared error (i.e., the quadratic loss function). The expected value of this function, the mean squared error (i.e., the risk function), is

$$E[(\theta^\wedge\text{-}\theta)^2] = E\{[\theta^\wedge\text{-}E(\theta^\wedge)] + E[(\theta^\wedge)\text{-}\theta]\}^2$$

$$= E[\theta^\wedge\text{-}E(\theta^\wedge)]^2 + 2E[\theta^\wedge\text{-}E(\theta^\wedge)]\cdot[E(\theta^\wedge\text{-}\theta)] + E[E(\theta^\wedge)\text{-}\theta]^2$$

$$= E(\theta^{\wedge2})\text{-}E(\theta^\wedge)^2 + 2[E(\theta^\wedge)\text{-}E(\theta^\wedge)]\cdot[E(\theta^\wedge)\text{-}\theta] + [E(\theta^\wedge)\text{-}\theta]^2$$

$$= \sigma_{\theta^\wedge}^2 + [E(\theta^\wedge)\text{-}\theta]^2.$$

The quantity, $B = E(\theta^\wedge)\text{-}\theta$. is the bias of the estimate, and the quantity, $\sigma_{\theta^\wedge}^2$, is the variance (i.e., precision) of the estimate. As mentioned elsewhere in this book, we believe that the best definition of accuracy is the sum of these two types of estimates (i.e., accuracy = small bias + small variance).

Nested Desirable Properties of a Point Estimator

The following five types of estimators are considered desirable.

1. Unbiased Estimators

An estimator, $\theta^\wedge$, is said to be unbiased if

$$B = E(\theta^\wedge) - \theta = 0.$$

2. Consistent Estimators

The sequence of n estimators, $\theta^\wedge{}_n$, is consistent in the sense of convergence of the quadratic loss function, $(\theta^\wedge{}_n - \theta)^2$, if

$$\lim_{n\to\infty} E[(\theta^\wedge{}_n - \theta)^2] = \lim_{n\to\infty} \{ \sigma^2{}_{\theta^\wedge} + [E(\theta^\wedge{}_n) - \theta]^2 \} = 0.$$

3. Efficient Estimators

Let $\theta^\wedge{}_n$ be an asymptotically unbiased estimator of θ, and consider the variable, $n^{1/2}(\theta^\wedge{}_n - \theta)$. From the central limit theorem:

- Its sampling distribution is normally distributed.

- Its mean is zero.

- Its variance is the variance of $\theta^\wedge$ (i.e., $\sigma^2{}_{\theta^\wedge}$).

Now, $\theta^\wedge$ is an efficient estimator of θ if

$$\sigma^2{}_{\theta^\wedge} = E[(\theta^\wedge - \theta)^2]$$

is less than the variance of any other unbiased estimator.

The sample mean is an efficient estimator of the population mean of a normal distribution because every other estimator has a larger variance.

4. Best Asymptotic Normal (BAN) Estimators

A sequence of estimators, $\theta^\wedge{}_1, \dots, \theta^\wedge{}_n, \dots$, is a BAN estimator if it has the following three asymptotic populations:

- **Asymptotically Normal**. The distribution of the random variable, $n^{1/2}(\theta^\wedge{}_n - \theta)$, approaches the normal distribution with mean = 0 and variance = $\sigma^2{}_{\theta^\wedge}$ as n $\to\infty$.

- **Asymptotically Unbiased**. That is,

244

$$\lim_{n\to\infty} P[(\theta\hat{}_n - \theta) < \varepsilon] = 1 \text{ for all } \varepsilon$$

where P is the probability function, and $0 < \varepsilon$.

- **Asymptotically Efficient**. There is no other sequence of estimators, $\theta^*_1, \ldots, \theta^*_n, \ldots$, having the above two properties, and also,

$$\lim_{n\to\infty} \{[E(\theta\hat{}_n - \theta)^2] / E[(\theta^*_n - \theta)^2]\} > 1$$

for all θ in some open interval.

5. Maximum Likelihood (ML) Estimators

If one cannot obtain the desired estimator, the maximum likelihood method can be used to obtain an estimator that is a subclass of the BAN estimators.

Maximum likelihood estimators are also estimators of sufficient statistics. That is a statistic (i.e., a statistic that contains all information about the estimator that can be obtained from the sample). When these statistics are substituted for the parameter in the density function, the maximum likelihood estimator (if it exists) is the "best" estimator. Suppose g is the joint density of the sample values $x_1, \ldots, x_n$. Then,

$$g(x_1, \ldots, x_n|\theta) = f(x_1|\theta) \cdot \ldots \cdot f(x_n)| \theta).$$

Let

$$L = f(x_1|\theta) \cdot \ldots \cdot f(x_n)| \theta)$$

where L is called the likelihood.

The natural logarithm of L is

$$\ln L = \ln[f(x_1|\theta) \cdot \ldots \cdot f(x_n)| \theta)].$$

Then,

$$(\delta \ln L/\delta\theta) = [1/f(x_1|\theta)] \cdot [\delta f(x_1|\theta)/\delta\theta] + \ldots + [1/f(x_n|\theta)] \cdot [\delta f(x_n|\theta)/\delta\theta] = 0.$$

From this, θ can be obtained in terms of $x_1, \ldots, x_n$.

Figure A-1 is a Venn-type diagram that depicts the relationship among desirable properties of a statistical estimator.

Figure A-1. Venn-type diagram depicts the relationship among desirable properties of a statistical estimator. Best asymptotic normal (BAN) estimators have many desirable properties, but maximum likelihood (ML) estimators have the most desirable properties.

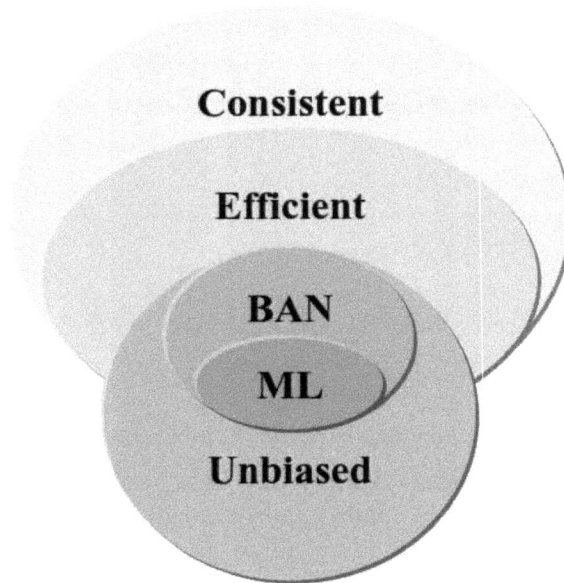

The following are the five sections for deriving the Freedom function.

A.1 Assume that the Trials Deviate Randomly within Samples

A.2 Assume that Dependence within Populations Depends on the Relative Order of the Variables

A.3 Assume that Dependence Decreases Monotonically with Respect to K

A.4 Assume that Dependence Allows the Sampling Covariance to Converge to Zero

A.5 Assume that Dependence within Populations is First-order Markov Dependence

The general formula of the sampling covariance of two distributions is derived in equation A-1. Then, assuming no knowledge of dependence between observations, seemingly reasonable and general assumptions of dependence are imposed to arrive at equations A-3, A-5, A-6, A-7, and A-11.

The Sampling Covariance

Suppose $x^\wedge$ and $y^\wedge$ are the maximum likelihood estimates of the means, μ_x and μ_y, from samples of size n for two hypothetical populations. Suppose also that E[ ] is the expected value of the bracketed quantity. Then the covariance of $x^\wedge$ and $y^\wedge$ is

$$cov(x^\wedge, y^\wedge) = E[(x^\wedge - \mu_x) \cdot (y^\wedge - \mu_y)]$$

246

$$= E[(1/n) \cdot \Sigma^n_{i=1} x_i - \mu_x] \cdot [(1/n) \cdot \Sigma^n_{i=1} y_i - \mu_y]$$

$$= E[(1/n) \cdot \Sigma^n_{i=1}(x_i - \mu_x) \cdot (1/n) \cdot \Sigma^n_{i=1}(y_i - \mu_y)]$$

$$= (1/n^2) \cdot E[\Sigma^n_{i=1}\Sigma^n_{j=1}(x_i - \mu_x) \cdot (y_j - \mu_y)]$$

$$= (1/n^2) \cdot E[\Sigma^n_{i=1}(x_i - \mu_x) \cdot (y_i - \mu_y) + \Sigma^n_{i=1}\Sigma^n_{j=1}(x_i - \mu_x) \cdot (y_j - \mu_y)]$$
$$(i \neq j)$$

$$= (1/n^2) \cdot \Sigma^n_{i=1}E[(x_i - \mu_x) \cdot (y_i - \mu_y)] + \Sigma^n_{i=1}\Sigma^n_{j=1}E[(x_i - \mu_x) \cdot (y_j - \mu_y)]$$
$$(i \neq j)$$

$$= (1/n^2) \cdot [\Sigma^n_{i=1}cov(x_i, y_i) + \Sigma^n_{i=1}\Sigma^n_{j=1}cov(x_i, y_j)]$$
$$(i \neq j)$$

$$= (1/n^2) \cdot [n \cdot cov(x, y) + \Sigma^n_{i=1}\Sigma^n_{j=1}cov(x_i, y_j)].\ ^{201} \quad (A\text{-}1)$$
$$(i \neq j)$$

This is the expression for $cov(x^\wedge, y^\wedge)$ when no assumption is made about the relationship between x and y.

A.1 Assume that the Trials Deviate Randomly within Samples

By definition,

$$\rho_{xy} = cov(x, y)/(\sigma_x \cdot \sigma_y), \text{ and } \rho_{xiyj} = cov(x_i, y_j)/(\sigma_{xi} \cdot \sigma_{yj}).$$

The correlations, ρ_{xiyj}, express cross-correlation between the x's and the y's, but with a lag $|i\text{-}j|$. One would expect the correlations to be highest when i = j and to diminish as $|i - j|$ increases. At least, one would expect that

$$|\rho_{xiyj}| \leq |\rho_{xy}|.$$

The first, and a plausible assumption for $cov(x^\wedge, y^\wedge)$ is to replace ρ_{xiyj} with the product of ρ_{xy} and the harmonic mean of ρ_{xixj} and ρ_{yiyj}. That is, assume that

$$\rho_{xiyj} = \rho_{xy} \cdot (\rho_{xixj} \cdot \rho_{yiyj})^{1/2}.$$

---

[201] If sampling is from real (finite) populations of size N and is without replacement, multiply this expression by (N-n)/(N-1).

Although this expression is somewhat intuitive, it can be proven if it us assumed that x_i, x_j, y_i, and y_j deviate randomly about their means. Let

$$x_{ik} = \mu_{xk} + e_{ik}, \; x_{jk}, = \mu_{xk} + e_{jk}, \; y_{ik}, = \mu_{yk} + e_{ik}, \text{ and } y_{jk}, = \mu_{yk} + e_{jk} \qquad \text{(A-2)}$$

where

$$E(e_{ik}) = E(e_{jk}) = E(e_{ik} \cdot e_{jk}) = 0.$$

Then

$$E[(x_{ik} - \mu_x) \cdot (x_{jk} - \mu_x)]$$

$$= E[(\mu_{xk} + e_{ik} - \mu_x) \cdot (\mu_{xk} + e_{jk} - \mu_x)]$$

$$= E(\mu_{xk}) - \mu_x^2$$

$$= E[(\mu_{xk} - \mu_x)^2]$$

$$= \sigma_{\mu x}^2.$$

Now,

$$\rho_{xixj} = E[(x_{ik} - \mu_x) \cdot (x_{jk} - \mu_x)] / \{E[(x_{ik} - \mu_x)^2 \cdot E(x_{jk} - \mu_x)^2]\}^{1/2}$$

$$= E[(\mu_{xk} - \mu_x)^2] / (\sigma_{xi} \cdot \sigma_{xj})$$

$$= \sigma_{\mu x}^2 / \sigma_x^2.$$

Similarly,

$$\rho_{yiyj} = \sigma_{\mu y}^2 / \sigma_y^2, \; [202]$$

and

$$\rho_{xiyj} = E[(x_{ik} - \mu_x) \cdot (y_{jk} - \mu_y)] / \{E[(x_{ik} - \mu_x)^2] \cdot E[(y_{jk} - \mu_y)^2]\}^{1/2}$$

$$= E[(\mu_{xk} - \mu_x) \cdot (\mu_{yk} - \mu_y)] / (\sigma_{xi} \cdot \sigma_{yj})$$

$$= \rho_{\mu x \mu y} \cdot \sigma_{\mu x} \cdot \sigma_{\mu y} / (\sigma_x \cdot \sigma_y)$$

$$= \rho_{\mu x \mu y} \cdot (\rho_{xixj} \cdot \rho_{yiyj})^{1/2}$$

$$= \rho_{xy} \cdot (\rho_{xixj} \cdot \rho_{yiyj})^{1/2}.$$

Note that

---

[202] The correlations, ρ_{xixj} and ρ_{yiyj}, are nonnegative under the assumption of random deviation.

$$\text{cov}(x_i, y_j)$$

$$= \sigma_x \cdot \sigma_y \cdot \rho_{xiyj}$$

$$= \sigma_x \cdot \sigma_y \cdot \rho_{xy} \cdot (\rho_{xixj} \cdot \rho_{yiyj})^{1/2}$$

$$= \text{cov}(x, y) \cdot (\rho_{xixj} \cdot \rho_{yiyj})^{1/2}.$$

Now, equation A-1 becomes

$$\text{cov}(x^\wedge, y^\wedge) = (1/n) \cdot \text{cov}(x, y) \cdot [1 + (1/n) \cdot \Sigma^n_{i=1} \Sigma^n_{j=1} (\rho_{xixj} \cdot \rho_{yiyj})^{1/2}]. \text{[203]} \qquad \text{A-3}$$
$$\text{(i} \neq \text{j)}$$

where n is the sample size.

A.2 Assume that Dependence within Populations Depends on the Relative Order of the Variables

Although the correlations, ρ_{xixj} and ρ_{yiyj}, have values dictated by the distributions, without knowledge to the contrary, it is reasonable to assume that dependence within each distribution depends upon the number of observations between the ith and the jth observations (i.e., between x_i and x_j and between y_i and y_j).

If it is assumed that dependence between each pair of x's and y's depends only upon k = |i-j|. Then

$$\rho_{xixj} \equiv \rho_k(x), \text{ and } \rho_{yiyj} \equiv \rho_k(y).$$

Due to the first assumption, $\rho_k(x)$ and $\rho_k(y)$ are nonnegative for all k = 1, ... , n-1 where n is the sample size (i.e., random clusters around zero).

Now,

$$\text{cov}(x^\wedge, y^\wedge) = (1/n) \cdot \text{cov}(x, y) \cdot \{1 + 2\Sigma^{n-1}_{k=1} (1-k/n) \cdot [\rho_k(x) \cdot \rho_k(y)]^{1/2}\} \qquad \text{(A-5)}$$

where n is the sample size.

---

[203] The variance of x^ (or y^) is
$$\text{var}(x^\wedge) = \text{cov}(x^\wedge, x^\wedge) = (1/n) \cdot \text{var}(x) \cdot [1 + (1/n) \cdot \Sigma^n_{i=1} \Sigma^n_{j=1} \rho_{xixj}].$$
$$\text{(i} \neq \text{j)}$$

A.3 Assume that Dependence Decreases Monotonically with Respect to K

Under this assumption,

$$\rho_{k+1}(x) \leq \rho_k(x), \text{ and } \rho_{k+1}(y) \leq \rho_k(y) \text{ for } k = 1, 2, \dots, n-2.$$

Then, it can be shown that

$$cov(x^\wedge, y^\wedge) \leq (1/n) \cdot cov(x, y) \cdot \{1 + (n-1) \cdot \{2[\rho_1(x) \cdot \rho_1(y)]^{1/2} - [\rho_{n-1}(x) \cdot \rho_{n-1}(y)]^{1/2}\}\}$$

or

$$cov(x^\wedge, y^\wedge) \leq cov(x, y) \cdot \{2[\rho_1(x) \cdot \rho_1(y)]^{1/2} - \lim_{n \to \infty}[\rho_{n-1}(x) \cdot \rho_{n-1}(y)]^{1/2}\}\}$$

$$\leq cov(x, y) \cdot [\rho_1(x) \cdot \rho_1(y)]^{1/2}. \quad (A\text{-}6)$$

Hence, under this weak condition of dependence (that decreases with respect to k), the sampling covariance is not guaranteed to converge to zero with large samples.

A.4 Assume that Dependence Allows the Sampling Covariance to Converge to Zero

If greater precision is to be obtainable from larger samples, it is necessary to impose a condition upon $\rho_k(x)$ and $\rho_k(y)$ that is stronger than that just imposed.

Let

$$\rho_k(x) = a_\xi/k^\xi, \text{ and } \rho_k(y) = a_\eta/k^\eta \text{ where } 1 \leq a_\xi \cdot a_\eta.$$

$$cov(x^\wedge, y^\wedge) = (1/n) \cdot cov(x, y) \cdot [1 + 2(a_\xi \cdot a_\eta)^{1/2} \cdot \Sigma^{n-1}_{k=1}(1-k/n)/k^{(\xi+\eta)/2}] \quad (A\text{-}7)$$

where n is the sample size.

The integral test for convergence shows that $cov(x^\wedge, y^\wedge)$ converges to zero when $0 < (\xi+\eta)$.[204]

The following definition is often used. It results in less dependence (and faster convergence than this definition).

---

[204] if $(\xi+\eta) = 0$, $cov(x^\wedge, y^\wedge) = cov(x, y) \cdot (a_\xi \cdot a_\eta)^{1/2}$.

A.5 Assume that Dependence within Populations is First-order Markov Dependence

If dependence between all pairs of consecutive random variables is equal, dependence is said to be first-order Markov dependence. This is equivalent to assuming that dependence is exponential in k:

$$\rho_k(x) = \rho_{k-j}(x) \cdot \rho_j(x) = \rho_1(x) \cdot \ldots \cdot \rho_1(x) = \rho_1^k(x), \qquad \text{(A-8)}$$

and

$$\rho_k(y) = \rho_{k-j}(y) \cdot \rho_j(y) = \rho_1(y) \cdot \ldots \cdot \rho_1(y) = \rho_1^k(y)$$

where $j = 1, \ldots, k\text{-}1$.

Then,

$$\text{cov}(x^\wedge, y^\wedge) = (1/n) \cdot \text{cov}(x, y) \cdot \{1 + 2\Sigma^{n-1}_{k=1}(1\text{-}k/n) \cdot [\rho_1^k(x) \cdot \rho_1^k(y)]^{1/2}\} \qquad \text{(A-9)}$$

where n is the sample size.

For simplicity of notation in the following derivation, let

$$\rho_1 = [\rho_1(x) \cdot \rho_1(y)]^{1/2}.$$

Now, the factor in braces in (A-9) becomes

$$c_n^2(\rho_1) = 1 + 2\Sigma^{n-1}_{k=1}(1\text{-}k/n) \cdot \rho_1^k$$

$$= 1 + 2\Sigma^{n-1}_{k=1}\rho_1^k - (2/n) \cdot \Sigma^{n-1}_{k=1}k \cdot \rho_1^k \qquad \text{(A-10)}$$

where

$$\Sigma^{n-1}_{k=1}\rho_1^k = \rho_1/(1\text{-}\rho_1) - \rho_1^n/(1\text{-}\rho_1) = (\rho_1\text{-}\rho_1^n)/(1\text{-}\rho_1),$$

and

$$\Sigma^{n-1}_{k=1}k \cdot \rho_1^k = \rho_1 \cdot d[1/(1\text{-}\rho_1)]/d\rho_1 - \rho_1 \cdot d[\rho_1^n/(1\text{-}\rho_1)]/d\rho_1$$

$$= [\rho_1/(1\text{-}\rho_1)^2] \cdot [\text{-}n \cdot \rho_1^{n-1} \cdot (1\text{-}\rho_1) + 1 - \rho_1^n].$$

Now, (A-10) becomes the Freedom function:

$$c_n^2(\rho_1) = 1 + 2[(\rho_1\text{-}\rho_1^n)/(1\text{-}\rho_1)]\text{-}(2/n) \cdot [\rho_1/(1\text{-}\rho_1)^2] \cdot [\text{-}n \cdot \rho_1^{n-1} \cdot (1\text{-}\rho_1)+1\text{-}\rho_1^n]$$

$$=1 + 2[(\rho_1/(1-\rho_1)]\cdot[1-(1/n)\cdot(1-\rho_1^n)/(1-\rho_1)] \qquad \text{(A-11)}$$

where n is the sample size.

Due to the first assumption, $0 \leq \rho_1$, and then $1 \leq c_n^2(\rho_1)$. Also

$$\lim_{n\to\infty} c_n^2(\rho_1) \equiv c^2(\rho_1) = (1+\rho_1)/(1-\rho_1),$$

Figure A-1 is a graph of (A-11), the Freedom function for first-order Markov dependence.

If this factor is to be used for the covariance, $0 \leq \rho_1$ (i.e., due to the assumption of Section A.2).

If this factor is to be used for the variance, $-1 \leq \rho_1 \leq 1$.

Finally, equation (A-9) becomes

$$\text{cov}(x^\wedge, y^\wedge) = \sigma_{x^\wedge y^\wedge}^2 = (\sigma_{xy}^2/n)\cdot c_n^2\{[\rho_1(x)\cdot\rho_1(y)]^{1/2}\}.$$

$$\text{var}(x^\wedge) = \sigma_{x^\wedge}^2 = (\sigma_x^2/n)\cdot c_n^2[\rho_1(x)].$$

$$\text{var}(y^\wedge) = \sigma_{y^\wedge}^2 = (\sigma_y^2/n)\cdot c_n^2[\rho_1(y)]. \qquad \text{(A-12)}$$

QED

Appendix B Measures of Autocorrelation

This appendix describes autocorrelation from three perspectives:

B.1 Sample Graphs of Autocorrelation

B.2 A Measure of Constancy

B.3 Conditions for Negative Autocorrelation

B.1 Sample Graphs of Autocorrelation

We have created many sample graphs of autocorrelation to illustrate how observations affect the following features:

- orientation,
- number of observations,
- constancy (i.e., shape), and
- slope.

The four features are listed in Table B.1-1 and illustrated by 16 graphs of autocorrelation in five figures.

Table B.1-1 features of autocorrelation depicted in each figure

	Figure	Letter Identification
Orientation	B.1-1 B.1-2 B.1-3	W, Z R, S G, H
Number of Observations	B.1-4 B.1-5	R, S α, β, E, F, M, N
Constancy (i.e., Shape)	B.1-3 B.1-4	G, H, P, Q C, D
Slope	B.1-5	

Correlation and Constancy

As seen in the following graphs, the shape of the correlation graph indicates morality. Correlation is independent of orientation, but it increases with the number of observations.

Constancy is strongly associated with autocorrelation.

A sequence of observations rarely forms a straight line, which would cause the autocorrelation to approach 1 as the number of observations approaches infinity. In fact, a sequence of observations often meanders or jogs back and forth.

Figure B.1-1 Orientation: Correlation is independent of orientation.

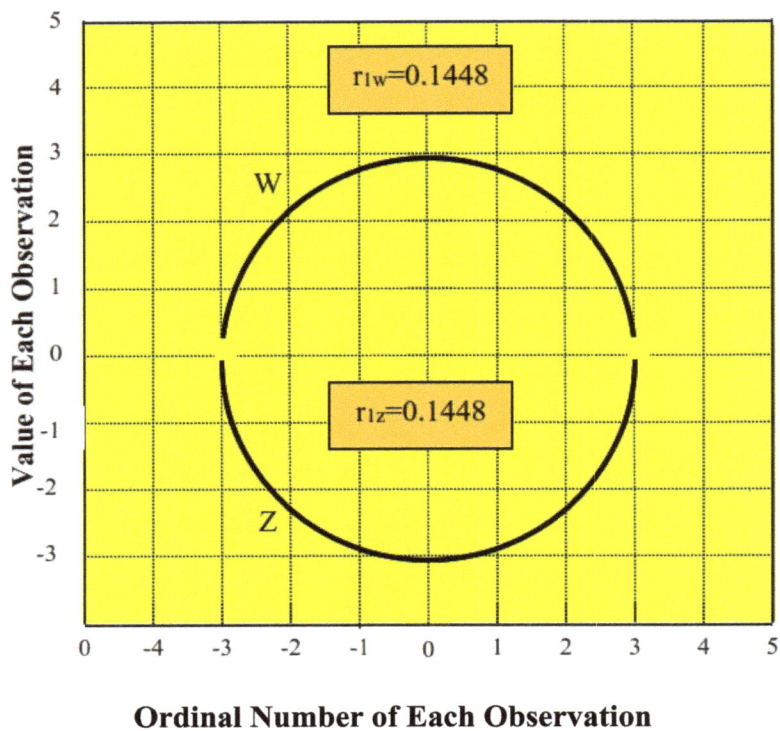

Ordinal Number of Each Observation

Figure B.1-2 Orientation: Correlation is independent of orientation.
Number of Observations: Absolute value of correlation increases with
the number of observations.

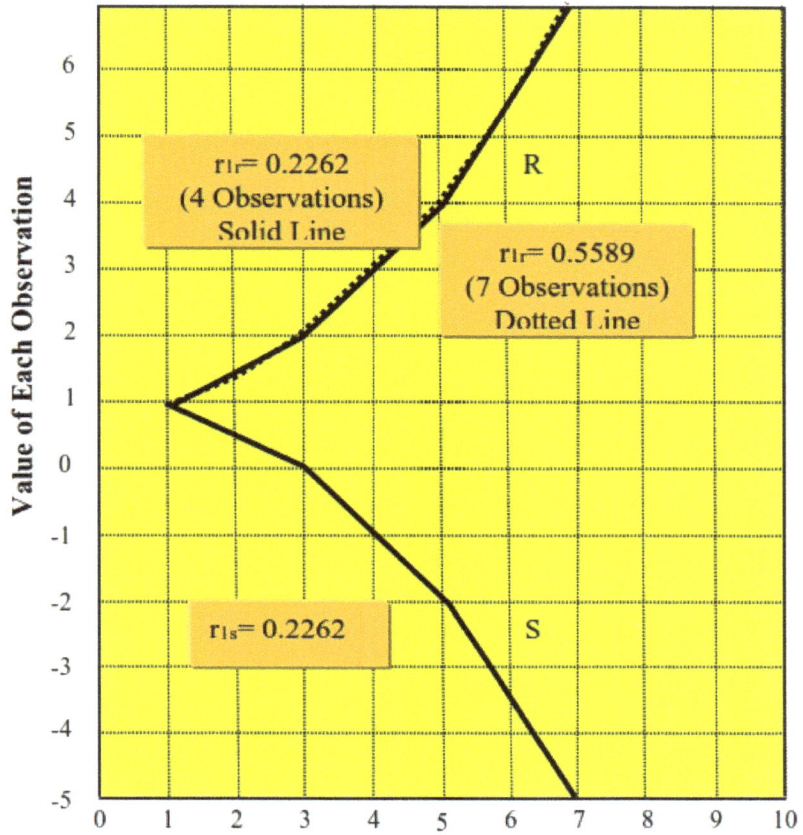

Figure B.1-3 Orientation: Orientation can affect the autocorrelation.

Constancy (i.e., shape): Total inconstancy causes extreme negative autocorrelation.

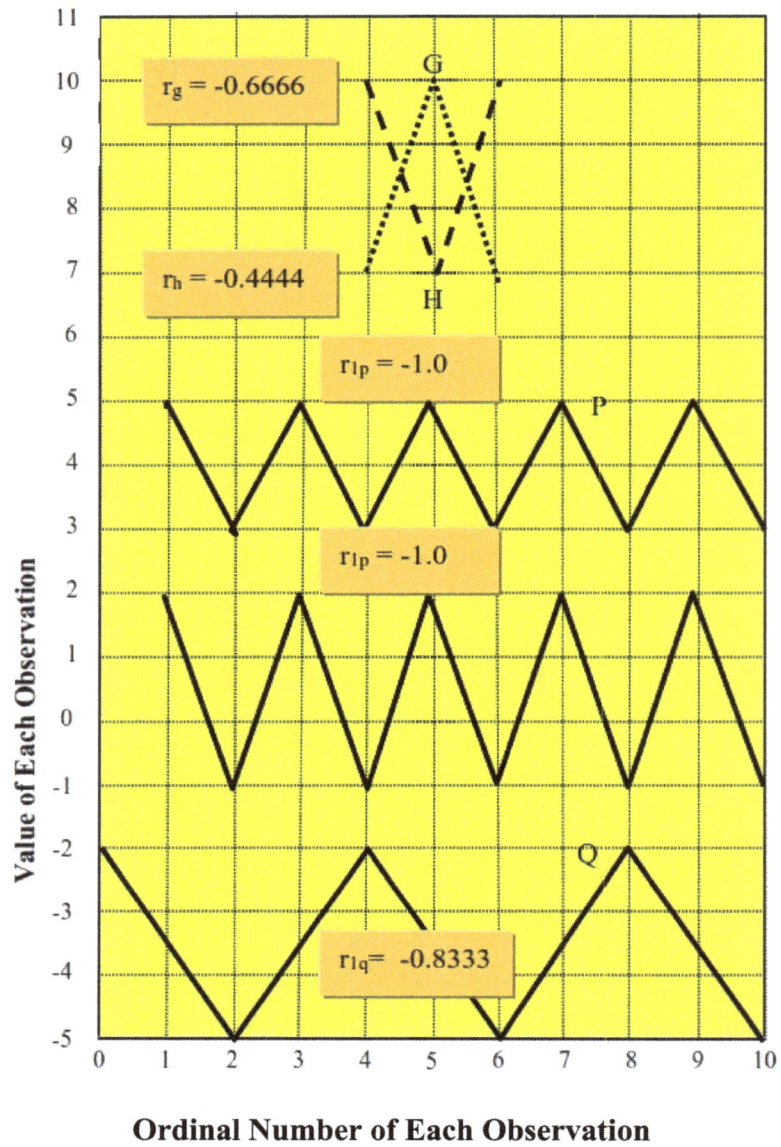

Figure B.1-4 Constancy: Autocorrelation increases when observations are more uniform.

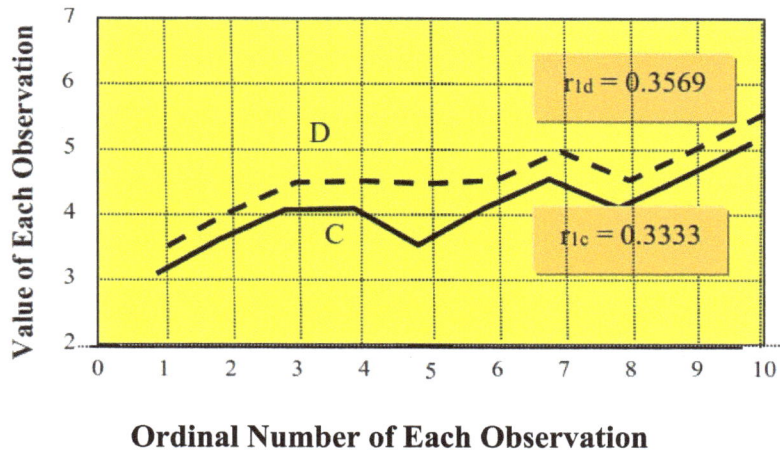

Ordinal Number of Each Observation

Figure B.1-5 Number of Observations: Absolute value of autocorrelation increases with the number of observations.
Slope: Autocorrelation is independent of the slope of the graph.

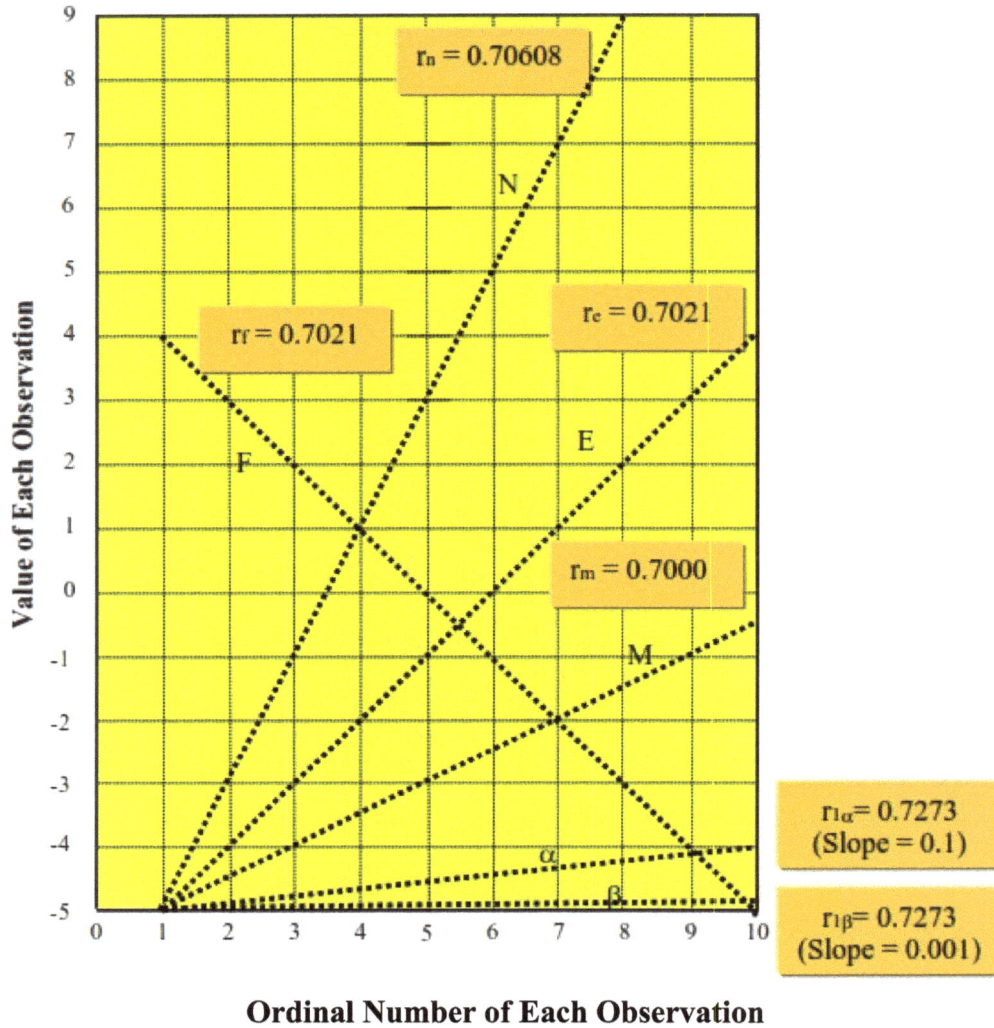

Ordinal Number of Each Observation

B.2 A Measure of Constancy[205]

The autocorrelation tends to be closer to 1 the straighter the sequence of observations and the larger the number of observations in the sequence. It is reasonable that the autocorrelation is greater if the sequence of observations is relatively constant.

A geodesic is a curve representing the shortest path between two points on a surface. On the surface of the Earth (an oblate spheroid), the great circle is the shortest distance between two

_____

[205] Consistency of an individual's propensities is not the same as constancy of observations from the individual's behavior.

points when measured on its surface. If there is no surface or if the surface is a plane, the geodesic is a straight line.

A sequence of observations rarely forms a straight line - which would cause the autocorrelation to approach 1 as the number of observations approaches infinity. In fact, a sequence of observations often meanders or jogs back and forth. We can associate an autocorrelation that is less than 1 with a sequence of observations that is less than uniform.

B.2.1 General Formula

Specifically, we can define constancy as the ratio of two distances:

- the distance between the first value of the sequence, x_i, and the last value of the sequence, x_k, and

- the distance that is the sum of the distances between each of the k-1 consecutive value of the sequence.

That is,

$$con(x_i, x_{i+1}) = [(x_1 - x_k)^2 + (y_1 - y_k)^2]^{1/2} / \{\Sigma_1^{k-1}[(x_i - x_{i+1})^2 + (y_i - y_{i+1})^2]\}^{1/2}$$

where

$con(x_i, x_{i+1})$ = constancy of the observations in a sequence.

k = number of observations (i.e., the sample size).

x_i = i^{th} observation in the sequence of k observations of the phenomenon.

x_{i+1} = $(i+1)^{th}$ observation (i.e., lag 1) in the sequence of k observations of the phenomenon.

y_i = i^{th} observation in the sequence of k observations of the phenomenon.

y_{i+1} = $(i+1)^{th}$ observation (i.e., lag 1) in the sequence of k observations of the phenomenon.

Σ denotes the sum of the observations i = 1, ... , k.

y_1 = first abscissa value of the kth observation in the sequence.

x_1 = first abscissa value of the kth observation in the sequence.

y_k = last abscissa value of the kth observation in the sequence.

x_k = last abscissa value of the kth observation in the sequence.

B.2.2 Special Formula

Notice that, if each value of the sequence is defined at a consecutive integer from 1 to k on the abscissa, we can simplify the definition of constancy so that

$$con(x_i, x_{i+1}) = [(x_1 - x_k)^2 + (k-1)^2]^{1/2} / \{\Sigma_1^{k-1}[(x_i - x_{i+1})^2 + 1^2]\}^{1/2}.$$

In either case, the value of constancy is in the interval, $0 \leq con(x_i, x_{i+1}) \leq 1$. If the sequence is constant, it equals 1, and if it meanders widely or jogs frequently, it is near 0.

What is the shape of the sequence of observations if behavior is moral or immoral? The shape is irrelevant, but it is a question most everybody would like to know because the shape of a sequence of observations could immediately identify the value of the coefficient.

When applied to behavior, a sequence of observations is moral if and only if the autocorrelation is positive. The definition of constancy is similar to the definition of efficiency.

B.3 Conditions of Observations for Negative Autocorrelation

It would be convenient if a behavior could be identified with an equation known to result in a particular negative autocorrelation.

The autocorrelation coefficient is negative if the covariance is negative. That is, the autocorrelation is negative if

$$cov(x_i, x_{i+1}) = \Sigma_1^{n-1}(x_i - \mu) \cdot (x_{i+1} - \mu) < 0.$$

The autocorrelation coefficient is negative also if

$$\Sigma_1^{n-1}(x_i \cdot x_{i+1}) + (x_1 + x_n)\mu < (n+1)\mu^2.$$

Appendix C Traditional Classification of Morality

Moral theorists define three dominant moral theories, two senses of morality, and two standards of morality.

Definitions of Three Dominant Moral Theories

Currently, moral theorists define moral theories by emphasizing one or more of three elements of a moral situation:

- **Deontology.** Deontology favors the *rules* of a moral situation (e.g., "Do the means justify the end?");

- **Consequentialism.** Consequentialism favors the *outcome* of a moral situation; and

- **Virtue Ethics.** Virtue Ethics favors the subjective *virtue* of the acting person - and deemphasizes the theories of deontology and consequentialism.

Senses of Morality

Moral theorists consider two senses of morality, the descriptive sense and the normative sense:

- **Descriptive Sense.** Theorists who believe there are multiple codes of conduct also believe they should be described.

- **Normative Sense.** Theorists who believe there is a single universal sense of morality among rational people also believe morality is normative.

Standards of Morality

Moral theorists consider two standards of morality:

- **Objective Standard.** If an individual expresses a morality that comes from a standard (of some kind), it is considered objective.

- **Subjective Standard.** If an individual expresses a morality that is an opinion, it is considered subjective.

This traditional classification of the innate morality is discussed in Section 4.5.

Glossary

Accuracy. Accuracy measures how well estimates represent a true value. Accuracy is the expected value of the random squared error. Accuracy is the sum of two quantities: the square of bias and the square of precision.[206]

$$\text{Accuracy} = (\text{Bias})^2 + (\text{Precision})^2.$$

Accuracy is achieved if and only if the estimates provide a small bias *and* great precision (i.e., a small value). The smaller the value of this sum, the greater the accuracy.

Amygdala. two almond-shaped bodies, one on each side of the brain. They have many connections to warn of significant situations, particularly those related to memories, the sense of smell, social interactions, and survival.

Binary States. many situations or activities naturally have two states, called binary states. For example, binary states are on or off, up or down, inside or outside, true or false, etc. In terms of economics, binary states are production or consumption, supply or demand, responsibility (i.e., risk) or reward, etc. In our modern world, political control and technology can cleave the natural binary states into two unnatural unary states. This book discusses how political control separates responsibility from reward and how technology separates production from consumption.

Capital. Capital is knowledge and its manifestations. Capital is a factor of production that began with the first tool. It now consists of financial, human, intellectual, and physical capital. Capital allows productivity to exceed unity.

Capitalism. an economic system characterized by relative freedom from government control and by private ownership for profit with respect to trade and industry

Communism. a political theory, derived by Karl Marx, advocating class war and leading to a society in which all property is publicly owned and each person works and is paid according to his/her abilities and needs[207]

Constant/Consistent. These two words are similar, but consistent is usually reserved for elements that agree logically.

---

[206] Many believe that accuracy and precision are synonymous, but precision is only one of the two components of accuracy: bias and precision. (Bias is sometimes called *trueness*.)

[207] Abilities and needs are independent and can lead to conflicting results.

Correlation. dependence or association is a statistical relationship, whether causal or not, between two random variables, say x and y. Correlation coefficients measure the agreement of the association between two variables. The sample correlation coefficient is

$$r_{xy} = s_{xy}/s_x s_y$$

where s_{xy}, s_x, and s_y are the sample covariance between x and y, the sample variance of x, and the sample variance of y, respectively. The population coefficient is

$$\rho_{xy} = \sigma_{xy}/\sigma_x \sigma_y$$

where σ_{xy}, σ_x, and σ_y are the population covariance between x and y, the population variance of x, and the population variance of y, respectively.

The correlation coefficients, r and ρ, are defined in the interval, $-1 \leq r, \rho \leq 1$..[208]

Density Dependence. the dependence of population growth on the population density

Dependent. two or more conditions that tend to occur together – either with or against.

Dependence Factor. Activities are often dependent - such as from cooperation or competition. Dependence affects the variance of a statistical distribution. The variance can be corrected if it is multiplied by the dependence factor. The dependence factor is

$$c_n^2(\rho) = 1 + [2\rho/(1 - \rho)] \cdot \{1 - (1/n) \cdot [(1 - \rho^n)/(1 - \rho)]\}^{[209]}$$

where dependence is assumed to be consistent with a first-order Markov chain;

ρ = autocorrelation of lag 1, where $-1 \leq \rho \leq 1$; and

n = number of participants, where $n \geq 1$.

The value of the correlation coefficient depends upon the similarity or dissimilarity with which individuals compete or cooperate

Dorsolateral Prefrontal Cortex (dlPFC). The dorsolateral prefrontal cortex does not mature until adulthood. It is a functional region of the neocortex rather than a clearly defined structure. The dlPFC communicates with the neo-cerebellum, posterior cingulate, posterior parietal cortex, premotor cortex, and retrosplenial cortex. These communications provide mutual regulation between these five structures and the dlPFC. The dlPFC also provides two extremely important

---

[208] If the trials are independent, the correlation coefficient is zero. However, if the correlation coefficient is zero, the trials are not necessarily independent.

[209] $c_n^2(\rho) = 1$ when either $\rho = 0$ or $n = 1$.

types of functions, executive and decision-making. Since dlPFC decision-making does not communicate with (emotions from) the amygdala, its decisions are logical (i.e., not emotional).

Ecosystem. a biological community of organisms that interact and their physical environment.

Entropy. a thermodynamic quantity representing the unavailability of a system's thermal energy for conversion into mechanical work - often interpreted as the degree of disorder in the system. It is an individual's potential demand for energy- an energy debt

Environment. a set of conditions that influence an individual/society but does not include the individual/society

Evolution. the change in the characteristics of a species over many generations that relies on the process of natural selection

Expected Value of the Random Squared Error The *expected value* of the random squared error is

$$E[(\hat{w}-w)^2] = [E(\hat{w})-w]^2 + \sigma_{\hat{w}}^2.$$ [210]

Where $\hat{w}$ is a random variable.

Factors of Production. land, labor, capital, and (usually) entrepreneurship that produce goods and services

Fascism. Fascism is a political system that is often led by a dictator. It regiments the economy and usually encourages an aggressive nationalism. Fascism is similar to socialism with some characteristics of capitalism: Roughly, socialism provides direct control, and fascism provides indirect control (through state intimidation of owners). Fascist states group businesses from the same industry into a cartel. Labor and management are represented on the same boards - subject to the state. Where fascism was practiced, state control caused domestic commerce to be so inefficient that protectionism was considered necessary.

Feudalism. a cooperative relationship of labor for land in medieval Europe (between the 9th and 15th centuries). Feudalism usually emerged from the decentralization of an empire. Specifically, a set of legal and military customs created a system of holding land (i.e., fiefs) in exchange for service or labor: The king (or lord) owned the land (hence, the word, landlord). He leased some land to barons, who subleased some land to knights, who further subleased some land to serfs.

---

[210] Notice that the random squared error does not explicitly refer to the mean or variance, but its expected value does.

Usually there were reciprocal duties between the king (or lord) and the tenant. For example, knights would supply the king (or lord) with military service in the form of armed horsemen.

Fiscal Policy. the aggregate of policies of the executive and legislative branches of the Federal government regarding the government's input (i.e., revenue and borrowing) and output (i.e., spending)

Free Market. an economic market or system in which prices are based on competition among private businesses and not controlled by a government. A free market is relatively free of control. The freedom from a free market allows the requirements of successful behavior to be available (i.e., appropriate degrees of competition, independence, or cooperation, effective selection, accurate selection, and efficient behavior).[211] Consequently, a free market economy is a moral economy. (See Moral Economy.)

Freedom. the ability to behave morally

Freedom Function. $F(x) = (x-1)/(x+1)$, where x is the the degree of freedom and $F(x)$ is the morality

Genotype. an individual's genome

Group. a number of humans that live together, usually fewer than 100 family and friends Groups are important because evolution is thought to act on the group level rather than the gene or individual level.

***Homo* sapien.** the primate species in which modern humans belong

Independent. An item is independent of a second item if it is viewed in the same way regardless of the existence of the second item.

Industrialism. An economic system that emphasizes manufacturing

Labor. a factor of production. Until capital (i.e., tools), labor from organisms produced themselves only - for the consumption by other organisms. That is, productivity was unity. (After capital, labor produced products and services.) Labor does not have the ability to increase productivity above unity; humans have remained practically unchanged.

Level. A condition of a characteristic

---

[211] The requirement, self-interest, is inherent in the individual; it does not depend on external situations such as markets.

Limbic Brain. The limbic brain evolved with the first small mammals approximately 250,000,000 years ago to control fight-or-flight responses. Since it records many types of memories including "good" and "bad" experiences, it is responsible for emotion in humans. The amygdala are located in the limbic brain. The limbic brain, along with the neocortex, is the seat of our decisions - often unconscious decisions.

Market Freedom Function. $T(a) = (1-a)/(1+a)$, where a is the degree of accuracy and $T(a)$ is the morality of the market

Mathematical Model. an isomorphic construction of the phenomenon it is modeling. A mathematical model allows the phenomenon to be analyzed and measured.

Mercantilism. a national economic policy in the 16th-18th centuries that was designed to maximize the trade of a nation and to maximize the accumulation of gold and silver. Trade was viewed as a zero-sum activity.

Moral Behavior. Behavior that increases the probability of freedom

Moral Economy. An economy is a moral economy if and only if it is a free market economy. That is, morality is successful behavior with respect to freedom, and morality for a society can exist only in a free market economy.

Moral Hazard. In the 17th century, the moral hazard concept was realized to be inherent to the insurance industry. By virtue of the insurance contract, the insured reduces his/her risk. Hence, the insured tends to become less responsible - and the risk for the insurer increases. Correspondingly, this hazard can occur when responsibility for an act is either inadequate or misplaced; one party acts, but another party is responsible for the consequences of the action (i.e., the risk from the action and the responsibility are independent). The moral hazard exists for the responsible party. For example, taxpayers are responsible for the actions of a bank that is "bailed out" by the government (i.e., using taxpayer's money). See Binary States.

Moral Propensity Space. the dimensions and range of values of moral propensities

Morality.

- **Two Dictionary Definitions.**
  - **Independent of Society.** a doctrine or system of moral conduct or a particular moral principle or rule of conduct).
  - **Dependent on Society and Permanent within the Individual.** a code of conduct that regulates interactions within complex societal groups; it is permanent within an individual.

- **Our Definition.** Morality is successful behavior for individuals in a society with respect to natural selection. Morality is inextricably linked to the environment that designed the individuals and society to conform to that environment.

Multi-level Morality. Morality is successful behavior with respect to natural selection for the individual, group, species, or ecosystem.

Natural Law. a system of rights that is considered by some to be common to all humans and derived from nature.

Natural Selection. the process (i.e., variation, heredity, and differential reproduction) whereby organisms better adapted to their environment tend to survive and produce offspring. Over generations, organisms are designed to conform to that environment. Natural selection is the primary method of evolution. This book divides natural selection into three independent types, depending upon criteria (i.e., environmental protection criteria, pathogen-predator criteria, and prey acquisition criteria). Prey acquisition criteria (i.e., closely related to economies).

Naturally Opposing States. two states that balance each other in nature. Consume-produce in the food cycle, on-off, up-down, Newton's Law of Motion, etc.

Neocortex. Since the neocortex (i.e., "new bark") is the newest layer of the cerebral cortex, it is the outermost layer. The neocortex comprises 90% of the cerebral cortex; it is the "grey matter." The neocortex first appeared with the evolution of larger mammals and primates 75,000 years ago. The neocortex is responsible for abstract thought, attention, consciousness, culture, imagination, information processing, language, logic/reason, and memory. It has almost unlimited learning abilities.

Optimal Environment. The optimal environment for an individual or society is the environment that designed it.

Phenotype. a manifestation of an individual's genotype

Production. the value of goods and services produced by an economy. The value is usually measured by the gross domestic product (GDP). It is the final market value of all goods and services produced domestically during a stated period (usually one year or a fraction of one year).[212] GDP is a measure of the standard of living in a governmental jurisdiction.[213] The nominal GDP is the current GDP, and the real GDP is the nominal GDP that has been adjusted from previous inflation and deflation. The GDP can be expressed as the sum of expenditures:

$$GDP = (\text{Consumer Spending}) + (\text{Government Spending}) + (\text{Investment})$$
$$+ [(\text{Exports}) - (\text{Imports})].$$

Productivity. Productivity is production divided by the amount of a relevant resource - such as hours worked, number of consumers, etc.

Propensity. A propensity is an inherent tendency to behave is a particular way.

Reptilian Brain. Since the reptilian brain is the oldest of the three layers, it formed directly on top of the spinal cord. It is quick, constant, and reflexive. It controls the body's vital functions and motor control. (Reptiles evolved 315,000,000 years ago.) The two structures of the reptilian brain are the brain stem and the cerebellum.

Risk. risk of activity with respect to an asset:

$$\text{Risk} = (\text{Probability of Loss}) \times (\text{Value of Asset}).$$

Socialism. an economic system characterized by social or government ownership of the means of production

Species. the largest group of organisms in which any two individuals of mating types can produce fertile offspring, typically by sexual reproduction

State Capitalism. an economic system characterized by state ownership of the means of production. However, the state allows businesses to be *operated* by institutional investors (rather than by bureaucrats) and provides some control and subsidies.

---

[212] In 2014, the Bureau of Economic Analysis (BEA) began to publish a measure of economic activity that is an alternative to the Gross Domestic Product (GDP). It is the Gross Output (GO). Whereas the GDP is the output of final goods and services, GO is the output of new goods and services (i.e., total of industry's value-added and intermediate inputs - the supply chain). As measured in 2015 by the BEA, GDP was $18.1 trillion, and GO was $31.6 trillion.

[213] The gross domestic product is a convenient measure of production. Not all production is desirable: government, crime, trials, lawyers, defense, accidents, climate damage, pollution, etc. Velocity is a vector that measures speed and direction. Perhaps a vector should be designed that measures production and direction (i.e., "good" production, "bad" production, etc.). See *The Little Big Number* by Dirk Philipsen.

Statistical Inference. *Statistical* inference (also called either statistical estimation or sampling) is the process of drawing conclusions about the general (i.e., the population) by drawing one or more samples from the population (i.e., random subsets of the population).

Thermodynamics. the relationship between temperature, thermal (heat) energy, and other forms of energy. Energy is transferred to a region of lesser energy.

Trait. a specific level of a characteristic of an organism

Triune Brain. an organizing metaphor that describes the structure and functions of the human brain as the instinctive reptilian brain, the emotional limbic brain, and the reasoning neocortex

Unsuccessful Behavior. behavior that diminishes the probability of success. This book discusses three types of unsuccessful behavior practiced by governments:

- biased values,

- inappropriate responsibility, and

- unfair practices.

These types of unsuccessful behavior apply to individuals as well as organizations.

Ventromedial Prefrontal Cortex (vmPFC). The ventromedial prefrontal cortex (vmPFC) is part of the neocortex that communicates sensory information between itself and many structures in the brain - especially the amygdala. The vmPFC is involved with important decisions: It compares *emotion and logic* to make moral judgments.

About the Author

Martin J. Miles is a retired mathematician, author, inventor, investor, and business owner. He was employed as a mathematician by the National Institute of Standards and Technology (NIST), the National Oceanic and Atmospheric Administration (NOAA), and the National Telecommunications and Information Administration (NTIA) for 36 years doing research of the environment, digital networks, and telecommunications. He also had a 14-month research contract with the University of Wyoming to develop methods to evaluate the performance of digital networks. He has authored 10 books, more than 40 technical reports and lectures, and has been the subject of about 40 media articles. He has discovered, and had published, two mathematical theorems. He has been granted a patent with 67 claims that determines the logical way to combine the probabilities that a number of items of evidence prove a conclusion. He was the lead author of a six-volume report that is the American National Standard (and the de facto world standard) method to evaluate the performance of digital networks. He has a bachelor and a master degree in mathematics from the University of Colorado - including at least 53 credit hours in biology, chemistry, and physics.

He has two children and seven grandchildren.

Other Published Books

- *The Miles Chart Display,* 1971, Convex Industries, Inc.

- *The Miles Chart Display of Popular Music,* 1977, Arno Press (New York Times, Inc.)

- *The Encyclopedia of Real Estate Formulas and Tables*, 1978, Prentice-Hall, Inc.

- *Real Estate Investor's Complete Handbook,* 1982, Prentice-Hall, Inc.

- *Investment Math Made Easy,* 1986, Prentice-Hall, Inc.

- *The Vest-Pocket Real Estate Advisor*, 1989, Prentice-Hall, Inc.

- *Performance Evaluation of Data Communication Services: NTIA Implementation of American National Standard X3.141*, 1995, NTIA Report 95-319 (1, 2, 3, 5, 6)

- *The Nature of Economics,* 2019, Title ID: 9180729,